MANAGEMENT OF SPORT
AND PHYSICAL ACTIVITY
(THE CASE METHOD APPROACH)

Earle F. Zeigler
Ph.D. D.Sc., LLD., FNAK

TRAFFORD
2012

Order this book online at **www.trafford.com**
or email orders@trafford.com

Most Trafford titles are also available at major online book retailers.

Printed in the United States of America.

ISBN: 978-1-4669-1301-1 (sc)
ISBN: 978-1-4669-1302-8 (e)

Library of Congress Control Number: 2012901315

Trafford rev. 01/23/2012

 **www.trafford.com**

North America & International
toll-free: 1 888 232 4444 (USA & Canada)
phone: 250 383 6864 ♦ fax: 812 355 4082

DEDICATION

This book is dedicated to those graduate and undergraduate students who studied management with me at The University of Michigan, the University of Illinois, and The University of Western Ontario (in that order chronologically). We introduced the Harvard case plan of instruction to them and offered it to the broader the field of sport and physical education management in the 1950s and 1960s for the first time.

CONTENTS / CONCEPTUAL INDEX

PREFACE

This text is divided into four parts. Part 1 introduces the reader to various aspects of the Harvard case plan of instruction as it might apply to students having a course experience in sport and physical activity management. It includes chapters that serve to introduce students and instructors to one person's employment of, and "enhancement of", the "case method" of learning management and human relations.

Parts 2 and 3 are collections of actual cases related to the management of sport and physical activity education. The cases in Part 3 include situations strong elements where involving ethical consideration are present. Part 4 summarizes the overall experience for the student prior to a course's final examination.

Under what was termed (historically) the Harvard Case Method, students read, analyzed, and then discussed "real life" administrative problems like those they would have to face in their future careers. The emphasis was on careful analysis and "digging" for facts. The instructor is very important with this approach, but he/she does not dominate the discussion or seek a predetermined goal. He/she may serve as (1) a resource person, (2) an evaluator of progress, (3) an informed member of the group, (4) a discussion chairperson, and (5) a summarizer.

The student will find that no new supply of "knowledge" is included–one that must be learned. Here instead is an approach to the learning of management, however, that the prospective manager of physical activity education and athletics has not yet met to a truly significant degree. This text can be used by itself at either undergraduate or graduate levels of instruction, or it may be used as a laboratory manual in conjunction with a more traditional, knowledge-oriented text. (For example, the author's *Management Theory and Practice in Physical Activity Education (Including Athletics)* was published in 2010 with this in mind by Trafford Publishing, Bloomington, IN. <www.trafford.com>)

Down through the years of the twentieth century, the case method of instruction attracted favorable attention steadily and increasingly in business, law, educational administration, and the social sciences. The author is convinced that it should be used much more intensively and much more knowledgeably in sport and physical activity management as well than at present.

Many who have managed programs, and who have perhaps taught "the management course" in the professional program, have felt the new for an improved approach to the subject at hand. We have played with the concept of "democratic management". In our courses we have tried group discussions, committee work, group projects, different types of readings, term papers, and possibly case analysis to a limited extent. Although all of these techniques have been helpful, and have served to break away from the traditional, monotonous, unilateral type of teaching (the lecture!), student reaction has not been such as to provide evidence that these courses have been most worthwhile.

The author learned early on in his career as a teacher of this subject that so-called traditional teaching methods were inadequate. He felt that there had to be a better way, As a result of a great deal of reading, conversation, and experimentation, he came to believe that serious consideration should be given to the Harvard case method of teaching management and human relations in our field. The author soon thereafter found it to be the ideal method in a democratic country.

Through the case method of teaching, students apply their understanding and imagination to management problem that actually have been faced by professionals on the job. For the first time the student takes part actively in the search for a rational course of action based on the relevant facts available. He or she will develop attitudes and learn to analyze the problems critically. Ultimately we hope that the prospective manage will develop the self-reliant judgment necessary for success as a manager of sport and physical activity.

Certain questions are included at the end of each case presentation. Ideally, they would not be employed as they tend to be directive. Further, we do not suggest that these are the only ones to be asked, In fact, they may not even be the best ones. They are merely those suggested by the person who submitted the case, and in some instances by the author of the text.

Part 1 serves to introduce and orient the student (and may serve as a review for the instructor) to the case method teaching. A course such as this is not a place where secrets are kept from the students. They should know what is going on at all times. First we discuss the general concept of management, emphasizing that there are even today few specific rules in the field.

Then the student is presented with an analysis of learning by the case method, as well as an analysis of teaching where it is employed. Since the cases have been selected to include most of the problem areas in the management of sport and physical activity education, the third "selection" of Part 1 offers summary "knowledge statements" defining the main areas. They are offered as "currently useful generalizations" that are generally recognized as being valid at present. (This chapter of "knowledge statements is also included in the more orthodox 2010 text written by the author as mentioned above.)

In Part 2 the actual cases for discussion are offered. There are 30 of them of varying length and complexity. Each case is listed under a "management problem heading". *It is important to note, however, that a case is often more than what it may appear to be on the surface.*

In Part 3, after first including a discussion of use of the case method of analysis when the addition of an ethical dimension to the problem appears to be present, a number of short cases divided into three categories of problems areas is included : *environmental, personal,* and *professional* cases that have an ethical orientation. Students who go on to become managers will face all three types of such problems in their lives.

In Part 4, the final section, the author "wraps it all up" with a brief, but fairly detailed analysis of the essence of what the case method approach has offered in this text. The goal, or primary objective, of the text was to provide information and experiences that would help the user become a successful manager. Give it a "good try"! You won't regret it…

Earle F. Zeigler

PART I: ORIENTATION TO THE CASE METHOD

Selection 1
What Is a Sport and Physical Activity Manager?

> Note: Throughout this text the terms "management" and "administration" will be used interchangeably. Please understand, also, that–although the term "she" is used here and there throughout the text–when I use the term "he" anywhere in the text–I am NOT showing gender bias! To always use "he/she" is so cumbersome and often incorrect within the narrative being told.

What is a sport and physical activity manager? Is he/she the "boss"? Is he the one who gets people to do what they would rather avoid? Does he "sugar the pill"? Does he organize a department, division, or program so that the work will get done? Does he implement the planning of his principal, the superintendent, the school board or board of directors? Is he working toward a goal that his staff is aware of? Does he keep the staff "sullen but not mutinous"? He may dangle offers of rewards to the underpaid teachers, coaches, or associates, if they will economize at every turn. He may be concerned about the welfare of the individual staff member, but he never lets him know. Perhaps he never has conflicting loyalties. This he can't forget-he is paid to be a "watchdog" for his superiors.

The "Strong" Manager

A "strong" manager gives the impression of efficiency every time he/she is seen on the job. His decisions are clear and correct. His superiors lean on him heavily, because he has such a strong personality and is so well prepared for meetings. His system of communications is excellent, insofar as changes in policy and procedure are concerned. There is never any doubt on the part of the staff member, because this administrator has issued a covering memorandum anticipating the changing situation. This man picks his teachers carefully; he demands excellence; he fights for high salaries.

The "Fairly Friendly" Manager

Perhaps the administrator is known as "fairly friendly." She is a hard worker, but she has an interest in his staff as people and is kindly even when she must discipline them for inefficiency. She is respected and also liked by her fellow workers. She is always ready to discuss problems. When they arise, she appoints committees to bring forth recommendations. She generally acts on these suggestions, but she does not evade responsibility. If a faulty recommendation is acted upon, she stands clearly as the administrator in charge of the program. She had the power to reject the recommendation of the committee, but she allowed it to go through. She is at fault and she accepts the blame.

The "Weak" Manager

Our manager might be a person who "puts up a big front" (or not!) but actually has no courage "when the chips are down." He never calls meetings of staff members, because he believes in individual action. He confides to small groups of staff members that "John" (he calls the dean by his first name) told him that the board wanted a particular policy carried out "such and such" a way. He acts like a "big shot" to the "team members", but they know that "his bark is worse than his bite." When certain segments of the staff call informal meetings to discuss a subject and invite him to be present, he never shows up, although he has promised to attend. If one of his superiors is to be there, however, he is right there talking about "my staff" or "my team." Staff members wonder how he got to be an administrator, but they know that little can be done about it now; they work around him and manage to do a fair job, considering the circumstances.

The "Friendly" Manager

It might be that the administrator's personality radiates throughout his department. He has a friendly department; a relaxed atmosphere prevails. He rarely seems hurried, and he always welcomes the opportunity to chat with staff or students. He is reluctant about recommending the dismissal of a staff member, but he occasionally refers to a Mr. X who left "for the good of the team." On rare occasions he speaks sternly, but when he has made his point the sternness seems to vanish. He is anxious to be friendly with all.

He is professionally minded, as shown by his interest in the state and national associations.

The "Conservative" Manager

The manager might be a former staff member who had always been a good "politician." He was promoted when his predecessor resigned to take another position. This man is quiet and very attentive to his position. He sees his responsibility somewhat differently than the last administrator, and spends more time on matters pertaining to the local institution rather than promoting state and national professional organizations. He is careful to maintain his relationship with the staff as the representative of the principal—and ultimately of the board; yet, he often presents staff grievances sincerely and effectively. Because he is anxious to keep in touch with competitive athletics, this administrator continues to coach one sport. He enjoys this contact with the students. When speaking outside the school, he is careful to avoid any publicity that might be viewed unfavorably by his superiors. He could in no way be considered a dictator, but he does believe in the line relationship pattern that has existed for many years.

The "Democratic" Manager

Another administrator is at least as friendly as any department head in the school. She says she is interested in democratic living and her friends would agree with her. She greets whomever she meets on the school grounds. She chats with the janitors and the locker room attendant occasionally, and can be seen listening intently when they discuss problems connected with their work. Both students and staff come to her with their problems. When she must criticize a staff member or student, she tries to ease the way by pointing out that she made a similar mistake once, and then quietly and sincerely telling the individual what she believes the difficulty to be. After this 'lecture," the staff member or student is encouraged to present his side of the story, and then they discuss the problem further. When people leave these sessions, they generally feel that they want to work a little harder to live up to the confidence that this administrator has placed in them.

This person encourages both staff and students to offer constructive criticisms. All departmental policy is decided through democratic procedure. The manager considers himself a chairperson at these meetings, although he does speak to the various issues raised without the formality of leaving the chair. Once, when a program change was recommended, there was a difference of opinion and it was necessary to take a vote on the issue. Because the vote ended in a tie, and because he wanted to encourage a staff minority to continue to show interest in "change for improvement," he broke the tie by voting for the change. This "democracy-in-action" approach is evident throughout the entire program and has stimulated a forward thinking staff. Staff members are given responsibilities and the authority to carry out their duties without interference. Students and parents find this attitude contagious, and the entire program reflects the inculcation of the "principles" of democratic living.

This man (or woman) works diligently himself, but he takes time for family living and a hobby. He delegates various duties to other staff members, whom he treats as co-workers. In staff meetings he stimulates many discussions about the direction in which the program seems to be heading. He is anxious to have the various staff members improve themselves professionally and has encouraged the idea of staff study projects. He is not afraid to praise his staff members when the occasion arises both within and without the school. Many people feel that the department would slip back seriously if this administrator were to accept another appointment. He insists that someone else could step in and assume the job easily, because there are no "secrets" for a successor to learn by bitter experience. Actually, the department has made considerable progress in the past few years. Many of the other staff members have been responsible for much of this progress.

> Note: It should be made clear that it is dangerous to categorize managers in the preceding manner. No one can be made to fit into a particular mold, although the examples given here were of administrators as seen through the experience of the author. Each administrator is inescapably unique, however, and meets situations as he sees them at the time.

Do We Operate According to Principles?

Traditionally, departments seem to have operated on the basis of a group of unexpressed major and minor principles. Such principles of sport and physical activity management do seem necessary to the formulation of operational policies. The department may even function in such a way that a "philosophy" is clearly evident. Moreover, certain over-all principles of education exist beneath the specifics of the professional field. Still deeper, a consistent and logical philosophy of life and/or religion should be the foundation upon which the whole system rests. Unfortunately, emergencies and practical considerations, as well as individual personalities and autocratic administrative patterns, constantly force a department to make exceptions to its prevailing "philosophy." At times the program takes on the appearance of a patchwork that bears little resemblance intrinsically to the principles upon which the department thinks it is operating. Should the administrator and the staff members then resign? This is an interesting postulation, but quite often impractical.

If a department or program is to function on the basis of certain long-range aims, realizable objectives for year-to-year progress are a necessity. These aims and objectives should be clearly stated for all to see, especially the principal, dean, president supervisor, owner, board of directors…. Each spring, when the next year's budget is being presented, these aims and objectives can be enumerated on a priority basis. Those objectives that have been largely realized can be noted, and the remainder listed again for another year. Actual budget expenditures can be based on these immediate or long-range goals.

From the discussion thus far the reader might be able to suggest what management or administration is. Or, to approach the subject negatively, we know all the things that an administrator should not be. By a process of elimination, then, we may arrive at a fairly acceptable definition of what he should be. Positively and rather broadly conceived, a manager (in this field) should be one who employs wise leadership in such a way that a complex unit functions effectively, making possible maximum learning or involvement on the part of the students, participants—whatever…. But these are just words: what's behind them?

There is no doubt but that administration or management could be greatly improved if its real nature were better understood. This is true because many administrators operating in terms of conflicting underlying assumptions. It is for this reason that we first examine the administrative process more closely. Following this, we must scrutinize the forces used in administration to help us see how they may be employed more effectively for "energizing" and "shaping" the process. Lastly, we should consider the subject matter by which the process may be learned.

Five Major Divisions of Managerial Process

Traditionally the five major divisions of the managerial or administrative process have been seen as planning, organizing, directing, coordinating, and controlling. As we examine the process we ask ourselves, "What makes it go?" It appears to be a mechanism that is very much alive. The forces are authority derived from law; knowledge, gleaned from observation and study; and social usage, determined from life in our culture and stated as either cultural standards and specialized as our professional ethics-these are the available forms and sources of energy.

Further Steps to Success

Subsequently, we must discover what knowledge is requisite to success as an administrator. We must learn what skills are needed on the job. Lastly, and of utmost importance, how can the novice develop the character or personality traits necessary to implement his knowledge and skills? This last question, to the author's way of thinking, is that which must be resolved first. Why? Because it is just at this point that we should realize how much the case method of teaching administration has to offer. The user will be very satisfied with the various degrees of knowledge and skills will necessarily result from the interest that is generated by this problem-solving approach.

Terms Synonymous with Management

When the terms management or administration is used in the educational field, we associate it with such words as superintendence, direction, planning, supervision, organization, regulation, guidance, and control. In common usage we think of it as the process of directing people in an endeavor.

The Typical Approach

The typical approach to administration is to ascertain those principles and operational policies upon which we can base our own theory and practice of educational administration. Administration (or management), in its simplest form, could probably be likened to a football coach blowing his whistle to call the players together at the beginning of practice. To carry the parallel further, we realize that the coaching of a football team involves different types of activity. The more complex the activity, the more specialization becomes necessary. Thus, the manager (coach in this discussion) must devote long hours to planning, organization, and coordination, in addition to his functions of directing and controlling on the basis of the plan thus evolved.

What Is Management?

A student of management becomes aware that a substantial body of literature has been written on the subject. There are those who maintain that management is a science or is rapidly becoming a science, although many still refer to it as an "art." The author is more inclined to accept it as a developing social science.

If a specific action pattern could apply to all situations, it would be relatively simple to select a set of guiding principles. However, the type of management one employs can vary greatly. There is a need for a new pattern of rules in almost every situation. It is for this reason that it is generally recommended that those learning how to administer should understand theory of management based on evidence and develop his or her philosophy of administration. Such an approach obviously gives credence to an "emerging science of administration" school of thought.

Inductive Versus Deductive Approach

We may approach a study of management in two ways. We can work from what we believe are facts leading to general truths or concepts-an *inductive* approach. Or we can start with what appear to be established facts and pry into their nature and truth to "identity" the true nature of the situation at hand-a deductive approach. A combination of both methods is often attempted. Generally, the inductive method is best applied to the study of administrative practice, while the deductive procedure is employed with the theory of management

The success of the case method of teaching management would appear to negate the value of the deductive approach and place the inductive procedure in a position of primary importance. Furthermore, complex human relations enter every administrative situation, and play havoc with the thought that management is *rapidly* becoming a science. In the inductive approach, a great deal of stress is placed on the necessity of taking into account all the facts pertinent to a problem area. The case method maintains that we can never know all the facts. Our task is to function effectively on the basis of those relevant facts available to us. Because of the complexity of human personality, the number of facts applying to all situations may be very few indeed.

Can Both Approaches Be Used at the Same Time?

A manager may feel that he (or she) is presently using both approaches. Each acts as a support for the other as well as a check on the validity of the technique. This assumption on his part doesn't tell when to use the one as opposed to the other. nor does it let him know how far to go with either approach. In addition, use of the two approaches could throw his staff into turmoil. Picture the department head as a person who sees his role as that of a decision-making administrator concerned primarily with the department's policies. This is a task he can carry out without consulting the other members of the staff beforehand. This type of action implies that authority is applied according to management principles obtained from a study of the theory of management. On the other hand, in certain situations the department head might find that he needs the considered opinions and support of his colleagues within the department. On these occasions he gives the rest of the staff an opportunity to vote on a particular issue. The department head, perhaps inadvertently, is developing an "oscillating theory" of administration by considering and abiding by the views and opinions of the various staff members.

> (Note: This reminds the writer of the anecdote where the husband says: "My wife and I get along fine. We agreed that I would make the "big" decisions, and she would make the "little" ones. It's odd, however. There haven't been many big decisions to make that I can recollect...")

Do you believe it is possible to use one approach at one time and the other on another occasion and achieve uniformly happy results? Could it be that this dilemma is the "root of all evil"? Is such a dual approach the reason we can speak about our "democratic administrative" approach and still realize that we are a long way from achieving this ideal?

Case Plan of Instruction Ideal for This Field

Other texts treating sport and physical activity management have typically reflected a more traditional approach. The author believes that the field should of necessity align itself with progressive trends. Textbooks that abound with "underlying principles" should not shape our programs unless there is solid evidence to support their employment in practice. Our field has not yet discovered whether management is an art or a social science; consequently, we have covered only superficially the "energizing" forces used by the manager. We have dealt largely with the subject matter—the knowledge and some of the skills by which the process must be learned.

The main idea of this volume is not to point out possible deficiencies in previous "traditional" approaches. It is to suggest how greatly the management process is governed by the personality of the administrator. It is just this problem of "human relations" that may rule out forever a completely scientific treatment of administration. The author believes that the best path to success as a manager is through the medium of the case method of learning about human relations and administration.

Selection 2
Learning by the Case Method

What is the objective of a course in administrative or managerial practice? The primary objective is undoubtedly to increase each student's capacity to work effectively with others. The ability to lead on many occasions, to follow in other situations, and to cooperate at all times is essential. You can be helped to develop a beneficial attitude and a point of view toward administrative practice. The case method approach will help to give you a frame of reference in which you can develop. In this way you will be actually preparing yourselves for positions of responsibility in the field of sport and physical activity. You will be working with others in a plan to accomplish objectives and aims that have been devised through group effort.

"Team Effort"

You who have had a level of experience in sport can realize much more fully than others that group effort means, literally, "team effort." A team can best achieve its goal by unselfish, cooperative play by each of its members. Each individual has to carry out his duties to the best of his ability. You may desire personal prestige and gain, but, above all, it is most desirable for you to make your own interests secondary, striving to do your share in the drive for eventual team victory.

Factual Knowledge Is Important

The importance of factual knowledge cannot be minimized. An administrator must possess a large store of facts about his work and must also realize where to find information. Such knowledge, however, is not the main attribute of a good administrator. The important qualities are the ability to work cooperatively with others; the ability to think and act responsibly; and the ability to provide an "atmosphere" where co-workers will have opportunities to work effectively and with true satisfaction as members of the group.

Developing a "Managerial Frame of Mind"

Students need to develop a "managerial or administrative frame of mind." This cannot be achieved by only hearing lectures, reading, and discussion of various assignments, although this method certainly gives some increase in understanding. Through the case method of instruction, student and instructor meet new "problematic situations" in management constantly. These situations cannot help but be characterized by facts, half-facts, and opinions.

If you hope to find "the answers" in this book on sport and physical activity management, you will be disappointed. You will find a certain number of opinions, which may be correct in those situations to which they apply. Your answer may be *an* answer, but you cannot state unequivocally that it is *the* answer. Mature administrators can recall the many problems they have encountered. Many of them may have studied selected "principles" of management in their undergraduate and graduate careers. How many times were they able later to lift these "principles" out of context and apply them directly to the problem at hand without considerable adjustment? How many of these principles were they forced to bypass because of the practical considerations of the moment? The manager may start action "according to the book," but what happens thereafter depends upon the many unforeseeable factors that always enter any situation.

A Supplement to Experience

Of course, the case method of teaching human relations and administration is not an infallible substitute for experience. But it does expose the student to a variety of cases taken from the field he/she is preparing to enter. As the group faces these concrete situations, it is the responsibility of the instructor to guide each member in such a way that he arrives at a solution by constantly examining and re-examining all the relevant facts that are known.

With this approach you are not asked what you believe about the importance of sport and physical activity in society or in the educational system. Answering from your background in a course on principles, you might say: "Competitive athletics under competent leadership should be an integral part of every school's educational program." Has such "experience" really helped you to act in a given situation? Consider the following example.

You are presented with an actual case situation where a particular school principal has made the statement that "athletics is all right in its place." Furthermore, this principal has control of the budget, and he tells the athletic director that no "regular school funds" are going to be diverted to an extra-curricular activity the beneficial result of which is questionable. To back his stand further, the principal knows that certain influential members of the school board agree with his position 100 per cent. Certain other relevant facts, half-facts, and opinions are made known to you about this school in question. Now, what do you think? If you were the athletic director, to whom would you turn for support? Would you resign on the spot? Not if you want another job... Would you begin to criticize the principal publicly at every opportunity? Would you try to curry favor with the chairman of the school board, whose son happens to be a second-string fullback on the football team? What can you do? One thing is certain: You cannot spout your principles of sport within physical activity education, or what chapter three of your sport management text said was the place of athletics in the secondary school. Furthermore, you can't "play God" and fire the principal summarily in order to clear the way for your plans.

No Fixed Formulas

A word of warning is necessary, particularly if you are beginning to believe that the case method approach to the teaching of management has merit. Possibly no other method of learning is more demanding of your time, effort, and interest. There are no ready-made general theories one can apply to all situations. A certain amount of confusion and frustration will often result from your efforts. The instructor, too, may have certain misgivings. You may ask, "What kind of a technique is this case method?"

After a few months of hard work-perhaps even sooner-you will begin to "see the light." Perhaps for the first time you will feel the satisfaction of independent, concrete, responsible thinking. You will realize that fixed formulas and established principles are next to useless in specific situations. What is generally needed in each situation, on the other hand, is a step-by-step pattern to bring the various factions at least partly into harmony so that some progress can be realized.

Instructor Needs Restraint

An instructor may find the need to exercise restraint, because he may "know the answers." That is, he may think he does because of his greater experience. It is difficult for an instructor steeped in the traditional pattern to realize that he can't fall into the trap of giving you the answer to the problem being discussed, because after all there probably isn't any *one* solution to it!

Two Main Purposes of a University

Let us approach the matter from a different tangent. It is generally accepted that the two main purposes of a university are teaching and research. That there should occasionally be a bit of conflict between these two divisions, with the university administrators in the middle, is inevitable. Faculty members sometimes feel that certain administrators are determining policies in such a way that it would seem as if deans and presidents were interested in only their own purposes. Conversely, administrators may complain that the faculty members are shortsighted if they don't realize that boards of governors, trustees, or regents actually decide the issues that in turn govern the actions of the administrators.

To narrow this problem down, it is probably true that there are relatively few research people on most university faculties who do not do any classroom teaching at all. In addition, research-minded professors do not usually make the best teachers, although this is not necessarily true. Conversely, the best teachers do not usually make ideal "researchers"; again, this is not a foregone conclusion.

A Third Category: The Manager

Between the researchers and the teachers there stands a third important category of university employee that has developed as universities have grown tremendously in complexity-the manager or administrator. Many universities choose their administrators, below the level of president, from among the ranks of successful teachers or researchers. *Strangely enough, it would appear that at times the administrator/manager is chosen because he or she has been on the staff for some time and has excelled at neither teaching nor research endeavor.*

The Best Method of Preparing Administrators

The thesis of this text is that administrators or managers can be best prepared by the case method of teaching. Certainly, they cannot become qualified for these important duties because of their eminence as teachers in the traditional pattern, where intelligent statements and "practical advice" are offered to the students for consumption. In addition, it is self-evident that research specialists generally are not interested in diverting their time from research pursuits to administrative work. Furthermore, it goes almost without saying that a person who has not excelled at either endeavor does not have much to offer unless he has a "gift" for dealing with people or has had special training. It could be that this latter individual might have just the sort of intelligence and personality that would lend itself to preparation through the case method approach for an administrative position. Of course, one would not recommend automatically that maladjusted "teachers" and "researchers" be drawn into administration.

All Are Administrators, But to Varying Degrees

No matter whether we are considering administration at the higher, intermediate, or lower levels of education, all faculty and staff members have managerial responsibilities to varying degrees. This is one more reason why the case method of teaching human relations and administration seems particularly good. It represents, the author believes, the best possible method of implementing the concept of "democratic administration" that was brought to the fore in this field in the twentieth century. In addition, we are recommending that it be implemented further in the twenty-first century!

Can the Delay Be Made Worthwhile?

Anyone who has made even a cursory study of the history of higher education on this continent realizes that the period of preparation for a manager, as well as for a teacher, has lengthened enormously within the past hundred years. For example, Dio Lewis offered the first ten-week course designed to prepare teachers of physical education in Boston in 1861. In some areas today, a secondary school specialist must have five years of preparation above grade twelve to be certificated. A few individuals desirous of bettering themselves take at least three but probably more years more of graduate study in order to acquire the doctorate. This lengthy period of professional preparation delays students from entering the field of education and earning a livelihood. The task of teachers in professional schools is to make this delay worthwhile for the most important person in the educational picture-the student. When consideration is focused on the professional preparation of managers, the MBA degree has become a sine-qua-non. How is the problem best handled in sport and physical activity management?

Traditional Approach Found Wanting...

Why can't those responsible for professional education simply choose prospective physical activity education teacher/coaches more carefully and then give them the knowledge, skills, and principles that experts have gathered and included in the many texts available? In principle this approach appears to have great merit for any position, but educational psychology has shown that mere lecturing to students does not prepare them to administer programs. (The same logic applies to those who would be managers.) For that matter, typical tests, term papers, curriculum syllabi, occasional brief discussions, trips to swimming pool filtration plants, or any of the various other devices employed have also failed to meet the need completely. Why is it that graduating professional students often approach their first positions with many misgivings?

It was probably such shortcomings that led to the introduction of student teaching and fieldwork experience into the curriculum of professional groundwork. These brief experiences help, but rarely do they give students the opportunity to think and to reason about managerial problems. Unfortunately, it is too wasteful of time and money for students to learn everything through the "school of hard knocks."

The Innate Urge to Give Advice

Many instructors have an innate urge to tell their juniors just what the score is. They have been "through the mill," and they want to tell students what they will encounter on the job. Consider the case of the young teacher who complains that the principal doesn't listen to his solution for a problem connected with scheduling. The instructor would generally suggest that this young man immediately either "talk turkey to the old bird" and let him know that he has some good ideas about this problem, or better still, suggest that the teacher "ad-prac" his way through the situation by praising the principal and then indirectly leading him to adopt the teacher's idea as his own. These thoughts may arise in the instructor's mind because people told him what was "right" in his early days. Perhaps the instructor's older friends have suggested ways of obtaining objectives by flattery and other devious means. Now, he wants to play the role of elder wise man.

Instructors Can't Tell How to Do It

Naturally, better teachers really do have a sound background of facts and experiences. They have faced most of the problems that students will encounter. Many times teachers do know what students should do or say in a given situation. In fact, the teachers must have been successful earlier in their methods of solving problems, or they probably would not be holding their present positions.

Nevertheless, the sad fact remains that no amount of theoretical or factual knowledge passed on by the competent teacher can give the student wisdom and judgment about how to act most effectively as an administrator or manager. You must develop and use your own knowledge, your own wisdom, and your own insight to penetrate a difficult situation involving human relations.

Let us assume that the young teacher mentioned above heeds the well-meaning advice and tells his principal clearly and strongly how the problem should be solved. What are the chances that the principal will accept the teacher's advice? Would you wish to wager on the chance that the recommendation is accepted?

Case Plan Emphasizes Democracy in Action

Instruction by the case method has a democracy-in-action flavor that can never be approached by the dictatorial method of "telling." You, as a member of the class, begin with the same facts as the instructor-the case. Your task is to analyze the known facts and arrive at a solution systematically. Each one in the class has exactly the same opportunity to offer a solution to the administrative problem area under discussion. All contribute to the development of a set of "principles" that will govern policy formation in this particular case. Actually, not even the instructor knows the answer. There is no set of answers that can be consulted. It is quite possible that, because of the way the case has been presented, or for some other reason, the best answer has not yet come to light.

Instructor Leaves Limelight

Through this method of instruction, a new set of personal relations precepts will appear to each participant. The spotlight does not fall on the teacher as the star performer. You begin to transfer your attention to all the other personalities in the group. In this class all are equals; hence, you must know what each is thinking. To achieve this there must be the chance for freedom of expression. Only through this means is there a hope of arriving at a mutually satisfactory solution. Because each student realizes that he/she is a part of this process, he thinks more and is anxious to "try his wings." You begin to realize that others will come up with suggestions that you had not even considered. You acquire experience in expressing your own thoughts to an extremely critical audience.

You may wonder just what the instructor does in this approach. There is no set formula for conducting classes by this method. He/she generally introduces the method and assigns the cases to be read for class discussion. He becomes an important member of the group. He asks pertinent questions. He offers his own considered opinions occasionally—perhaps when some class member requests his contribution. If the students have many logical arguments and opinions to offer, the instructor must be alert to understand and evaluate each contribution. He may be hearing certain reasoning about a particular problem for the first time. You, the student, are in a position where you don't necessarily have to parrot the instructor's views to get an "A" in the course. But you do have to justify your stand against all comers. If you fail to win your point, you must be ready to accept a compromise or even to act on the basis of majority opinion.

Students as Discussion Leaders

With a mature group the instructor may want to give individual students the opportunity to "chair" certain discussions. The instructor might even choose to sit outside of the "traditional circle."

(Note: Students face each other in many classes by sitting in a circle. In larger groups, the same effect may be accomplished by the use of swivel chairs in the classroom.)

Students who lead discussions for the first time tend to be quite "directive" or even dictatorial in their approach, but the rest of the class will usually not be denied. They tend to take over and make it a real group discussion. The chairperson should be careful to see that each person has a chance to express his opinion. Hand raising is often used to let the chairperson know that a person wishes to speak, although this may not be necessary in a small class.

Most Students Expect Answers

Most students have come to expect that the answers will be handed to them. This new approach will thus come as a shock. You may find that you have no background from which to draw certain material. In fact, the strain of such active thinking may be great, especially when your arguments rarely escape being challenged. On the other hand, you may find that group opinions do not always form readily. You may want to ask the instructor to give you his conception of the "correct answer" under such conditions.

Typical Student Undergoes Three Phases

The student new to the case method approach may undergo three clearly recognizable phases: First, he/she realizes his inability to think of all the suggestions that will come from his/her fellow students. He has read the case carefully and prepared his answers or solutions, perhaps in written form. Sometimes he types out the solution to a case on one page and lists the "currently useful generalizations" arising from this situation on another. To his surprise, in class he encounters a multitude of opinions and interpretations that he hadn't even considered.

About half way through the course, students can generally accept help from others in good grace. Realizing that they can't know it all, they draw more heavily on the ideas of others. Although competition for grades can be keen, no one should be worried about giving or receiving assistance.

If all progresses well, intelligent students should realize toward the end of the course that their instructor might think he has the answer, or he may truly seem to have the best answer. But what is most important, they understand that they are entitled to their own opinions, so long as they are ready to substantiate their facts and to argue their opinions logically. The aim in this approach, of course, is the development of an intelligent administrator or manager, a person capable of wise self-direction and ready to accept advice from his fellows without having to fall back on the authority of his position to achieve sound results.

Case Plan Not Perfect

Although great things can be expected from the case plan of instruction, it is far from perfect. There is a great difference between thinking about an administrative problem constructively and cooperatively on the one hand, and being responsible for a decision that may radically affect the success of an important program of physical activity education (including athletics) on the other. The author believes, however, that this approach is the best substitute for actual experience that has yet been devised. Understanding, judgment, and independent thought are the rewards to be gained from a careful application of this plan.

Importance of Class Atmosphere

The "atmosphere" in the class is all-important. This point cannot be stressed too much. It involves such intangibles as the relationship between you and the teacher. The instructor may quickly begin to call you by your first name. It is not necessary that you address him so familiarly. The main point is that you both feel that you are discussing a problem as equals. Only then will the student feel free to express all his ideas about a subject. Occasionally, generally when asked, the instructor will express his own ideas. Each time he does so, remember that his ideas are only those of one man analyzing a situation-albeit an intelligent, experienced observer.

Thus, you will learn to express your own ideas. Equally important, you will gain respect for the opinions of others. Everyone in the class, including the instructor, can't help but gain from this interaction.

Students Learn to Analyze

It is very important in this plan of instruction for you to learn how to analyze situations carefully and completely. Although some may do this automatically, many in the class will read through a case quickly and rather carelessly. Some may even wander far from what appear to the majority to be the central issues of a problem, but the instructor will ask 'leading" questions to keep the class on the right track.

Your instructor will probably ask you to "write up" cases of all types that you may have observed or experienced. This is extremely valuable experience in many ways. Perspective is developed which can be most helpful. In writing a case, you may give an over-all interpretation after the basic "reporting" has been finished. It is advisable to interpret the case from the standpoints of the various people actually involved in the situation. Such a case writing assignment is best concluded with a summary statement of your own proposed solution to the problem.

> Note: A good job of reporting is necessary for a good case.
> You should report what you have seen and heard, and no
> more. H you find the material interesting, quite probably
> others will be interested also. Develop a case logically and
> sequentially. You can never know or give all the facts.

The general complaint of beginning students is that they do not have enough facts to arrive at a reliable solution. This may be, but often you will get a different slant on the problem when your instructor inquires if you have really utilized those facts that you do have at hand.

Beware of "Story-Telling"

When you analyze a case, do not waste time in story telling. For oral recitation, memorization of the case does not necessarily help, because you may refer to the written facts of the case at all times. You could make such a reference in a regular life situation, so why not here? If you aren't prepared when the instructor calls on you for an opinion, he will quickly pass on to someone who wants to speak. Many instructors give grades for class participation, and a consistent lack of preparation will surely be noted. It makes little sense to offer an ill-considered opinion to cover up for poor preparation.

Some cases will have happened in such a way that definite stages are apparent. Chronological sequence of occurrences is usually very important in a report. After a preliminary analysis, it is possible to consider the relationships among the various participants in the case. At this point the class is ready to examine any strong attitudes or beliefs of the people involved as evidenced by their statements or actions. The group can also try to determine what changes have taken place in a pattern of incidents and what caused these changes to occur. Each student might then be ready to postulate his own solution to the problem—that is, if such a solution is possible. Don't be afraid to use your imagination at this point. It will often lead you to new interpretations of the facts that you had not previously thought of.

Subjective Opinions vs. Objective Facts

Keep in mind that you must judge between a subjective opinion and an objective fact as well as between relevant and irrelevant material. If a coach states, for example, that the athletic director was unreasonable to think that the team could get along with such poor equipment, you, as a careful analyst, must determine if the director really was being unreasonable. Could it be that the coach used poor judgment in making such a remark? When asked to penetrate more deeply into such statements, some cynics in the class may feel that time is wasted in such imaginative speculation. Gathering together the various possibilities and re-examining the fragmentary evidence in the situation may assemble into a pattern just the sort of material you will want to have at hand later, when facing an actual life situation.

The truism "things are never as simple as they seem to be" is at the heart of the case plan of instruction. Each person involved in an administrative problem is inescapably unique, for no two people see the same situation in exactly the same way. When you realize this, your own discernment will greatly improve. In addition, you will be on the way to a better understanding of human relations in this complex human world.

When a Case Is Not What It May Seem to Be

You may find it trying to realize that few cases are what they appear to be on the surface. Every student will analyze the problem through the "colored glasses" of his own background and present attitudes. One student may look at things as either black or white. In one case, the coach will be his fair-haired boy, while the principal is the "rat." Such a student's opinion is generally that if the principal is fired, everyone will live happily ever after. A second student may be accustomed to having the instructor think for him. If this student offers an opinion to which the instructor nods and smiles, he feels he has the right answer. Still a third student may be looking for the approval of his classmates. Instead of expressing what he really feels, he says what he thinks the class wants to hear. An occasional student will go to the other extreme, "wandering off into the night." At first, his feelings may be hurt when group opinion tends to force him back onto the well-lighted street of accepted fact. Of course, such a person may become stubborn and even disrupt the class. You must ask yourself whether students who appear to be going off on a tangent should be held in tight check.

Some Students Talk; Others Don't...

One of the facts that we discover upon beginning this method of instruction is that some students talk a great deal more than others.

Does this mean that these people are the most intelligent in the group? This is not necessarily so. Many times these students are only the ones who, by nature, tend to express themselves more than others. After the first test, you might be surprised to find that the person who spoke in class only when spoken to subsequently wrote the best paper. You might be further surprised to find that the student who was always ready with a quick answer has analyzed the test problem only superficially.

Each discussion simply cannot follow any specific pattern. There is no "pat" answer. Two groups discussing an identical case may decide on diametrically opposed solutions.

Practical Suggestions for the Student

1. Don't try to copy a friend's solution to a case simply because he is known as a good student.

2. Find out what the problems are before you try to give any answers.

3. Don't reject a classmate's idea summarily if you disagree. Don't accept his theory at once if you concur.

4. Work at developing your powers of perception and discrimination.

5. Develop a point of interest if it seems important to you.

6. Pay attention to what is said-it may prove worthwhile.

7. It is often easy to detect the biases of others; to be able to realize your own prejudices is most difficult.

8. If you feel discouraged and frustrated with the case approach, discuss your feelings frankly and fully.

9. Don't force the instructor to give an answer, just so that you will go away "happy."

10. When all else fails, read the case again.

Selection 3
Currently Useful Generalizations
for
Physical Activity Education
(including Sport)

The words "currently useful generalizations" may sound "anemic" in the description of what physical activity education is all about within education at all levels. However, it does seem realistic and pertinent to include here what we generally accept as "our" responsibility" within the overall educational program. Hence, you will find concise summaries (i.e., "currently useful generalizations") concerning the management or administration of physical activity education (including athletics).

If the tenor and essence of this material seems reasonable, generally speaking, the credit should go to many of the administrators working in this area whose experience and insight have enabled them to gather and report a significant body of knowledge. Any deficiencies that may seem apparent when you attempt to apply these "generalizations" to specific problems may be caused by this author's inability to reflect correctly what many leaders have said and written, or by the peculiarities of the particular situation to which you are trying to apply them. The following statements may therefore sound authoritative and definitive; hence, you must challenge them as you strive to apply them subsequently.

Consider the total physical activity education program including both intramural and extramural athletics. You may be able to suggest several additional categories, or to combine or eliminate some of the following areas that are recommended as a point of departure:

> Aims and Objectives
> Health and Safety Education (related)
> Physical Activity Education Classification
>   or Proficiency Tests
> The Required Program
> Intramural Athletics
> Interscholastic or Intercollegiate
>   Athletics
> Voluntary Physical Recreation

The Individual or Adaptive Program
Facilities and Equipment
Public Relations
General Administration
Evaluation

Aims and Objectives

The determination of aims and objectives seems basic. A philosophy of life should coincide with a philosophy of education. Thinking should be logical and consistent, and these beliefs should not conflict too much with practice in physical activity education (including athletics). Professional educators in this area should be operating on the basis of the "currently useful generalizations" for which they stand. If one calls principles "generalizations," this does not mean that he or she does not believe anything. It does mean that he/she will base actions taken according to what appears to be best at the moment.

> (Note: for the remainder of this section to avoid awkwardness, I will use "he" instead of "she", but I trust the reader will understand that I am not thereby "downgrading" in doing so.)

It is most often practical to work from specific objectives toward general aims. Expediency may cause a physical activity educator to sidetrack some of his beliefs, but this does not mean that he must perforce lose sight of what he believes to be ultimately right. It is difficult for those in the field to agree on one basic philosophic stance to cover everything. Obviously, there will always be at least several schools of thought. Although various beliefs should be expressed in a substantial way, truly definitive philosophies of physical activity education (including athletics) are rare.

Although physical activity education has indeed made a solid effort to achieve a stronger scientific base, science and philosophy still have complementary roles to play in aiding the field to find its proper place in the educational system. Philosophy considers the basic problems of physical activity education (including athletics) in a systematic fashion. Philosophical thinking enables the professional worker to view his field as a whole. He will not see himself merely as an athletic coach, a physical conditioner, an organizer of intramural sports, or an athletic director.

Philosophy helps the professional to fashion a mental image of what his field should be. It is prospective in the sense that it forms a vanguard; it should lead actual practice. A philosophy, of course, must be practical, or it would be worthless. An instrumental philosophy would necessarily imitate science in part, but only as it serves as a plan for action. *Science describes a field as it exists; philosophy pictures it as it should be.* Philosophy is an excellent complement to science; it reaches and points toward the world of tomorrow.

A philosophy of physical activity education, typically as a part of an over-all educational philosophy, has a relation to the general field of philosophy. A prevalent view is that which holds a philosophy of life basic to a philosophy of education. To the former is assigned the establishment of fundamental beliefs; to the latter, their application to a specific field. A basic philosophy outlining specific aims and objectives could help physical activity education greatly and in many ways. This is true because there are now many serious conflicts dangerously splitting the field within education and "outside" in society at large. Yet all factions might readily agree that it is important for the administrator of physical activity education to strive to form a sound philosophy.

Health and Safety Education (Relationship to)

Physical activity education by its very nature is intimately related to the health and safety education program of an educational institution. Typically there are three aspects to the latter as follows:

Health Services. Health service today implies determining the student's health status, informing parents of any defects that exist, educating parents and offspring in the prevention of common defects, aiding the teacher to detect symptoms of illness, and helping to correct defects which are remediable.

It took many years for boards of education to realize that schools must be concerned with more than illiteracy. The new educational era demands that the school take unto itself practically all of the child's problems. Today, if conditions are ideal, the physician, medical specialist, nurse, dentist, psychologist, psychiatrist, nutrition expert, janitor, and teacher all have a part in the over-all job of keeping the child healthy.

Boards of education are increasingly taking the responsibility for health services. There are, however, many civic leaders who favor board of health control in this area. Cooperation between the two boards seems advisable on many occasions, but such an arrangement usually has its weaknesses. The fact that it is quite difficult for either agency to set policy which encroaches on the other's sphere of operation indicates that the responsibility for the health of the child should not be divided at this level.

"Medical inspection" was the now-archaic term formerly used for the medical examination of today. What is the school's responsibility for health appraisal? What type of medical examination should there be? Who should look after the correction of remediable defects? What is the relation of psychological services to the school health program? Who should maintain the health and accident records? What is the best plan for emergency care?

The medical examination itself serves more functions than is generally realized. In addition to diagnosis of defects and subsequent notification of parents, the school health authorities should strive to secure correction of remediable defects by careful guidance of the children involved. Each child must be helped to develop a scientific attitude toward bodily ailments. Having established the importance of the medical examination, ask your some questions about the actual examination the children receive. Is the parent invited to be present so that the physician can explain the results? Is the teacher present to learn more about the child for future guidance? Is the examination sufficiently complete and detailed? Too often, physicians are so rushed in the performance of their duties that the child receives only a more-or less perfunctory check-up.

It cannot be argued that a carefully maintained health record is superfluous in the development of a child. To be sure, limited budgets may restrict the adequacy of any such record. On the other hand, it is extremely important that the child receive the services of various educational experts. To get a complete picture of the child, youth, or young adult many things must be known about his environment, disease record, scholastic ability, social adjustment, and health practices. Health services should be involved with the appraisal, correction, and protection of children and youth throughout their years in the educational system.

Health Instruction. Health instruction is the second of three subdivisions of health and safety education. There are many questions to be answered here. Should health instruction classes be scheduled separately? What should a course in health include? What about the introduction of controversial subjects such as sex education? What should be the role of the physical educator in the field of safety education? Should driver education be included? Who should teach health-the physical educator, the health education specialist, a physician, or the science teacher? What attention should be given to mental health? Is a health coordinator necessary in a school?

The health instruction class has been a perennial problem. Facts about health have become a considerable part of the knowledge of how to live. Most important, of course, is that health education should be an influence in favor of "clean living." Although people know that regular medical checkups are advisable, they usually maintain their bodies in much poorer condition than they do their cars. Most people have their cars' oil changed regularly; yet, they insist upon waiting for pain before going to the physician.

Down through the years, health instruction has generally been taught somewhat poorly. Just as in the case of earlier "physical training," parents realized that health courses were, in many instances, next to useless. Even today they must still be convinced that most physical activity education teachers are anxious to incorporate the modem problem-solving approach into the teaching of health. Here is one area where the case method of instruction might be employed to advantage. Health instruction is more than just the teaching of principles and facts of healthful living; it is more than merely drawing the various systems of the body on the blackboard and explaining them superficially. Health education should have as its goal the integration of this book-knowledge with actual living achievement. This is no mean task-to motivate children and youth to use the facts to help them live at their best in order to be able subsequently to serve most.

Healthful School Living. Healthful school living itself can be subdivided into three categories: the conditions of the school environment, the conditions of the classroom experience, and the conditions of school organization. With so much school construction in all stages of development, the school building itself demands serious consideration. The taxpayer and parent must be shown that the demands of health and those of architectural beauty do not inevitably clash. And if they do, the students themselves should have first priority. The school plant must be both hygienic and beautiful if the student is to have the best educational opportunities. Although plans should be made for schools to be close to the geographical center of population, due thought should also be given to adequate size of building and surrounding area as well as to hygienic environment and the student's safety.

Conditions of the classroom experience are important, also. And what about the problem of discipline? Should the teacher dominate the students by sheer will power, or should the children be helped to develop their own standards of behavior? The end of all discipline would seem to be intelligent self-direction. Should such factors as undue fatigue, success and failure, noise and excitement, "sedentariness", the hygiene of reading, and individual differences be considered?

The actual conditions of school organization play an important role in healthful school living. Is there a proper balance in the school among work, play, rest, and the taking of nourishment? For example, do we realize the educational potentialities of the school lunch by considering the adequacy of the cafeteria, time allowed for eating, economics of the project, student participation in conduct rules, and health supervision of the lunchroom employees?

Is the course curriculum properly divided, keeping in mind that the students are more efficient mentally in the morning? What supervision is there over the health of the individual teacher? Should the general tone of the child's day be "hurry"? Modem society is so rushed that a conscious effort should be made to slow down the daily tempo of the school program.

Physical (Activity) Education Classification (or Proficiency Tests)

After the examining physician has informed the physical activity education teacher if the child is healthy, almost healthy, in need of adaptive work, or fit for only passive exercise, the teacher should test and classify the normal individual according to the objectives of the school's program. Testing and measuring are necessary in order to prove to administrators, supervisors, students, and the public that many students are physically and recreationally "illiterate." These tests provide classifications for the following purposes:

> (1) To serve their individual needs.
> (2) To promote fair competition between individuals and groups.
> (3) To facilitate instruction.
> (4) To assemble individuals of like interests as well as of like abilities.
> (5) To insure continuity in the program from year to year.

A battery of physical activity education classification tests should include items that the department considers that most students should be able to pass within the time allotted by the school to physical activity education requirements. Every effort should be made to hold the tests used to the desirable standards of validity, reliability, objectivity, simplicity, standardization of procedure, duplicate forms, and "worthwhile ness". Certain test items are often considered to be of greater importance to the development of the individual than others. If the student fails any part or all of the battery, he or she might be required to select activity in the order that the department feels is best for him. For example, if a young man failed tests in swimming, body mechanics, motor fitness, leisure skills, and self-defense, he might be required to correct these deficiencies in the order that the department of physical activity education deems best. A similar battery of tests with differing emphases should be constructed for girls and women with priorities determined according to the department's stated philosophy. It is recommended that this philosophy should reflect the thinking of the best leadership in the field, educational administration, the staff of the physical activity education department, the parents, and the students themselves.

It might be wise to permit the incoming student to begin with some form of physical recreational activity, so that he will develop good attitudes concerning the continuing value of this type of activity. It is suggested that the activity he chooses coincide with some deficiency demonstrated by the classification tests.

The department should consider classification and proficiency tests in the following categories:

    (1)   Cardio-vascular efficiency.
    (2)   Age-height-weight.
    (3)   Motor fitness.
    (4)   Body mechanics.
    (5)   Self-defense
    (6)   Aquatics & life saving
    (7)   Dance
    (5)   Skills and appreciations.
    (6)   Health and sports knowledge.

Obviously, the work of the administrator/manager of physical activity education has only begun when tests have been selected and administered. When the tests have been carefully scored, rated, and appraised, the program needs of all the students can be evaluated. Testing can also aid in measuring the progress of the students and in grading.

The Basic Required Program

The conditioning program. If the student has not met the standards of the cardio-vascular and motor fitness tests, it is necessary to raise the general level of condition. Forcing an individual to follow a long, conditioning program, including such exercises as calisthenics, pulley-weight manipulation, rope climbing, and running, may frighten him away from physical activity education for many years to come. On the other hand, allowing the student to engage in any sport he desires may result in a continuation of the ineffectiveness displayed in the classification tests. It would seem logical to follow the middle road by selecting a combination of activities from each of these categories. The emphasis should be placed on motivating the student to participate with interest in all the phases of a complete physical activity education program based on sound health and safety education principles.

The student's needs may be met best through the following activities:

(1) General body-conditioning: through exercises, weight training, jogging, and swimming, and a course in body mechanics (if needed).
(2) Aquatic activities stressing the development of an all-round ability in the water, including distance swimming, life-saving, water safety, stunts and skills, and water wrestling.
(3) Tumbling and stunts.
(4) Wrestling and self-defense instruction.
(5) Sports participation of an individual, dual, and team nature stressing the acquisition of individual skills.

A conditioning program for a definite period of, say, six to twelve weeks might include activity in at least three phases of the above.

The sports instructional program. A student showing a fair level of conditioning in the cardio-vascular and motor fitness tests might be referred immediately to sports instruction, but only for, perhaps, the first six weeks of the school year. With excellent instruction, interest can be aroused. In subsequent units, sports instruction can be coordinated with the other areas of instruction in which the student may have been shown to be deficient.

In the sports instructional program it is wise to schedule a yearly plan for all the various individual, dual, and team sports to be offered. A unit in a sports activity should be a planned sequence of learning and should take from twelve to thirty lessons for completion, depending on the difficulty of the activity. In planning a teaching unit, consideration should be given to (1) objectives, (2) learning experiences, (3) subject matter, (4) instructional methods, (5) a list of equipment and facilities needed, and (6) adequate means of evaluation.

The elective program. The elective program is actually a part of the physical activity education requirement. In this way it differs from the voluntary physical recreation program. "Elective" means that a student who has met all the standards set for the required program is permitted at some stage of the academic year (or perhaps for his total course) to select from suggested activities a physical activity education plan to suit best his needs and interests. Credit should be given for this activity, and definite instruction, supervision, and guidance should be offered if it is to be considered a regular part of the course of study. If possible, the student should meet with an adviser to help determine the objectives of his program.

> Note: A department should give consideration to the question of a student maintaining proficiency in certain phases of the entire required program over the years (e.g., maintaining a minimum level of cardio-vascular conditioning).

Intramural Athletics/Extramural Competition

A fine intramural athletics program is most important in the achievement of a balanced overall program in physical activity education. Intramural athletics has improved significantly at the college and university level over the years. However, at the high school level the surface has barely been scratched. More help is needed in this area to fulfill the educational responsibility adequately. If the average student has a sound experience in competitive sports, he is likely to have a favorable "image" of physical activity education. High school boys and girls are the "public of tomorrow" that will decide whether physical activity education is worthy of financial backing at all levels of the educational system.

Accepting as a premise the fact that competitive athletics is a desirable part of the total program, the intramural program provides recreational opportunity for leisure as well as another chance for the student to develop social contacts and group loyalties. As a result, the student should develop an appreciation of, and a lasting interest in, physical recreation. Healthful exercise and organic development must be considered as specific objectives.

> Note: Program administrators should keep in mind that "extramural athletic competition" may be desirable on selected occasions within the aegis of the Intramural Program. This would be separate and distinct from the varsity program.

Interscholastic and Intercollegiate athletics

Interscholastic and intercollegiate athletics, along with intramural athletics, are integral to the total program. Under ideal conditions *(i.e., if all students have the opportunity to take part in intramural sport)*, qualified athletes should have the opportunity for such fine educational experiences. The chairperson or head of the department should be responsible for the program that should be financed by institutional funds. It is recommended that all gate receipts be placed into the general school or college fund.

Unfortunately, there have been many problems in this aspect of the program to harass the administrator/manager. What is the present status of the inter-school program? Are more stringent controls needed? What should be the principal's or dean's relationship to athletics? Are the health and safety of the participants being fully considered? Is insurance coverage adequate for any emergency? How should athletics be financed? What about the use of radio and television in athletics? What purpose do tournaments serve? Should a student be declared ineligible for competition because of poor grades in scholastic work? Should similar athletic competition be encouraged for girls and young women? Should any interschool competition be encouraged at the elementary and junior high levels? At the university level, what about professionalism, the level of gambling, and the role of alumni? How should the overall program be evaluated? These are but a few of the questions that must be answered.

Because participation in athletics is entirely on an elective basis, it is actually a part of the program of voluntary recreation. Class credit in physical activity education should be given for team participation, however, but this should not take the place of the existing requirement. Team participation should never take the place of body mechanics instruction, self-defense instruction, aquatics, etc., unless duplication is involved (e.g., a member of the swimming team should not be required to take basic aquatics training).

A student who falls below the normally acceptable academic standards of the institution might be asked to discontinue athletics just as he might be asked to discontinue other "extracurricular" activities. Each student's case should be considered individually.

All sports are "major" sports to the individuals taking part in them. Each sport offered should have a varsity team with sound coaching. In colleges and universities freshman teams should be operated with limited schedules involving very little traveling. This recommendation is based on the orientation needs of the freshman year.

Organized practice should be held only during the season in which the sport is played. However, for reasons of expediency and because football is a "unique phenomenon," spring practices in that sport may be held on the college/university level. However, they should be limited to a maximum of twenty sessions.

Coaches should be regular members of the school, college, or university faculty, with salaries and tenure similar to those of other teachers. Because of their ability as teachers in the sports they coach, the coach in higher education should be involved as an instructor for these sports in the major program of the physical activity education department.

Voluntary Physical Recreation

This is the area in which the department can make a most lasting contribution. "Recreation assists man to become an artist in living." Physical recreation is that facet of the total recreational offering that relates primarily to the department of physical activity education and is so popular with children and young people. Physical activity educators have a responsibility to encourage students to develop healthy attitudes toward other areas of recreation-social recreational interests communicative recreational interests, aesthetic and creative recreational interests, and "learning" recreational interests. Often the "motor moron" is ridiculed, although he may be the class "brain" and an accomplished musician to boot. However, this individual is no more to be ridiculed than the proficient athlete who may be tongue-tied or confused when he is addressing a group. Both of these types are "more to be pitied than censured." Young people such as those described have both been exploited to a degree by either over-zealous, protective parents or thoughtless coaches. If "intelligent self-direction" is the aim of education, how truly uncultured both these young people are!

> Note: This judgment may seem a bit harsh, and it is possible that young people may not be happy at first exploring other facets of the recreational kaleidoscope. They can be helped to widen their activities, however, by example as well as by precept. When the athlete sees the coach enjoying himself in another sport or attending an art exhibit or a concert, he is likely to follow suit. However, teachers are often so busy providing recreational opportunities for others that they don't take time to enjoy recreation themselves.

How should recreation education (i.e., preparation for future leisure involvement) be interpreted? Is recreation entertainment or part of the educational curriculum? What type of planning is needed to adapt school facilities for recreational purposes?

The Individual or Adaptive Program (Special Exercise Prescription)

This phase of physical activity education is perhaps the most neglected. There is a definite need for this type of remedial work, although those who "control the purse strings" and/or administrators often do not feel it is important enough to merit a sufficient appropriation. This activity was once called medical gymnastics, and subsequently corrective exercise. The latter was shortened to correctives. This specialized area of physical activity education may well be called the individual program, the adapted program, adaptive physical education, or special physical education.

Earlier studies show a very low percentage of normal posture among students. A very large percentage have rounding of the shoulders, while more than half of them have increased antero-posterior spinal curvature. There is an ongoing need for body mechanics instruction and corrective exercise. If physical activity educators do not help this situation in the formative years, the situation becomes almost hopeless toward the end of the high school experience. Obviously, this task is a matter that should be handled in a cooperative manner by physicians and physical activity educators.

Directors' ideas of health and correction are frequently very limited. Nevertheless, every administrator should recognize definitely what movements, techniques, and skills in their departments may have deleterious effects. They should remember that upwards of 75 percent of their students have faults in posture and consequently are using "bodily machines" that are out of correct alignment. The result is slow injury to joints, ligaments, and muscles. Hence, a basic need arises for fundamental corrective positions for all activities.

Even the posture of athletes is bad. Coaches and teachers should explain to athletes that their performance can be improved through normal joint alignment. This is, of course, most important at the elementary school level, where such rapid growth and "excessive discrepancies" in structural relationships occur. It should also be stressed that in addition to the possible benefits in health and physical efficiency, one's appearance will also be improved through normal joint alignment. From what has been said, it should be evident that the field of physical activity education must either do something about body mechanics and adaptive work or inform educational administrators and the public that it cannot do anything, or hasn't been allowed, or hasn't the facilities, or isn't interested in this phase of the work.

Facilities and Equipment

The question of adequate facilities and equipment for physical activity education is often a vexing one. Recommendations made in the past were often overlooked or modified to the point where the resultant facilities are not adequate for the task. Physical activity educators do not know all the answers about facilities and equipment. They could not possibly understand all of the engineering and architectural problems involved. They do understand, however, the problems they are likely to encounter after the gymnasium or the pool has been in use for some time. The task seems to be one of developing ways of forwarding such information to the attention of the architects involved in the planning.

Communities face almost insuperable odds in their attempts to finance education. This means that physical activity educators should be careful to avoid demands for unreasonable size in new gymnasia, locker rooms, and other facilities. With the tremendous growth in the school population, however, the needs cannot be underestimated, as these essential parts of a school building are going to be in use for a long time. Careful study and close coordination are necessary to insure that the public's money is spent to best advantage. When communities are short of classroom space, swimming pools that are going to be called "lakes" or gymnasia the size of airplane hangars are out of the question. Economy and adequacy are two words that may cause conflict unless the needs of physical activity education (including athletics) are made known in such a way that all concerned will appreciate the problems.

The question of combining an auditorium and a gymnasium is a perplexing issue. "Gymtoria" are certainly better than nothing, but in the final analysis they are not completely practical. Why the physical activity education program, on the one hand, or that generally carried on in the auditorium on the other, should suffer from interruption is a question that is difficult to answer. Supplying both facilities costs a great deal of money, but formal education should not have to get along with inadequate facilities. If physical activity educators work constantly to make their programs truly worthwhile, and sound public relations are carried out, the public is given a better idea of what the field is trying to accomplish. Under such circumstances, the money necessary to do the job should be forthcoming sooner or later.

Greater care seems to be needed in purchase and care of equipment. Money is easily wasted in poor planning and improper care of equipment. Equipment should be purchased locally to the greatest extent possible with the business being shared among the sporting goods stores in the locality. Asking for the submission of "tenders" is time-consuming, but such an effort to standardize equipment purchasing is highly desirable. A program should use quality equipment; yet, dealers should not be asked to forego a fair mark-up when they solicit school business. Professional physical activity educators should not expect "hand-outs" or prejudicial treatment simply because they control large equipment purchases.

A good equipment man is invaluable to a high school, college, or university. Careful storage of equipment is nothing more than common sense and good business. Proper procedures for the control and issuance of expensive equipment are highly desirable.

Public Relations

If this is an era of "new conservatism" because of the overall economic situation, physical activity educators must redouble their efforts to improve relations with the public. People are influenced more by actions than by what a group says it is trying to accomplish. Physical activity educators must be able to prove that children and young people are being helped to lead more effective lives through their participation in physical activity education. Although equipment and facilities in this area are at least as costly as those for any other subject area, the public will not complain if it is given full value for its tax dollar.

Although teachers and coaches are busy with their many duties, they should take the time to concern themselves with public relations. Very few people are aware of the aims of modern physical activity education. Physical activity educators (including coaches) still face "aristocratic irresponsibility" on the part of traditionalists who would relegate them to the "frill" category. The public should know how much money is spent on intramural athletics for the many, as opposed to how much goes for interschool and/or intercollegiate athletics for the few. At the same time, the gate receipts of major sports should not be slighted. This money is a great help and is often used to finance intramural programs.

Continuous, reliable, responsible public relations will develop an informed public that will not mutter about "fads" and "frills." The administrator/manager of the physical activity education program should know what is news in his area and then make certain that it is presented to the various media in an interesting manner. Sports writers are allies in this venture; their influence is very great. The coach must be willing to devote some of his time to public speaking and must be adequately prepared when he speaks. A few basic talks about the various phases of the overall physical activity education program, including athletics, can be made to stretch a long way, but they must be developed with an eye to presenting the content of the message in the most entertaining manner.

Exhibitions and demonstrations of physical prowess and skill have been used often as public relations devices. Generally, these techniques are excellent, but they can be artificial and quite formal. To some, children must move like robots to show parents and the public that something is being accomplished in physical education periods. When this type of presentation takes place even some physical activity educators lose their sense of perspective. Rather than giving such stylized demonstrations, they might well present the actual teaching of the techniques that lead to proficient performance. This is most interesting to parents, since it informs them of what happens in daily classes. Despite the various devices that are employed to further public relations, perhaps the best means of satisfying parents is to show them that their children are receiving as much individual attention as possible, and that they are progressing. A satisfied, happy student is the best "broadcasting station" that has yet been encountered.

Professional Preparation of the Physical Activity Educator/Coach

This topic, of course, is the primary task of the university teacher, but elementary and secondary schoolteachers and administrators are experiencing the results of the product that is being produced by the professional courses at the college or university. When deciding upon course changes, university professional educators may take a narrow approach. It is necessary to study (1) the past development, (2) the actual job situation teachers are going to face, and (3) the society in which teachers will live in order to get the realistic picture necessary to the development of sound curricula.

What is a physical activity educator? In undergraduate and graduate work there has appeared to be some confusion. In many facets of professional preparation, however, physical activity education is setting a desirable pattern for teachers in other subjects to follow. Many areas still need attention, however.

First, the status of the major student in physical activity education/kinesiology must be raised in the minds of the public and other teachers. By and large, physical activity education majors will need a broader educational background. This deficiency shows up in many ways. This problem has developed partially because there is too much knowledge and skill to be mastered within four undergraduate years.

Second, ways must be discovered to bring the people involved in various specialties within the field into a closer relationship. "A house divided against itself cannot stand." All professionals can help this situation by working to promote greater unity within the profession.

A third problem is that of "passing courses" just to graduate. The traditional subject-matter approach to learning has sometimes stifled initiative. The professional student takes a set number of courses and goes to college for a required number of years. Upon graduation, the "teacher" or "program administrator" is presumably sufficiently educated and competent to engage in his profession. A "competency approach" would help to eliminate the ineffectual, repetitive teaching that many standard professional courses have been charged with offering. It is important to develop a more effective way to measure teaching/managing ability as determined by specific competencies. These competencies should be developed through selected experiences with subject matters as resource areas.

Because of the complexity of the total field, many relationships within the field are unclear. What is the relationship between physical activity education and school recreation? Must physical activity education leave adaptive physical education to the field of physical therapy outside of the educational environment? Where does school health and safety education fit in? Health education is too important to leave in the hands of the busy physical activity educator/coach along with numerous administrative responsibilities. Should there be recreation specialists in the school systems to supervise *all* the so-called extra-curricular activities? Where do athletics belong anyhow? Why should the department of physical activity education below university level make decisions about athletic matters when the entire school is concerned? What about the use of coaches who aren't qualified physical activity educators? Can one person meet all of the foregoing responsibilities and many more within the school, college, and university, or should there be continuing efforts to promote even further specialization?

Many people in the public seem to believe that anyone with a good personality, a typical educational background, and some excellent sports skill can teach physical activity education. There is no real need for him or her to study in the areas of anatomy, physiology, kinesiology, physiology of exercise, psychology, tests and measurements, and adaptive exercise. The teacher/coach should simply keep them busy, manage affairs of various kinds, have some forward-looking ideas, and develop an overall first-class program. Physical activity educators simply must decide if such a casual, slipshod approach will yield the increased status many seem to want.

Lastly, there needs to be a fuller understanding of "democratic administration." What departmental decisions should be shared? Should a department head go along with decisions of the total staff? Can administrators superimpose their will upon others and achieve optimum results? Staff members who have been allowed to grow and develop in an atmosphere where democratic spirit prevails have an esprit de corps that students will find contagious. People are great imitators, and physical activity education graduates tend to follow the prevailing pattern of their undergraduate institutions.

General Administration

General administration is a sketchy area, a catchall for problems that do not fit logically into any of the other subdivisions in this selection. Administration or management of any educational program is the responsibility of the personnel involved in conducting the program. In the larger community of persons, there will be people who are interested in, provide support for, and ultimately approve or disapprove of the program itself.

Depending on how the task of an administrator is conceived, it can be simple or complex. If an administrator or manager is "the boss," matters will be quickly expedited. However, there may be a significant staff turn–over. On the other hand, if staff members are regarded as co-workers, much time may be consumed in discussing this or that phase of the program. However, in the latter situation the staff will be happier and may thus do a better job. On balance, there appears to be a logical middle path between dictatorship and anarchy that will in the final analysis result in optimum staff growth.

Relationship to the Teaching
and Recreation Professions

Most people feel unable to devote sufficient time to carrying out their responsibilities in the many professional organizations whose functions often · appear to overlap. Many teachers have failed to fulfill their obligations here, thus making the burden heavier on those who are more conscientious. Professionals in the field of physical activity education (including athletics) must take care not to forget their fundamental responsibility to the teaching profession as a whole. Allegiance is owed to the National Education Association, as well as to the American Association for Health, Physical Education, Recreation, and Dance. To promote the goals of general education, as well as to secure higher status for physical activity education, a much greater effort should be made in this area of professional service.

What about the relationship between physical activity education and the recreation profession? Cooperation among the various areas of recreation, parks, physical activity education, and athletics is highly desirable. The strength that can be gained from unity is enormous. Yet, often these groups appear to be "fighting for the use of the same bodies." The physical activity educator should not be *competing* with the recreation profession but there will be overlap in the area of s-called physical recreation.

If there are sharp differences between the position of physical activity educator and that of recreation superintendent, a solid effort to determine a working relationship can be mutually beneficial. And what about the concept of the community school? This and many other questions wait to be answered through cooperative effort. The following analogy may help to clarify the entire problem. Both professionals are playing on the same team! The physical activity educator takes his turn as the pitcher quite early in the game, but not before the recreation director "pitches" to the preschool child. Sometimes the physical activity educator is batted out of the box very soon. In many elementary schools he never gets beyond the warm-up stage. Under normal circumstances, the recreation director—to continue with baseball jargon—must pitch from the fourth inning on in this game that includes each "player's entire life." Neither physical activity educator nor recreation director can forget that there are eight representatives of other fields on this ball club-adult education, commercial recreation, private agencies, and others. Look to them for support and guidance. The status of the two professions, the physical activity educator as a professional educator with management responsibilities, and the recreation director as a professional person who manages also, will grow as the worth of the overall program increases.

Evaluation

Many respected educators still say that there "is so little for the mind" in modern education, because they believe that misguided Deweyites hold the fort. Careful scrutiny of school programs might give the opposite impression: "There is 'far less for the body' in schools, colleges, and universities. Every year classification and proficiency tests indicate that students generally are woefully weak, misshapen, and uncoordinated. Evaluation is that aspect of the "subject matter" physical activity education where many professionals falter. What is there to measure? If measurements were taken, whom would it influence? Only in relatively few schools are physical activity education grades figured in with "academic" averages.

Is physical activity education an art, a social science, or a pure science? At present, it doesn't fit neatly into any category. The field was once one of the liberal arts, but in the Middle Ages it was torn from this lofty perch. Physical activity education appears to have deep roots in all three of the above areas depending on the angle from which it is viewed. One group stresses that it belongs to the humanities, because the aim there is to help young people achieve certain attitudes and appreciations that will enable them to lead richer, fuller lives.

A second faction will say that physical activity education has a great role to play in the social sciences-that is, students are helped to acquire desirable personality traits through participation in various types of physical education activities. There is, certainly, a concern with society as a group of interrelated, interdependent people, but it is doubtful whether it is wise to be affiliated with the humanities in the sense that the field would serve chiefly as a discipline and as an instrument of factual knowledge only.

Those who emphasize the scientific aspects of the program largely are anxious to gather as much systematized knowledge as possible through all possible avenues and types of research. Along with this, of course, there must be continual borrowing from mathematics and the physical sciences as well as psychology. The present trend seems to be to make progress through statistics (i.e., proving what is *right* through a coefficient of correlation). Certainly there must be borrowing from everywhere possible in order to get the best possible answers...

Immediate concern about a higher place for physical activity education in the curriculum hierarchy may help, but the aim should be to raise the physical fitness standards of all students–and thereby ultimately that of all citizens. Education "through the physical" is the correct slogan (and goal) so long as rugged, healthy bodies for boys, girls, men, and women are the end result. The development of physical attributes belongs uniquely to the field of physical activity education. This should never be forgotten!

For Consideration and Discussion

As an exercise, it is recommended that two students each make a 10-minute presentation, one telling to what extent his high school lived up to the characterization here of what might be considered a fine program of physical activity education and athletics, while the other explains the inadequacies of the program he/she experienced. Then a third student should be selected to conduct a short class discussion about the topic.

Selection 4
A Case Method Approach to Decision-Making
for Sport and Physical Activity Managers

The objective here is to provide the prospective sport and physical activity manager with information and a learning experience that will help to develop an understanding of one approach to decision-making. Broadly speaking, such understanding includes:

(1) defining the problem or issue that should be resolved (including whether one or more ethical issues is present);

(2) considering the possible alternative courses of action;

(3) making a decision as to which alternative is best (everything considered);

(4) implementing the decision in the most effective and efficient manner possible; and

(5) evaluating the results of the decision after a reasonable period of time has elapsed.

Specifically, the approach recommended for experimentation is an adaptation–based on long experience–of what is generically called the Harvard case method (or technique) of decision-making.

All creatures on earth, human and non-human, have been making decisions since the evolutionary process began. A problem arose and a decision had to be made–e.g., fight, run, or hide. A choice was made according to certain alternatives that apparently were present in the problematic situation. As social life became most complex, the decision-making process also became highly complicated as well. For example, what are the recommended steps that might be taken as an individual seeks to make a rational decision? Also, what relationship do decisions have to the manager's value system? And where do (or should) emotions enter into the decision-making process? Further, can we establish a rough classification system for the various types of decisions (e.g., routine decisions), and under what conditions are decisions made (i.e., degree of risk)? Finally, what techniques have proven to be useful and valuable in the decision-making process?

An extensive body of literature on management theory and practice has developed since 1900. Management thought and theory has been characterized by steadily increasing complexity with the result that we now have what may be characteristically called a "management theory jungle." One of the several schools of thought that have been identified historically within this "morass" views management's primary function as decision-making. If decision-making is so important, the manager's task is accordingly to gather as much information as possible about a subject or problem at hand and make decisions based on an analysis carried out with the best qualitative and quantitative techniques available. In essence, the latter of these two (quantitative techniques) is what was called operations research earlier before and during the World War II era of the twentieth century. Since then there has been support for use of the title "management science" thereby aligning the field with the so-called social sciences.

Research has shown that human behavior in organizational settings manifests many similarities as one moves from educational institution, to retail store, to hospital, to welfare agency, or even to military unit. The evidence points to formal organizations exerting similar influence on the individuals functioning within their boundaries. The status hierarchy, for example, tends to cause dysfunctional effects wherever it appears. The resultant feelings emanating from satisfying and dissatisfying work are remarkably similar, also. Conflict between line and staff members of an organization erupts in the same manner, and this is especially true when subordinates have greater (or exclusive) knowledge and accompanying professional or technical efficiency than their hierarchical superiors. Admittedly, recent research suggests, and often recommends, newer types of organizational structures, but the bureaucratic organization and the types of individuals it "spawns," are still preponderantly operative.

If the above thought holds true, and the evidence is pointing that way, it can be argued that organizations sponsoring physical activity education, including sport competition and physical recreation are influenced by the same confluence of organizational and psychological variables that prevail in the other organizations cited above. This means that the decision-making process, and the manager's behavior as a decision-maker, function in similar "living organisms" where people (1) pursue goals; (2) seek personal identification; (3) encounter opposition; (3) react and adjust to stress; and (5) strive to "stay alive" by adaptation, development of power, and growth.

The manager's role has typically been that of guiding and directing the resources of an organization from the input stage to the thru–put stages and finally to output where objectives and goals may be achieved. Prior to decision-making at any stage of the process, the decision-maker must (1) receive information; (2) interpret and integrate it keeping many factors and influences well in mind; (3) consider alternative courses of action and make a rational choice; (4) execute the chosen course by appropriate action with the help of associates; and (5) evaluate along the way whether the implementation of the decision has resulted in effective and efficient action leading to positive results.

Managers in sport and physical activity settings are no different than any other managers in other settings. They too are continually faced with the making of decisions. The importance of making a correct decision is obvious; managers who make bad decisions usually suffer the consequences of their actions. (This is possibly truer if such decisions were made arbitrarily with no consultation.) Investigation and study have shown that the very large majority of managers in sport and physical activity settings are using intuition, judgment, and past experience to guide them in the decision-making process a great deal of the time. Inasmuch as a variety of highly useful models and tools are now readily available, but are not being used typically, this indicates a lack of understanding as to their possible effectiveness. It probably also indicates an inability to cope with them in a practical manner as well. To be fair to sport and physical activity managers, it should be pointed out that managers in other fields are typically not using these tools and models very well or at all either. In fact, even among those who are presumably well versed in their use, they are often neglected because of lack of time, lack of applicability to a particular real-life situation, and the ever-present difficulty of quantifying all of the variables involved.

Factors and Influences Affecting Organizational Output

Some of the factors and influences that may affect organizational output throughout the implementation of the total management process are, for example, a lack of a clear set of explicitly stated, immediate objectives leading to the achievement of planned long–range goals. Another factor influencing output might well be a degree of dysfunction arising from conflict between the formal and informal structure of an organization in a situation where workers are "out of touch" with the plans agreed to solely by the organization's managers. There may be a relationship here, also, between the leadership styles and personalities of the managers that negate open communication within the unit.

Years of involvement as a manager/administrator, as well as more than 55 years of experience with the case technique (of broader descriptive method) of teaching human relations and management, led me to include a few thoughts here about the complexity of any administrative situation (Zeigler, 2007). This is so because of the large number of factors that may be involved in any case situation where decision-making is involved (e.g., past experience, one's present situation, economic incentive, personal attitude). The work situation itself and any changes that are occurring add to the mix. The group code within the organization, which in turn is affected by community standards and societal values and norms, are fundamental factors as well. Management says one thing, but management does another–this too can have an impact. In some circumstances certain factors indicated above could be the most important determinants of behavior; in others they might well be relatively insignificant. The task as you analyze a problem is, therefore, to gain as much perspective as possible. However, while responding to the facts, half-facts, and opinions as you see, hear, and assess them, you should keep in mind that each person views a situation differently. Such a realization in itself should often cause managers to hold back at least temporarily before initiating direct action to meet a problem.

Here we are discussing the achievement of at least elementary competency in decision-making through the use of a case method technique used extensively in law and medical training since the turn of the twentieth century. It is also true that the case method has been used as a teaching technique by business schools dating back to the 1920s. A notable example of this is the Harvard Business School in the United States and the subsequent complete adoption of this instructional approach by The University of Western Ontario School of Business Administration in Canada. Teachers in professional training programs know that the need to develop knowledge, competencies, and skills on the part of students in professional training programs is obvious and ever-present.

A common complaint of students in such programs in sport and physical activity management or administration, however, is that adequate laboratory and/or field experiences are typically not available. And yet somehow this approach within professional preparation programs in physical education and athletics did not get introduced to the field until the late 1950s (Zeigler, 1959). Furthermore, oddly and interestingly, due mainly to several social influences (e.g., onrushing science and technology) and subsequent, prevailing educational essentialism, the case method technique of teaching human relations and administration is still not used in sport and physical education management to the extent that it ought to be—a personal opinion, of course.

Experience and past literature have shown that students react most favorably to this teaching technique because it promotes involvement and stimulates interest. Accordingly, because of the presumed need for a variety of teaching techniques in professional training, it is being recommended here for this burgeoning field of within management. This teaching method has such a great deal to offer that it deserves consideration for use more or less in all aspects of management training programs.

There is no fixed model, no infallible approach, or no standard pattern for the analysis of a case leading to improved decision-making. The tone of the analysis is important, because it is advisable that the manager avoids solutions that are primarily authoritarian if he or she wishes to improve human relations within the organization. Typically the manager in assessing any problematic situation should develop as complete a mastery of the facts as possible, while keeping in mind that any case is characterized by facts, half-facts, and opinions. For this reason it imperative that a case be considered critically and that any opinions offered be weighed very carefully.

Recommended Steps
in the Decision-Making Process

The manager should try to **DETERMINE WHAT THE MAIN PROBLEM IS AFTER ENUMERATION OF THE VARIOUS SUB-PROBLEMS (Step No. 1).** Formulating the best possible answers to the sub-issues or sub-questions helps to get to the heart of the analysis. A manager should strive to ascertain the exact question at issue, keeping in mind that it may be clear or obscured. Learning how to ask the right questions is basic to the art of administration.

> Note. If the main problem, or any of the sub-problems, is basically ethical in nature that aspect should be noted and included in the analysis. An elementary three-step approach to ethical decision-making is included immediately below.

As can be readily appreciated, whether personal, professional, or environmental ethics are involved, the making of ethical decisions in no way resembles an exact science. Some might deplore such a situation, but probably the vast majority would find it desirable and wholesome. Nevertheless, the current dilemma faced by sport and physical activity managers in our society should be deplored—a situation where typically one hardly knows where to turn for some sound basis upon which to formulate an answer to just about any ethical problem that arises. What occurs, therefore, is that young adults are making choices, are forming value judgments, are experiencing emotions, and in many ways are acquiring an implicit view of life based on a "sense of life" (what Rand [1960, p. 31] called "a pre-conceptual equivalent of metaphysics, an emotional, subconsciously integrated appraisal of man and existence").

It is important, therefore, to help students approach ethical decision-making in as explicit a manner as possible. Such an approach should be one that could be useful to them throughout their adult lives. Yet such an approach should be one that they could possibly build upon throughout their lives as well. Over a period of time, with the advice of Professor Richard Fox of Cleveland State University, Ohio, U.S.A., a three-step plan of attack for ethical decision-making was devised. It was explained in considerable detail by the present author in *Applied Ethics for Sport and*

Physical Activity Managers (2007). (It should be pointed out, however, that an instructor should make it very clear that this is only one approach with which they are being asked to experiment as they move toward greater sophistication in this vital aspect of their lives.)

This plan of attack in its entirety includes the following three parts:

Part A. Determine through the employment of a "triple-play" approach—from Kant to Mill to Aristotle—what the ethical or moral issue is in the specific case at hand. That is, proceed from a test of "universalizability" to A second test of (net) consequences, and finally to a third test of intentions.

Part B. Once Part A has been carried out, proceed with Part B, or the layout of the argument (recommended as a jurisprudential argument in S. Toulmin. *The uses of argument*. NY: Cambridge University Press, 1964). In doing this, insert the universalizability maxim for Toulmin's warrant, the net consequences result of the presumably unethical action for the backing, and the intentions test items as possible conditions of exception or rebuttal.

Part C. Thirdly, upon the completion of Parts A and B—if there is time and if human relations appear to have played a significant part in the case problem—the students were asked to work their way through an even more detailed, overall approach (Part C) to ethical decision-making (as adapted first from Manicas, P. T. and Kruger, A. N., *Essentials of logic*. NY: American Book Company, 1968 and then explained further in Zeigler, E. F., *Decision-making in physical education and athletics administration: A case method approach*. Champaign, Il: Stipes Publishing Co., 1982). There are eight steps to this overall approach of Part C as follows:

1) Determination of the main problem after consideration of the various sub-problems (including any with ethical implications).
2) Explication of any knowledge base, carry-forward information that may exist already in the mind of the student in connection with this sort of case problem (including ethical implications).

3) Analysis of the main problem through application of a "three-step ethical approach" (the three tests listed above as recommended by Fox); this is integrated with a layout of the argument (based on Toulmin's approach).
4) Analysis of the various personalities and their relationships.
5) Formulation of only those alternative solutions to the ethical problem that appear to be relevant, possible, and meaningful.
6) Elaboration of proposed alternative solutions involving framing warranted predictive statements (i.e., both pro's and con's).
7) Selection of the preferred alternative solution (including initial tentative testing of the proposed solution prior to actual implementation—i.e., especially important if the case is actually a true one to be resolved).
8) Assessment and determination of currently useful principles or generalizations for possible future use in similar situations.

(Note. These "principles" or "generalizations" should supplement K-B-C-F principles suggested in "b" above.)

Here the management trainee is being asked to read the case carefully outside of class and then to draft an outline of a case analysis using the headings listed immediately above. (These headings are followed in the sample case analysis below, also.) Then he/she carries out an actual case discussion with approximately five other people in the class for approximately one class period (90 minutes would be better if such an amount of time is available).

One member of the group of six should be selected to serve as chairperson for the discussion. The chairperson should not dominate the discussion or seek a predetermined goal. This person would serve as (1) a resource person (if this person had such knowledge), (2) an evaluator of progress, (3) an informed member of the group, (4) a discussion chairperson, and (5) a summarizer.

The next recommended step (Step No. 2) is named **KNOWLEDGE-BASED, CARRY-FORWARD GENERALIZATIONS**, admittedly a long, odd, and perhaps somewhat confusing designation. All that this is, however, is an effort to determine what is already known (the knowledge base) in regard to the handling of similar problems or issues that may be "carried forward" for use at present. Hence the question is: 'which principles or generalizations can be brought for possible use to the case under consideration at present?"

> (Note. Keep in mind that we are not for a minute suggesting that there are basic principles of management that could apply here *rigidly* as determinants of action to be taken in all case situations. We are saying that there are currently useful generalizations that may be carried forward for possible use in similar situations. Obviously, there's a world of difference between the former and the latter type of information or knowledge.)

Step No. 3 involves a careful **ANALYSIS OF THE VARIOUS PERSONALITIES** in the case and their relationships with each other. In situations where human relations are involved—and they are typically involved where qualitative decision-making comes into question—the interpersonal elements of a problematic situation can be vitally important.

At this juncture, brainstorming enters the picture, and it is time to **FORMULATE POSSIBLE ALTERNATIVE COURSES OF ACTION**—often as many as 8 or more (including variations). This is Step No. 4. Only plausible alternatives should be considered (i.e., that appear to be relevant, possible, and meaningful).

In Step No. 5, these alternatives for consideration should be "tested in advance," or elaborated upon, by the **FRAMING OF WARRANTED PREDICTIVE STATEMENTS** through the listing the pro's and con's of each, and then forecasting possible results if such-and-such an alternative were implemented as a solution (i.e., a decision to be taken).

In Step No. 6, the **SELECTION OF THE PREFERRED ALTERNATIVE** occurs (including initial tentative testing of the proposed solution prior to actual implementation).

Next in line (Step No. 7) is the **IMPLEMENTATION OF THE DECISION OR PLANNED COURSE OF ACTION** as the preferred alternative to be carried out according to plan as to time, place, and method of execution.

EVALUATION OF THE RESULTS is Step No. 8 that should be carried out after a reasonable period has elapsed.

Finally, in Step No. 9, any **KNOWLEDGE, PRINCIPLES, OR CURRENTLY USEFUL GENERALIZATIONS** gleaned from this latest experience should be added to the Knowledge Base Carry-Forward— possibly at the time the decision is implemented and then later revised (see Step No. 2 above) for possible future use in similar situations.

Next to last, to set the stage a bit further, over and above the recommended steps to be followed in case analysis, below are offered below some hints to keep in mind as you carry out your own analysis. These might be called "traps to be avoided":

1. Consider the "whole case" (i.e., don't jump to a rapid conclusion from inadequate data).
2. Don't always reason as the person who is the boss.
3. Don't always press for immediate action to be taken.
4. Don't memorize facts, conclusions, or principles from other cases.
5. Avoid solutions that are primarily authoritarian.
6. Don't be afraid to use your imagination, but weigh your opinions carefully.
7. Don't accept everything written or said as "gospel truth."
8. Don't make recommendations meaningless by over qualification; avoid phraseology with no meaning.
9. Don't regard each case as a wholly individual and

isolated, problematic administrative situation.

10. Don't develop a case of "retrospective should-itis" (i.e., he *should* have done that; she *should* have done this; they *must* do that. In other words, be prospective! The case tells what happened; now "where do we go from here?" How can the administrative process be improved?

11. Don't re-hash too much of the case (as it was written) in your analysis.

12. Keep the "tone" of your analysis constructive.

13. Avoid "either-or" thinking based on the invoking of immutable principles.

> <u>Note</u>. The author first became involved with this approach to teaching human relations about 55 years ago. Some of the above suggestions have been adapted from M. P. McNair and H. L. Hansen (1949). *Problems in marketing*. NY: McGraw-Hill, pp. 22-25.

Finally, I urge you, the reader, to keep firmly in mind that the objective of this method of analysis is to help you as a manager to develop POWER by providing an opportunity to think in a constructive, orderly manner when facing new problematic situations. When you, as manager, finally do propose a solution, try to make recommendations that will improve the management process for the future. Through this type of analysis you will develop your powers of discrimination and generalization. Such "powers" can be of inestimable value to you in the years ahead.

References and Bibliography

Boehrer, J. (1994). On teaching a case. International *Studies Notes* 19:13-19.

Christensen, C. R., Hansen, A. J. & Barnes, L. B. (1994). *Teaching and the case method.* 3rd ed. Boston: Harvard Business School Publishing Division.

Colber, J. A., Trimble, K., & Desberg, P. (1996). *The case for education: Contemporary approaches for using case methods.* Boston: Allyn & Bacon.

Copeland, M. T. (1958). The case method of instruction. In *And mark an era: The Story of the Harvard Business School.* Boston: Little Brown.

Corey, R. (1998), Case method of teaching, *Harvard Business School* 9-581-058, Rev. November 6, 1998

Easton, G. (1993). *Learning from case studies.* London: Prentice-Hall.

Hammond, J. S. (1976), *Learning by the case method,* HBS Publishing Division, Harvard Business School, Boston, MA, Case #376-241.

Herreid, C. F. 1997. What is a case? *Journal of College Science Teaching* 27:92-94.

Herreid, C. F. 1997/1998. *What makes a good case?* *Journal of College Science Teaching* 27:163-165.

Leenders, M. R. & Erskine. J. A. (1989). *Case research: The case writing process.* London, ON: Research and Publications Division, School of Business Administration, University of Western Ontario.

Lynn, L. (1999). *Teaching and learning with cases: A guidebook.* New York: Chatham House Publishers.

McAninch, A. R. (1993). *Teacher thinking and the case method.* New York: Teachers College Press.

Mackenzie, R.A. (1969). The management process in 3-D. *Harvard Business Review*, 80-87,

McNair, Malcolm P., ed. (1954), The Case Method at the Harvard Business School: Papers by Present and Past Members of the Faculty and Staff, New York: McGraw-Hill, pp. 139, http://www.questia.com/PM.qst?a=o&docId=28506390

Wasserman, S. (1994). *Introduction to case method teaching.* New York: Teachers College Press.

Zeigler, E. F. (1959). *Administration of physical education and athletics:* The case method approach. Englewood Cliffs, NJ: Prentice-Hall.

Zeigler, E. F. (1959). *The case method approach: Instructor's manual.* Englewood Cliffs, NJ: Prentice-Hall.

Zeigler, E. F. (1982). *Decision-making in physical education and athletics.* Champaign, IL: Stipes.

Zeigler, E. F., and Bowie, G. W. (1983). *Management competency development in sport and physical education.* Philadelphia: Lea & Febiger.

Zeigler, E. F., Bowie, G. A., & Paris, R. (1988). *Competency development in sport and physical education management.* Champaign, IL: Stipes.

Zeigler, E. F. (1992). *Professional ethics for sport managers.* Champaign, IL: Stipes.

Zeigler, E. F. (1994). *Critical thinking for the allied professions: Health, sport & physical education, recreation, & dance.* Champaign, IL: Stipes.

Zeigler, E. F. (2007) *Applied ethics for sport and physical education professionals.* Victoria, Canada: Trafford.

Zeigler, E. F. & Bowie, G. W. (2007). *Management competency development for physical activity education & educational sport: A laboratory manual.* Victoria, Canada: Trafford.

Selection 5
Midwestern University A:
A Sample Case & Analysis
(With an Ethical Dimension))

Earle F. Zeigler, The Univ. of Western Ontario
Robert L. Case, Sam Houston State University
Steve Timewell, The Univ. of Western Ontario

This sample case, (MIDWESTERN UNIVERSITY A), was an actual situation that occurred (with names and places now disguised). A detailed analysis of this case is offered below for the reader's use. It is designed to provide an experience in the application of the case method technique to problem-solving and decision-making in sport and physical activity education. Remember that the objective of this method of analysis leading to the making of a decision is to help you as a manager develop power by providing an opportunity to think in a constructive, orderly manner when facing new, problematic situations. Through this type of analysis you will develop your powers of discrimination and generalization. When you finally do make a decision and propose a solution, do your best to make recommendations that will improve the management process for the future.

This particular case and analysis included also a consideration of possible ethical implications. However, since this approach to the case method technique of decision-making in sport and physical activity management can be used very well without detailed consideration being given to the ethical aspects of any given case, we decided to leave that step out of this presentation initially so that it all wouldn't seem too complex. A brief section offering an elementary three-step approach to ethical decision-making will be included at the end of the case analysis below.

> Note. Williams Sanders is an instructor working on his doctoral degree at Midwestern University. On February 1, 2005, he sent the following letter to Prof. T.C. Collins, Chairperson, Department of Sport and Physical Education, Midwestern University:

Dear Dr. Collins:

As you know, Head Coach Courtney and I have just completed the teaching of PE 156 (Wrestling), a course that we have handled jointly for the past few years. This year I had developed a new grading scheme that we presented to the students at the first class period. We agreed that I would determine the written work to be completed, and the skills we were to teach were those that Coach Tom stresses typically.

Both of us graded students at various times during the semester on their ability at the skills. Tom asked me, as usual, to grade all of the written work. This I did, and all grades, including attendance, were listed on a large chart kept in Mr. Courtney's office. (Near the end of the term, incidentally, a number of the students were complaining to both Tom and me that he [Tom] had been marking them absent incorrectly.)

While grading the written work, I noticed that one student, a prominent Midwestern athlete, turned in someone else's class notebook (a regularly assigned project) under his own name. I actually remembered grading this particular notebook over Xmas vacation a year ago. He also handed in several other assignments at this time, ones that were actually due at the middle of the semester. He explained that injury during the fall season had prevented him from getting them in on time. Unfortunately, this was not his work either. I notified Coach Courtney immediately since he is, of course, technically my superior with professorial status. He suggested that I give him the papers and the notebook, and that he himself would confront the student and his coach together.

The following day Coach Tom informed me that, despite the young man's plagiarism, Courtney and Slaughter (the student's coach) agreed that the athlete should re-work his notebook and assigned papers. As punishment he would be asked to complete an extra assignment recommended by me. In this way his failing grade could be raised sufficiently so as not to make it impossible for him to get off academic probation. The student came to see me; received the extra assignment; and was to return everything to me when it was completed. Then I would change the grade if his work merited such revision.

My complaint is that I never saw the results. I asked Coach Tom about it, and he explained that he had received the work, graded it, and had misplaced it at home. I decided to check out the grade submitted and learned that this person, and many other varsity athletes, received a grade of A in the course, while others more deserving received B's and C's. Regretfully, I must charge Coach Tom with dishonesty and a lack of professional ethics.

Very sincerely yours,
William Sanders.
Asst. Coach

Analysis of Case
(Including Ethical Implications)

1. Sub-Problems (leading to determination of the Main Problem):

a. The seemingly evident plagiarism of the athlete—ethically wrong.

b. Courtney, despite pre-determined grading agreement with Sanders that the latter would grade written work, grades Sanders' written work himself and doesn't even allow Sanders to see the submission—ethically wrong.

c. Athlete evidently was using his "athletic profile" for a special privilege (i.e., to be able to get away with handing assignment in late)--ethically wrong.

d. The fact that upon examination Sanders discovered that various varsity athletes received A's in the course, while others that Sanders felt actually did better received only B's and C's—ethically wrong.

e. The fact that Courtney initially went to the athlete's coach to discussed the athlete's predicament (a person who was already on academic probation) and seemingly took his plagiarism so casually; one wonders whether they (Courtney and Slaughter) ever even intended that he should complete his work for the course—ethically wrong.

f. The very fact that Coach Courtney showed truly unfair advantage to a varsity athlete, allowing him to escape any punishment for an offense that some other student might be severely punished for, or even dismissed from the university—ethically wrong.

g. Sanders may have erred by accepting the "substitute plan" recommended by Courtney after the initial plagiarism had been detected and reported by Sanders to Courtney.

After extensive discussion, the MAIN ETHICAL PROBLEM was determined to be Sub-problem #f above (Courtney's Ethical Conduct)

2. Knowledge Base Carry-Forward

    (Principles or Generalizations generally accepted)

    a. Plagiarism is cheating, an unacceptable practice in higher education.
    b. Unless there are truly extenuating circumstances, we must live up to commitments we agree upon with others.
    c. Granting "special" privileges to some people and not to their peers is unfair and will create serious problems.
    d. Athletics is but one of many aspects of university life, and should be kept in proper perspective with the overall educational function of higher education.

3. Employment of the Three-Step Approach Related to Ethics

    a. Universalizability or Consistency (Test #1)
    Based on society's values and norms, and that universities are regarded as pattern-maintenance organizations where honesty and integrity are absolutely essential, proven plagiarism is most serious

    b. (Net) Consequences (Test #2)
    Proven dishonesty by teachers and coaches that is somehow not punished could seriously damage the university's reputation and place the institution's future in jeopardy

    c. Intentions (Test #3)
    The voluntary and/or involuntary nature of Coach Courtney's actions must be ascertained, and then appropriate action should be taken based on the findings (e.g., dismissal for cause)

4. Integration of Three-Step Approach with Argument Layout

Data	So, (necessarily)	Conclusion
Head Wrestling Coach Courtney		The department head should

is reported by his teaching assistant as having shown extreme favoritism to a tendered athlete from another sport, a man who is on academic probation and who has evidently committed plagiarism

make every effort to learn the true facts of the situation, and then should take appropriate action based on his findings (e.g., dismissal for cause

Since
Warrant

Unless
Rebuttal or Exception

Based on society's values and norms, and that universities are regarded as pattern-maintenance organizations where honesty and integrity are absolutely essential, an offense such as proven plagiarism is most serious

It turns out that Courtney actually did forget and did grade the manual himself which was excellent in all regards

Universalizability (Test 1)

and/or

Because
Backing

Courtney was under some external pressure; and felt that he simply had no recourse other than to provide help for the athlete who was on academic probation

Proven dishonesty by teachers and coaches that is somehow not punished could seriously damage a university's reputation and place the institution's future in jeopardy

and/or

Consequences (Test 2)

Courtney was old, near retirement, had an excellent record otherwise, offered an apology; corrected the well-intentioned error; thus, clemency was felt to be in order

and/or

It turned out that the

problem has been
exaggerated by Sanders
who had it in for Courtney
and perhaps hoped to succeed
to the position if Courtney
were dismissed

Intentions (Test 3)

Key: Argument Layout (Toulmin, 1964)

D =data (a statement of a situation that prevails,
including evidence, elements, sources, samples of facts)
C =conclusion (claim or conclusion that we are seeking to
establish)
W =warrant (practical standards or canons of argument
designed to provide an answer to the question. "How do
you get there?")
Q =modal qualifier (adverbs employed to qualify conclusions based on strengths of warrants—e.g., necessarily, probably)
R =conditions of exception (conditions of rebuttal or
exception that tend to refute the conclusion)
B =backing (categorical statements of fact that lend
further support to the 'bridge-like" warrants)

   5.   Personalities and Ethical Relationships:

        a. There appears to be a difference in the way that the coaches at
Midwestern University regard academic work and offenses and
infractions that might occur. Courtney evidently felt it was more
important for a top athlete to be eligible than to be honest, as did
Slaughter—but Sanders didn't agree.
        b. At least some athletes at Midwestern figured you could get
away with handing in someone else's work—or else this one wouldn't
have tried it. If this is true, this could affect a professional program
most seriously.
        c. Even if everything that Courtney said was true (e.g., he had
found it to be worth an A grade), what about the other varsity
athletes who Sanders felt was receiving grades that were too high
(relatively speaking, that is).

d. If Courtney had been under some external pressure to see to it that the athlete became eligible again, one would think that Sanders might be aware of this—but perhaps not.

6&7. Relevant Alternatives Open to One of the Participants:
Note. We have chosen to view the matter from the standpoint of Wm. Sanders, Asst. Coach)

a. Initially, Sanders should have taken a stand against Courtney when he first learned how the matter was to be handled. Perhaps he should have done so…

Pro—maybe he could have convinced Courtney to quickly retrace his steps and change what he had just done (i.e., submit a false grade, etc.).
Con—Courtney might have been angry at being challenged and would have attempted to somehow "cover his tracks".

b. After Sanders discovered the plagiarism, he should have quietly referred it to Collins and not become so openly involved.

Pro—by "playing it safe" his position might be more secure.
Con—his conscience might have bothered him because somehow in North American culture a "sneaky Judas" is especially condemned when an action becomes generally known.

c. Before taking any action (i.e., writing the letter), Sanders should have confronted Coach Courtney about this matter; he should also ask him to justify the especially high grades for all the tendered athletes (with lower grades for others); this would be somewhat more ethical than "going over his head" immediately.

See pro's and con's in Question #6 below (Preferred Alternative Solution).

d. Sanders could have contacted Coach Slaughter to discuss the situation. Slaughter's reaction might have provided additional evidence (one way or the other).

Pro—this would have to be handled most carefully. It could have caused him to get back to Courtney rapidly to call the whole affair off. It would also give Sanders a stronger case either way it turned out.
Con—Sanders would be "sticking his neck out" even Further, and this might cause a violent reaction from the authorities in the Athletic Association and perhaps injured Sanders' job standing and his future.

e. Sanders could check grades over the most recent years to see if there had been a pattern indicating that athletes were being treated in a special manner.

Pro—this might also strengthen Sanders' case or it might dissuade him from writing the letter if nothing seemed to have been wrong. It could also have been used in connection with #c above to help convince Courtney about the error of his actions.
Con—it might be difficult to get the former grade books without arousing suspicion on Courtney's part.

f. Once the complaint has been filed, Sanders should leave the matter at that and remove himself as far as possible from having anything to do with it (ethical?).

Pro—one is tempted to do this if possible, and it does leave the accuser somewhat less tainted by the whole affair.
Con—this possibility rarely develops, mainly because the accuser is needed as a witness and thereby is forced to take a stand.

g. Sanders should somehow get the information to Dr. Collins anonymously; in this way he might conceivably escape from any responsibility in the matter.

Pro—this could really be playing it safe, and it might work.
Con—Sanders' conscience would probably have bothered
him, and also receipt of such an anonymous accusation might well
be ignored.

6&7. Preferred Alternative Solution (Confront Courtney before
reporting him to departmental chairperson)

Alternative #c above:

Before taking any action (i.e., writing the letter), Sanders should
have confronted Coach Courtney about this matter; he should
also ask him to justify the especially high grades for all the
tendered athletes (with lower grades for others); this would be
somewhat more ethical than "going over his head" immediately.

Pro's	Con's
Would have gone through proper channels	By confronting Courtney there might have been some "backlash"
Courtney would have known that Sanders was aware of unfair practices and might be reporting him to the administrator	Improper grading might have led to Courtney's downfall and his possible dismissal anyhow
Sanders would have given Courtney a chance to explain what he had been doing by offering some rationale for it	If Courtney could not explain his actions, he would be working mightily to harm Sanders and have him "black-balled by the Athletic Assoc.
If Sanders could have convinced Courtney that his grading practices were ridiculous, then something might have been worked out before chairman was told	If an investigation had taken place—and Courtney somehow was innocent—Sanders would have been in a most maybe precarious position to say the least

8. Currently Useful Principles or Generalizations

> Note. In this case analysis provided as an example (i.e., MIDWESTERN UNIVERSITY), you should understand that the results of implementing Step No. 8 could, of course, not be carried out until a period of time had elapsed.

> > Note. These are recommended as a result of the case analysis, being added to the Knowledge Base Carry-forward in #2 above.

a. Keep in mind that there is a considerable range of opinion in this culture as to how ethical conduct is perceived.
b. It is most important that teachers/coaches set high ethical standards for themselves.
c. Every effort should be made to keep the lines of communication open with colleagues in a work situation.
d. When team teaching is being carried out, it is especially important to have the policies and procedures used spelled out most carefully in advance of the actual teaching situation.

Selection 6
Writing and Analyzing a Case

One of the most interesting experiences for student and instructor alike arises when the student writes and analyzes a case for the first time. Most students will tackle such a problem with unusual enthusiasm. They seem to feel that it represents a challenge to their intellect, testing their power of observation as well as their ability to tell a story in a factual manner. Naturally, experienced case writers write the best cases. It is amazing, however, to witness the care that most students will put into the preparation of a case that they have observed or experienced.

Generally a student should not report a case in which he/she is one of the leading characters, although this is not a fixed rule. When students have been directly involved in a situation, they have the facts well in mind. Certain prejudices will be evident in the reports, although students really try to present both sides of the picture despite any embarrassment they might feel. When a young teacher handed a case to the writer for the first time, he said: "I'm afraid you're not going to be very proud of me as one of your graduates. I think I mad several bad errors in judgment during the past year/" Actually I was proud of the fact that this young man made such a statement…

Students should be given the chance to write and analyze their own cases several times during the course. Not only will it give them an opportunity to write, an experience that is often sorely needed, but it also develops their powers of insight and analysis. When all of the facts, half-facts, and opinions of a case are down on paper for the first time, the student also has the chance to rewrite and polish his/her efforts. Then perhaps for the first time, he will be able to gain perspective about a problem that he may have reasoned through in a hazy fashion originally.

By writing cases, the student is able to compete with the others in the class. If the instructor wishes to reproduce the best cases for possible discussion by the class, it is wise to ask for the student's permission privately. If the student shows any sign of embarrassment at such a request, such reproduction should be deferred until a later date. A young man submitted a case in which his father was the leading character. Although he did his best to defend "Dad", it was quite obvious to the instructor that the class would sharply criticize the actions of his father. For this reason,. although his work represented a good case, it was not reproduced.

Toward the end of the course, the instructor will generally notice a marked improvement in the cases that are submitted.

A good case writer is a good reporter. This point was brought home to the writer when he prepared a particular case not appearing in the current text because of the national publicity it received. When the story broke in the newspaper of a large city, we decided that this particular problem situation might make an excellent case for discussion. We read the story first in time and later a detailed account in Sports Illustrated. We decided to follow through and obtain as many facts as possible. We wrote to several friends who had first-hand experience in the area of the case. We obtained copies of all available newspapers and devoted an entire evening to clipping various articles. It took several hours to read the articles carefully. After all this work, and after return letters from friends had arrived with additional information, we came to the conclusion that Sports Illustrated had included all the essential material for a case. The story had been written by a fine reporter.

Students may wonder whether a case they would like to report will be useful. One of the best advance tests of the usefulness of any case is the interest the student himself has in the problem. Business education instructors often run across "springboard cases," in which the central issue holds great meaning for most of the class. Such problems engender lively discussions of many of the related problems, which impinge on the main problem.

In writing a case, it is important to disguise the identity of the participants. Business school and other case writers secure releases from the organizations and individuals involved before using a case for class discussion. In writing this text we realized that to secure written releases for many of the cases would be virtually impossible, since educators generally are not familiar with the case plan of instruction and the manner in which cases are collected. We discussed the liability possibility with several lawyers, after explaining to them that all names in the cases had been changed. They asked if some statements included might be considered libelous. According to Webster's Collegiate Dictionary, a libel is "any statement or representation, published without just cause or excuse, or by pictures, effigies, or other signs, tending to expose another to public hatred, contempt, or ridicule." We explained that this would certainly not be the intent of a case writer, since effort is made to disguise the persons concerned and, furthermore, half-facts and opinions can usually be recognized as such. One lawyer suggested that so long as cases were factual, there would be no need to worry. For a case of this type, refer to the Baldwin University (Case #5 in the text) that pointed out also that anyone would be foolish to take a disguised case to court because of the notoriety that a trial would bring to the complainant. (Note: Ideally, of course, this technique of teaching should be developed to a point where written releases might be obtained from the institution concerned.)

Although some potential cases set up certain pitfalls in which an unwary student might get caught, and others give only little concrete evidence other than the statements of the complainants, the large majority can be readily analyzed in a systematic fashion. The focus in writing cases might include:

1. Relations among teachers and/or pupils and/or administrators.

2. An introduction of a change in the school pattern.

3. The administrative methods used in a school, college, university, or private agency.

4. A single conversation between two people, or three people, etc.

5. The experiences of a teacher, coach, or administrator.

6. Relations between a teacher and a supervisor.

7. Relations among students or a group of students.

Basically, the case writer should report just what he sees and hears– no more. He should obtain a broad perspective, yet look for commonplace statements and incidents, which hold significance for the readers of the case. In a chronological, sequential way, the case writer should tell what actually happened when. Be explicit! "The principal told the writer on November 7, 2008 that he thought Coach Jones didn't have the respect of the boys." Of course, the case writer can never know all the relevant facts.

We have included in this selection a case analysis written by a senior in business administration who was an excellent varsity swimmer. It describes this student's outlook on a situation in which he was one of the main characters. The case is about a situation that almost every coach has faced at one time or another —what to do with an athlete who has broken training rules. The young man presented the case quite briefly. Generally speaking, a good case might extend over anywhere from five to 40 or more double-spaced, typewritten pages. Sometimes it is advisable to divide long cases into a series of incidents.

After the presentation of the problem, this young man followed a formula for analysis that had been suggested to him. (Instructors may wish to deviate from this pattern.) First, there is a very brief interpretation of the problem. He then analyzes the case from the standpoint of (1), Doug, the coach; (2), Ron, the offending swimmer; (3), the other smoking members of the team; and (4), the nonsmoking members of the group. Finally, the young man gives his conclusion and recommended solution. Naturally, readers may find that they disagree with the case writer's analysis of the situation:

Analysis of Faber College Case

Interpretation. In this situation, the coach (Doug) may be considered the administrator of a group of athletes in which a training rule violation has taken place. The problem here seems to revolve around the theory of whether winning meets or consistency of principles is of more importance to a coach. A coach's purpose is not only to develop a winning team, but also to develop team unity and spirit. Each member of the team has an obligation to the team and to the coach. Unless each one obeys the training rules, works for the benefit of the whole team, and upholds his particular position on the team, he is not fulfilling this obligation.

Doug (the Coach). Following from the above relationship that should exist between team members and the coach, plus the relationship among the members themselves, it would seem that there was a lack of good administrative action by Doug. Initially, he was trying to stick to his own principles and rules that he had set up when he brought the problem into the open. However, by letting Ron swim when he had definitely stated in front of the other members that he would not, Doug went back on his word. He put the onus of winning ahead of his own character. When training rules are set up, the coach should take into consideration every possible violation of the rules and should absolutely stick to these rules when a violation has taken place.

Because Doug did go back on his word, he was not consistent in his handling of the problem. By discussing the problem with his classes, the head of his department, and the athletic director, Doug was perhaps seeking approval for his initial decision. This may show lack of faith in his decision. If he felt that he should discuss his problem with someone, he should have taken it to the athletic director even before he took it to the team. As it was, he was leaving himself open for criticism. Also, by allowing the team to vote on the eligibility of Ron, he took the chance of losing face. This is so, because he had already told them of his decision. At least, he received a verbal agreement from the offenders to stop smoking. As was seen later, however, this promise did not mean anything.

Throughout the entire situation, it would seem that Doug wanted to hold his position of authority. However, at the same time he sought approval for his decisions. It is apparent that he used rationalization a great deal to explain his actions. By changing his mind, seeking approval, and trying to act in a democratic way, Doug probably lost the respect and position of authority in the eyes of his team, as well as in the eyes of all the "outsiders" with whom he discussed the matter.

As the description of the case ended, Doug had just seen Ron and another team member smoking again in the cafeteria. Now Doug had to proceed most carefully to overcome the more serious problem and to regain his own position of authority and the respect of the boys. As smoking on an athletic team can be a major problem, Doug must abide strictly by the rules that he has set down; ignore them completely; have no rules of any kind; or suggest that the training rules be carried out. Everyone would then know what to expect, and he could be consistent in his actions.

Ron. Because he has the support of his teammates, Ron can be assumed to be the leader of the group within which there are internal groups—those who smoke and those who do not. Ron can also be considered as valuable to the total team effort because of his special ability as seen from his winning performances. He liked swimming as a sport. Before he made his appointment with the coach, Ron did a great deal of thinking about how he might change Doug's decision. By bringing the other smoking members of the team to the coach with him, he sought to achieve this end. To do this, Ron would have to be fairly certain of his position on the team and among the team members as well. He must have thought that he knew the characteristic behavior and personality of the coach reasonably well, also. Ron realized, however, that the only way to alleviate the situation was to promise that he would stop smoking.

Doug's change of heart did not solve the problem for Ron as was seen by his action the following week. The incentive factor and the threat factor as presented by Doug at two different times were not high enough or strong enough, respectively, to change Ron's attitude. The solution presented by the coach was actually no solution at all. Ron simply continued to violate the training rules.

Members of the Team Who Smoke. The position taken by the smoking team members in the situation is not too clear, but it would seem that they are somewhat in the same position as Ron. Some of them probably thought that a certain amount of smoking would not hurt their performance, because it had not seemed to affect Ron's performance noticeably. They did seem to have a sense of guilt, as they agreed to accompany Ron on his visit to Doug's office. By telling Doug that they should not be allowed to swim in the next meet either, they appeared to be willing to take their punishment. They did seem to have a sense of responsibility. With a little pressure from the coach and the other team members, they would very likely have given up smoking. Despite these factors in their favor, they were guilty of a violation of the rules and some administrative action should have been taken against them as well.

Members of the Team Who Don't Smoke. These members were not directly involved in the problem. Their vote of confidence in Ron appeared reasonable, as they wanted to see the team do well. In all probability, however, their respect for Doug decreased, because he did not hold to his original decision. By deciding to allow Ron to swim through a vote, they were simply agreeing with the coach's earlier decision that afternoon.

Suggested Solution. Doug should not have changed his original decision concerning Ron. If he was not certain of his theory and philosophy of administration, he should never have brought the problem into the open in front of the team. As it was, he way trying to be both authoritarian and democratic. By discussing the problem with people external to the situation, he was leaving himself open for criticism. As the solution was made, these people would tend to lose respect for Doug, also. He should have asked the team to vote before he made his decision rather than afterwards.

Doug must regain his "status" as an administrator and coach following the incident. A partial solution to this would be to talk to Ron and the other member seen smoking in the cafeteria, individually. Before he does this, he must decide which principles he will uphold, if any. He must ask himself whether winning the next meet is a most important factor. If Ron can be made to accept his guilt, the whole team might benefit by this realization on the part of an informal leader. By presenting either a strong incentive or punishment factor to Ron, Doug might achieve a successful solution.

Doug's best action would be to emphasize several ideas in his talk with Ron. First, he should stress the influence of Ron's actions on his own performance, and then he point out to Ron the influence that his actions might have on team morale and performance. It is difficult to see how Doug can take any action against Ron for his initial offense. He must take some definite action, however, as a result of the second violation that will stop Ron and the other team members from continuing such flagrant violation of the training rules. In this way Doug would regain his place of authority and respect in the group. Doug should be careful not to put any rulings across in such a way that he alienates the members personally. The decision to punish the young men should be handled as impersonally as possible. In this way a sounder relationship will be developed all around, although the team may lose a couple of meets they might have otherwise won.

Selection 7
Examinations and Grading

Examinations mean trouble for both students and teachers. At examination time one is tested, evaluated, or measured in some way. It is when the student is expected to prove that he has mastered a course.

But what is being tested? We are, many say, testing the student's knowledge. A pupil has knowledge if he can memorize certain facts, figures, and statements. Teachers lecture while students take notes. These notebook pages are typically "swallowed whole and regurgitated" at exam time. The teacher, who knows what he wants, sets the examinations—true-false, multiple-choice, matching, essay question, or another type. Some get "A's." Many pass. Some fail. What does it all mean?

Many of us have begun gradually to set up different criteria to help us learn how much students have learned in the courses we teach. There is more to the process of true learning than mere memorization of isolated data. Our examinations give the students a chance to work some of the facts into a meaningful pattern. Data and facts are necessary bases for critical thinking, but where and how do we strike a happy balance? If the aim of education is a person capable of intelligent self-direction in society as well as in his chosen field of work, how do we test our achievement of this aim?

In a case method examination it is difficult for the instructor to explain why a paper is "superior, satisfactory, or unsatisfactory." Grading by instructors is quite subjective, and there is room for disagreement among instructors as to the classification of grading possible. We lean toward the classification quoted above, but some might be willing to grade papers excellent, good, fair, and poor. Whether it is possible to follow the A, B, C system with pluses and minuses right down to F is debatable.

We must grade examinations written by students trained by a traditional system. In case method examinations the need is to develop examinations, which will show us whether students have truly, developed the ability to direct themselves capably in administrative situations involving a complexity of facts, half-facts, and opinions. It is no easy task for the instructor. We think the student would agree that it is a difficult task for him as well.

There is room for considerable variation in the actual makeup of the examination, although it should consist of the analysis of one or more cases. A format described by Fuller might be adapted to our needs in sport and physical activity management: a four-hour examination that might be shortened to three hours.

A written announcement outlining the purposes of the examination was handed out to the students approximately two weeks in advance. Students were given the opportunity to raise questions concerning this proposal during regular class time. Three cases were included:

The first case was given to the students the day before the examination. Students could spend the evening analyzing the case in small groups, or in any way they saw fit. This first case took up one hour of the student's time on the following day. A second case, given out as the students entered the examination room, was allotted an hour and a half in the examination formula.

The third case was given only one half hour before the examination sessions ended. The plan here was to force the student to make a fairly rapid analysis to show how his former way of thinking had, or had *not*, changed through the course experience.

The instructor who taught the course should grade the examinations. The identity of the students can be kept unknown by giving each student a number to place on his examination booklet.

The first time the author tried this type of examination, good students reacted in the way various sources had indicated they would. Good students were concerned with the problem of communication and the achievement of a common basis of understanding. They took a more carefully defined clinical approach to the managerial problems involved in a particular case.

They understood that on one could hope to learn all the facts in a given situation, and they realized that a person responds not to the facts, but to the facts as he sees them. They believed that the attitude of the administrator was most important in determining the behavior of the various staff members.

They stressed the point that action can be taken too fast in the light of possible reactions on the part of the subordinates concerned. They refrained from recommending "principles" of administrative action and suggested instead adoption of basic assumptions that had to stand the test of verification in specific situations.

One of these "basic assumptions" that they made was that all staff members, as well as the administrators, have good ideas on decisions and policies. They "assumed" also that staff members want to work for the achievement of the institution's purpose Without being driven, they realized that people's behavior is governed by many different factors—that one factor might govern their action today, a different one tomorrow. They understood that staff members might not always be affected by logical thinking. Hence, any given action on the part of a staff member might be taken in the light of the assumed favor or disfavor of the group.

Before considering some of the deficiencies of the poor student's approach, an example is offered of one student's solution of the Meadow High School Case (No. # 14). A college junior in a final examination wrote this analysis. His class had discussed relatively few cases during the year. His solution appeared to be the best in a class of twelve students.

Meadow High School

The Main Issue. The main issue in this situation is, I think, that there has been no established administrative policy regarding the purchase of new equipment. Apparently, the board of education had just bought all equipment from Mr. Dobson, a local dealer. They do not appear to have given any consideration to the relative cost of equipment, quality, and service provided. When Bob Change attempts to obtain good equipment, there is confusion and misunderstanding. First of all, they agree to allow him to have a free hand. Then they changed their minds and invoked the three-pronged policy regarding the purchase of new physical education equipment. I think, therefore, that the basic problem in this situation is the lack of standardized procedure.

Sub-issues.

(a) The service rendered by Mr. Dobson is a problem, which Bob faces. Apparently, Mr. Dobson isn't too concerned with the service, which he gives to the school. He sent goods of inferior quality both times with part of the order missing.

(b) A second sub-issue is the relationship existing between the school board, Mr. Dobson, and the vice-principal. Mr. Ross, the business administrator, is a good friend of Mr. Dobson's, also.

Analysis of Individuals and Relationships

(a) Bob Change: Bob was a fairly experienced physical education teacher. He had been teaching at least three years. He seems to have been very interested in doing a good job. We see this from the care he took in regard to the ordering of equipment. When the first inferior order arrived from Dobson, Bob should have told the principal then and not have let it go. This may be an indication of the fact that Bob did not realize the local situation in regard to buying. He should have found out.

When given a free hand in the purchase of equipment, Bob might have been wise to question this arrangement. Some control should have been kept by the school administration, and this might reside with the business administrator.

Bob made a mistake when he examined Mr. Dobson's equipment in the Board Room. All tenders should have been treated equally. Finally, Bob should have seen the principal when Dobson again sent a faulty order (because of line relationship within the system).

(b) Mr. Dobson: Dobson was very friendly with people on the Board of Education and the vice-principal. The fact that he delivered inferior orders is evidence of his lack of business integrity, or of extremely careless and sloppy handling of orders. He used what influence he had to bring business his way. It was reported that "he spoke to various members of the Board and tried to put pressure on a manufacturer." There appears to be no reason to doubt these actions by Dobson.

(c) Mr. Lord: Lord tried to help Bob by at least allowing him to go to the Board of Education meeting. Whether Bob should have gone or not is a good question. Possibly Lord, who was in between Bob and the Board, should have taken his suggestion forward. On the other hand, it was obvious that Bob would have been able to explain the situation better.

Mr. Lord: Lord tried to help Bob b at least allowing him to go to the Board of Education meeting. Whether Bob should have hone or not is a good question. Possibly Lord, who was in between Bob and the Board, should have taken his suggestion forward. On the other hand, it was obvious that Bob would have been able to explain the situation better.

After Mr. Lord took Bob to the Board meeting, no more is heard of the Principal. Bob believes that he is really interested in physical education. Although we cannot accept this as evidence, it does give some inkling of Mr. Lord's attitude.

(d) Mr. Ross: The Board's business administrator seems to be lacking in integrity. The fact that he allowed Dobson to show his sporting goods in the Board Room instead of with the other tenders seems to bear this statement out. We have the rumor also that he is accepting a "kickback" from Dobson. We don't know this to be true, but this gives us an idea of the impression he creates.

Solutions

(a) Alternative #1: Bob might resign as head of the department. The only argument for this solution is that Bob at least would not have to face similar struggles in the future. However, this is not a solution to the problem. The next department head would have to face the same problem, and Bob would have to go on using Dobson's inferior equipment in his work.

(b) Alternative #2: Bob might resign from the staff. This has the advantage that Bob would be completely out of the situation, but it is still not really a solution. His problem doesn't seem to warrant such a drastic action. He would just be running away from what he would consider a hopeless fight. Running away would not do him any good.

(c) Alternative #3: Bob and Miss Giles might approach the principal together and once more tell him of the situation. They could ask him to request that the Board draw up a definite standard procedure to be followed in connection with the purchasing of equipment in the future, one that that must be followed at all times. At the same time they could inform the Principal again that more inadequate supplies had been received from Mr. Dobson. If the Board is responsible for the procedure to be followed, Bob Change can do no more than report inferior equipment to his superior. Further action is not up to Bob.

The advantages to this solution are that Mr. Lord, from what we are told of him, is an efficient and helpful individual. We are told that he wants a "big, happy family." When he learns of the dissatisfaction that is present, he will probably help Bob and Miss Giles. If he is an efficient administrator, he will realize that the system used at the present is not producing the best results. He may try to correct the situation gradually.

Another advantage of this alternative is that the Board will have to take some action if Mr. Lord speaks to them about the ongoing nature of the problem. If Mr. Lord told them that the two teachers were very upset about the inferior equipment, the Board would be almost forced to consider some solution. Having just recommended that the school purchase better football equipment to prevent injuries, the Board appears to want to protect itself from public criticism. It would not help the Board's position to have the public know that the school system was paying exorbitant prices for inferior equipment.

A third advantage to this alternative is that it might have long–range results for standardization of purchasing procedure. Meadow High School hasn't been in operation too long, and evidently is having some difficulty with certain policies and procedures regarding the purchase of equipment. This solution offers the possibility of a long–range policy being implemented.

The disadvantage of this alternative is that the Board is very friendly with Mr. Dobson, or at least certain of its members are. Furthermore, Mr. Ross hasn't been very cooperative with Bob to this point. At any rate, the final decision should be up to them.

Recommendation: That Alternative #3 is followed in the hope that a definite policy for the purchase of equipment would eventually result. The Board has already introduced a scheme that has merit. Allowing Bob to purchase anything up to fifty dollars with the principal's consent seemed sensible. With any order from fifty dollars to two hundred dollars, the further confirmation of the business administrator was recommended. Over and above this, three written tenders had to be submitted by dealers in sporting goods. Perhaps this three-fold plan could be incorporated in any statement giving further clarification to the matter. At any rate, Bob could not go wrong by taking a long range approach and allowing this situation to "iron itself out" gradually. Bob should be firm about not accepting any orders with missing or inferior equipment.

Note: Poor students, as opposed to the way the solution proposed the situation should be handled, approached the situation in a different way. They tended to see things as either "black" or "white." Many of them accepted all opinions in the case as fact, while others discounted any statements or opinions as unverifiable. When some students found that they were making no headway in the analysis of a case, they "reasoned" that the case did not offer them enough information to gain insight from which they could arrive at a solution.

From the standpoint of the "science of meanings," most students' language and logic showed deficiencies. The words and the phrases that they used in their answers carried no real meaning. The instructor could not tell what thoughts they really intended to convey. They tended to say things like "the whole answer to this problem lies in the fact that the department head didn't establish good communications," or "that coach needs to lie on a couch and tell his troubles to a psychiatrist." One student seemed possessed with the idea that a departmental administrator has only two choices: either he gets efficiency, or he keeps his staff members happy.

It does seem that poor students try to operate on the basis that there are set principles of administrative action. This approach on the part of students is easily understood when one remembers courses like "principles of educational administration," "principles of sport and physical activity management," and others. Many administrators today are the products of all these so-called "principles" courses. Unfortunately, complex departments cannot be administered merely through the implementation of a set of principles. The logic of the principles may be indisputable, but the staff may not be ready emotionally to accept this or that carefully reasoned decision. It is most difficult to inculcate "principles" of good human relations into a society that has built up production to enormous heights. but which has also ignored the human element to a considerable extent.

Some of the statements of certain students are very revealing: "If he refuses to cooperate, fire him!" "Leaders resent it when their subordinates make suggestions." "If you can't get along with him, try flattery." "Put her in a job where she can do the least amount of harm." "Unmarried women teachers are emotionally unstable." "An administrator must be given authority to preserve efficiency." "Teachers will resent an efficient colleague automatically." "If sympathy doesn't work, discharge him." "What we need is a new chart of organization!" How many more could you add to this list?

Despite prior class experience with this "new" approach, many students will still come to examinations prepared to think, feel, and act in habitual ways. Only those students who have truly comprehended the lessons to be learned by the case plan of instruction will have learned a new behavior pattern. Since examinations involve greater pressure, poor students revert to their basic ways of thinking because they have not mastered this new approach. They concentrate on one small area of the total problem. They rarely show a new understanding of the administrative process to be invoked with the analysis of the problem in the case. They grasp for a solution and, because they are confused, resort to an authoritarian approach.

They see that a definite problem exists; hence, it must be solved immediately. They fail to see all of the alternatives. "Either the coach should be dismissed, or the "recalcitrant" put

94

on probation." They "play God" and arbitrate in heavy tones. But what does the second-string quarterback think? Who cares?

Some will qualify their statements to such a degree that their proposed solutions are meaningless. Others develop "should" complexes. "The coach should realize that he has been too strict with the boys." "The boys should understand that winning the Harvard game means everything." "The athletic director should be able to see that the coach is under great pressure."

These are but a few of the problems that instructors will meet as they try to face a basically subjective task in as objective a manner as possible.

Selection 8
The Instructor As a Counselor

Problems will arise that appear to be uniquely related to the case plan of instruction as it is employed in a course on human relations and management. Because this approach had never been tried in teaching the management of athletics and physical activity, there was no body of experience to guide us when it was first introduced (Zeigler, 1959). It was understandable that difficulties would arise at, say, the Harvard Graduate School of Business Administration, because the entering students are plunged wholly right into the case plan of instruction in the first year of the program there. In the field of sport and physical activity management, however, such a course would be only one of many students would be required to take in perhaps the third or fourth year of a major program in management. Hence we in our field would presumably not have to give special attention to counseling because of the introduction of the case method in one course in the program. Some students would have presumably have difficulty, but it would be of a relatively minor nature.

This writer's experience demonstrated very soon conclusively that our students "eat up" this method. They truly seemed to be ready for it, because they had already begun to question the "traditional approach" to teaching in other professional subjects as well as those employed in the arts and sciences. From this standpoint alone, it seemed necessary to keep other instructors on the staff informed as to the "why's" and "where fore's" of the case plan of instruction. One instructor on the writer's staff became quite antagonistic because the students questioned his didactic method of instruction.

In an early study at Harvard, Fox (in Andrews) discovered that the number of students finding difficulty with the case method approach at Harvard was directly proportional to the maturity and practical experience of those enrolled in the course. Approximately one third of an entering class seemed to make an adequate adjustment. About one third of the latter group was believed to have made a "complete adjustment." Many of them had excellent academic records beforehand, but, in addition, they had "unusual capacity to handle comparatively simple arithmetical problems, to express themselves clearly both orally and on paper, and to learn from experience."

A second group, about half of the entering class, generally each required between five and ten hours of counseling time. They seemed to have difficulty in grasping this new approach to learning as opposed to that practiced in typical "academic disciplines." Although some passed unnoticed until it was discovered at the end of the first semester that they were failing, most students became vocal about their problems earlier. Strangely enough, a number of the students experiencing difficulty had excellent prior academic records.

The third group, the remaining one-sixth of the entering MBA program, included 10-15 students in need of psychiatric assistance. The remainder of this group had serious problems with their social orientation. After realizing that they were not advancing with the rest of the group, they became confused and often angry. It took special counseling to help them understand that the case method would help them develop their powers of discrimination and analysis. These students needed to understand that "strengths and weaknesses" needed assessment to help them compensate as best possible. This adjustment took time, but it was time well spent because their very future in management depended on it. Getting these people "adjusted" was important because they had become an annoyance to those students progressing normally.

As it developed, a certain amount of counseling service was necessary for a large percentage of those seeking to progress normally. As it turned out, some professors were better equipped than others to fulfill this function. Students needed help in their efforts to relate to others, in the choice of a vocation, with their inability to fully understand the case method of instruction, with poor scholarly achievement in general, and with the resolution of financial problems.

Of course, counseling techniques differ. Basically, of course, counseling is much more than just a pleasant chat between two individuals. A counseling interview should have a definite purpose, and it is up the counselor to guide the interview in such a way that this purpose is accomplished. Either the student or the counselor may initiate the request for an interview. The counselor must develop a rapport with the student so that the student will be receptive to the points the counselor wants to make. With this approach, first interviews may not even include a discussion of the main problem. Subsequently, of course, the counselor tries to change the student's thinking about the basic problem.

We can appreciate that much counseling in the past has been incidental and unscientific, but down through the twentieth century these efforts have been improved. Counseling is a personal matter that implied a relationship between two people in which the counselor attempts to be of assistance to the counselee. There is no fixed limit to the length of a counseling session held in a well-kept, private office. The counselor should try discreetly in advance to learn as much information about the students assigned to him or her. After one or more discussion sessions, the student is left to make all pertinent decisions.

The development of so-called non-directive counseling added a distinctly new dimension to the area of counseling. By employing it, the counselor had to develop a set of attitudes about the importance of the individual. He/she had to believe that the "counselee" had the ability innately to make decision for himself. It was important, also, that the counselor realize that he should not merely adopt a passive role. If he were to do this, the counselee would feel not the counselor was not interested in his problem. The extent to which the counselor is capable of understanding a client's internal frame of reference and display empathy for the individual's concerns is debatable anyhow. Obviously the counselor should avoid any significant emotional entanglement.

What *is* important in the final analysis is that a learning process occurs, and that the counselee eventually sees himself as a more adequate person aware of outside experience. The individual should come to understand that he/she ultimately must be capable of deciding whether an experience is "good" or "bad." If this level of personal understanding is not achieved, a continuing psychological tension may well result. For psychological adjustment to take place subsequently, the person must arrive at a concept of self in which various sensory and visceral experiences are assimilated in such a way that basic harmony exists between his/her external experiences and how the individual sees himself functioning. In this way there should develop within a reasonable period of time a positively oriented adaptation to the individual's environment. In essence the person's "value system" would at that point "identify" with the value systems of well-adjusted people in the same society.

The reader can now see important it is, as did the writer many years ago, that through proper employment of the case method of instruction can contribute to assisting students to learn how to truly direct their own lives. In addition to becoming critical learners, they will learn how to evaluate the contributions of others. When new problem situations arise, students should be able to adjust intelligently, while at the same time utilizing effective cooperation with others to achieve a common goal.

There are still those "out there" who believe that the goal is the ability to repeat large amounts of factual material. At the same time, the educational system has developed individuals in the execution of numerous required operations of mental capacity. In addition, very often we have demanded that students reconstruct in class recitations, term papers, and examinations the same type of thinking that has been given to them in the form of class lectures and assigned readings.

With the case method of approach to teaching, the assumption is that we cannot teach people directly. We can facilitate learning, however, in a variety of ways. People are so constructed that they will learn that which they believe will be helpful to them in the future. They should not feel threatened by what we as instructors wish to convey. The individual's prevailing concept of self will then permit new ideas and experience to be incorporated within it. Here we are simply recommending these thoughts in relation to student counseling, but we believe further that they have merit for use in all aspects of the educational system.

> Note: A sample of an interview in which the non-directive
> approach to counseling was attempted can be found in
> the Lewis College case (see p. 188).

Selection 9
Opportunities for Case Method Research in Sport and Physical Activity Management

There are opportunities for research in human relations and management through use of the case-method technique of descriptive research. Although the three main methods (i.e., historical, descriptive, and experimental group method) differ a great deal in their specific applications, basically this clinical research technique would follow the same steps of: (1) observation, (2) recording observed data, (3) generalization to theory formulation, and (4) testing the new generalizations through further clinical observation.

Since little experimentation of this type has been conducted in this profession, prospective researchers would need to acquire some background in clinical research and case writing. Professors in universities offering graduate work in our field are typically competent in descriptive and observational techniques. Thus, they could easily adapt their thinking to the case-method technique approach of broad descriptive research.

Although a basic knowledge of statistical terms and techniques is essential, many students with no special talent along these lines may find the case-method technique intensely interesting. With this approach we are concerned with the analysis of qualitative factors that cannot be measured by statistics. Even coefficients of correlation have their limitations and can't measure everything in life!

Looking back almost a century, after the 1920s in America the rising industrial world—whether it knew it or not—needed a type of research geared to human relations problems inherent in the managerial situation. Harvard University's business school introduced the case-method approach and with its teaching assumed an eminent position. It is still most highly ranked today. Other business schools have since used "some" of the same approach but typically to a lesser extent.

PART TWO: PROFESSIONAL CASES

1. GLEDHILL HIGH SCHOOL
("Work Load")
(As reported by a department head)

Mr. Robert Turnbull, the principal of Gledhill High School, felt that extra-curricular activities were fine in their proper place. This is not meant to imply that he didn't like to see his school's teams win. Once when he felt that a basketball official had ruled unfairly against the Gledhill team in the closing minutes of a game, he rushed out onto the floor and proceeded to tell the official in no uncertain terms what he thought of him. After several technical fouls were called against the Gledhill team, the embarrassed coach finally led him off the floor.

Staff members generally recognized Mr. Turnbull as an unpredictable individual. When staff members wanted to see him about a problem, they would take care to determine just what sort of mood he was in on that particular day. One staff member recalls an incident in which Mr. Turnbull one day just about frightened some relatively innocent freshman "almost to death" for a minor infraction of the rules of the school. On the next day he dealt with a "hard-rock" delinquent youngster as if he were his "fair-haired" boy.

Mr. Turnbull prided himself on the fact that his high school had a high academic standing. First and foremost, he was what might be called an "academic man." He was due to retire shortly, after a long career in teaching and educational administration.

Staff members were quick to admit that he had a number of good sides to his personality. When he hired a teacher for a particular job, that person soon learned that his job was "his baby." Mr. Turnbull was not the sort of person to interfere with the running of a department on the slightest provocation.

Following the War, Gledhill High School had an enrollment of 700 students. During the War, athletic activities had been curtailed to a great extent. As a result, the extra-curricular program managed by the athletic department consisted of senior football, junior and senior basketball, intramural basketball, and senior tennis. Two physical education teachers and one other teacher, who coached basketball, were the only staff members available for the boys' athletic program. Both of these physical education teachers had not majored in the subject during college and they were anxious, because of their age, to "retire" to the teaching of other subjects in the curriculum.

Shortly thereafter, the boys' athletic program expanded to include junior and senior football, junior and senior basketball, volleyball, gymnastics, senior hockey, junior and senior track and field, and tennis, in addition to intramural volleyball and basketball and a school golf tournament. At the beginning of the next academic year, two new physical education teachers took over the department from the two "retiring" teachers.

George Thomas was named head of the boys' physical education department, and he was to be assisted by Frank Lloyd. George was a big, friendly individual with a lot of drive and a desire to develop an outstanding program. He was highly regarded by the state education department. The other coaches in the district respected him and his work. Later, he was elected president of the state branch of the national professional association.

As the athletic program grew, it became increasingly apparent to George that he and Frank needed some help with their many coaching duties. In addition to a full work load of daily academic and physical education classes, George was coaching senior football, senior hockey, senior and junior track and field, and the gym team. He also took responsibility for the supervision of all intramural athletics. Frank Lloyd, his assistant, coached junior football, junior basketball, volleyball, and tennis. When he could, he helped George with intramural athletics. Mr. Mahler, a history teacher, continued to coach senior basketball, as he had done before George and Frank were hired.

After discussing the matter at great length with Frank, George decided to catch Mr. Turnbull in a good mood and tell him that more help was needed. He explained to Mr. Turnbull what was happening. He mentioned also that although two new teachers had been hired that year, neither of these men was qualified nor willing to help with the extra-curricular program. Mr. Turnbull listened, but made no promises. George expressed the opinion to Frank after this interview that Turnbull still felt that athletics were largely the domain of the physical education department, and that was the way it was going to stay.

George Thomas's philosophy of physical education was such that it included an opportunity for most boys to take part in some phase of the varsity and intramural program. He was quite concerned that students should have the chance to learn leisure skills. With this end in view, George went to Mr. Turnbull later in the year and suggested that he use some of the money in his budget for the purchase of badminton rackets and golf clubs. Mr. Turnbull merely laughed. He explained that he felt any extra money should be used to develop further those interscholastic sports already in the program. He suggested that vertical rather than horizontal expansion of Gledhill's athletic effort would help produce more conference winners in the various senior sports.

Matters continued about the same for the next two years. Although interested in their work, George and Frank were becoming discouraged. One day, George figured out that he had spent 500 hours on extra-curricular work during the past academic year. At the next monthly meeting of the coaches in the district, he mentioned this fact and found that many of the other coaches were facing similar situations. After a lengthy discussion, a committee was formed to make a survey. When they had the facts, the executive of the coaches' association asked to present their problem at one of the regular meetings of the high school principals in the city. When the principals saw the chart that the coaches had prepared, a great many questions were asked. They tried to show that mistakes had been made in the computations. When the executive of the coaches' association left the meeting, the coaches felt that the principals had almost called them liars.

At the beginning of the next year, Mr. Turnbull hired three new male teachers. Not one of them was assigned any extra-curricular responsibilities. George, with his usual heavy workload, became discouraged. His wife began to complain because he had one team practice before school started in the morning and another after school closed in the afternoon. About this time, a principal from a nearby school approached Mr. Turnbull to say that he would like to offer George a position in his school. Although Mr. Turnbull didn't know about it, George had received another attractive offer from an insurance firm in the city. Both George and his wife were favorably inclined toward this latter offer. Mr. Turnbull talked to George about the offer of the department headship at the other high school with a higher salary.

About this time, the physical education teachers in the district became aware of the fact that teachers in Longden (a city of about 150,000, 120 miles away) were receiving extra compensation for handling extra-curricular duties. They discussed this at their monthly meeting. The Teachers' Association had considered this problem recently and had expressed general disapproval of this practice. On the other hand, the physical education teachers knew that they could not be forced to assume duties beyond their regular classes in the curriculum.

During the fall, George had an outstanding senior football team. The team was doing very well, but the pressure upon George was great. Things were beginning to get on his nerves and his usual genial disposition was beginning to disappear. Some of the boys on the team were temperamental and hard to handle. To make matters worse, George began to develop a series of skin rashes. His physician was not sure of the cause of this ailment, but he did point out that the stress and strain of George's work might be a factor.

The senior football team finally won the district championship. George was completely exhausted both mentally and physically. His academic class work was beginning to suffer. Mr. Turnbull informed George that Gledhill's football team had been invited to represent their section in the state tournament the next Saturday. Mr. Turnbull was elated. George also was happy and proud, but he wondered if he could stand the strain of another such week as the last. His rashes had been getting worse.

George's team did well in the tournament. The winner was determined by committee vote later in the day. Gledhill did not win, but they gave a good account of themselves. They were an outstanding defensive team, but they didn't have any exceptional "breakaway" runners on the offense. It was a rough weekend for George. He had the complete responsibility of the group, including busloads of cheering students, and he had to be everywhere at once even after the game was over.

Next Monday morning, Mr. Turnbull called George to his office. George still hadn't recovered from the hectic weekend. Mr. Turnbull commended him on the team's performance and then said that George had been doing so well with his guidance work that he had decided to give him more responsibility in this area. He made no mention of any plan to lighten George's workload in any way. George "blew his top." Mr. Turnbull also became quite upset and somewhat belligerent. When he saw that George was adamant in his refusal to accept any more assignments, Mr. Turnbull calmed down. Both people appeared quite upset by the interview.

There was a good deal of tension during the next few months, especially when George told Mr. Turnbull that he was going to drop senior hockey from the athletic program immediately, because he simply could not stand the pace and his health was being affected.

In February at the annual variety show, George met many of the students' parents. Several of the fathers said they were sorry that it had not been possible to have an interscholastic hockey team that year. Moreover, during the preparation for the show, he had told the other teachers that he would not be able to arrange for the usual gymnastics demonstration. George was a bit embarrassed.

As he was getting ready to go home, he overhead a conversation between Mr. Turnbull and an influential lawyer in the city. The lawyer, Mr. Garde, was quite upset that interscholastic hockey had been dropped. His son, Ray, was an outstanding player and missed the chance to play on the school team. Mr. Turnbull appeared quite embarrassed and tried to pass over the matter. Mr. Garde, however, pressed his point by remarking that Gledhill was the only school in the district conference without a hockey team.

Suggested Questions for Discussion

1. What insight into Mr. Turnbull's personality might you get from his action at the basketball game?

2. Do you think it is fair to type a principal as "an academic man"?

3. Do you think George should have discussed the developing program sooner with Mr. Turnbull?

4. What do you think of Mr. Turnbull's opinion that the responsibility of an athletic program is largely the task of the members of

the physical education department?

5. Do you think George was right in stressing the idea of leisure carry-over skills, in view of Mr. Turnbull's opinion that vertical expansion of athletics was the better policy?

6. What mistakes, if any, did the coaches' executive make in his method of presenting their case to the principals? Why do you imagine that the principals didn't seem to believe him?

7. If you were George, would you make a point of letting Mr. Turnbull know that you were thinking seriously of taking the other school's offer in order to pressure him for more help? Should George have told Mr. Turnbull about the offer from the insurance firm?

8. Do you think that George and Frank should have gone to see Mr. Turnbull and pointed out that they were thinking seriously of dropping all extracurricular activities because their contracts would allow them to take such action?

9. Should George have refused to take his team to the state football tournament because of his health?

10. Why do you suppose that Mr. Turnbull asked George to assume further responsibility in the guidance program without lightening his load in some other way?
11. Was George right in "blowing his top"?

12. Should George have decided to drop senior hockey competition?

13. What influence would Mr. Garde's criticism have on Mr. Turnbull's opinion of the athletic program?

14. Should George have submitted his resignation after the "heated interview" with Mr. Turnbull?

2. Dixon College
"Staff Selection")
(As reported by a department head)

In the spring, Professor Cobb asked the administration of Dixon College to allow him to add another male staff member to the department of physical education. Although the scope of the physical education program had been increasing, the administration still hesitated to grant this request. Professor Cobb discussed the situation with Mr. Slaughter, the athletic director, who would be using the new appointee part-time as a coach in football and wrestling. Mr. Slaughter agreed to speak to the president to emphasize the need for another man. One week later, the dean called Professor Cobb and told him to begin looking for a junior staff member.

Dixon College had an enrollment of about 2500 students. There was a one-year requirement in physical education for all students, in addition to voluntary programs in intramural and intercollegiate athletics. A major program leading to the Bachelor of Science degree in Physical Education had been started five years before the beginning of the case.

The new department member was to have responsibilities in various phases of the physical education and athletic program. The appointment was to be at the instructor level, with an annual salary starting at $42,000. After a two-year probationary period, teachers were generally promoted to the assistant professor level if their work was satisfactory. This promotion meant that the position was "permanent". There was no tenure in the generally accepted use of the term.

The dean and the president were interested in a man with a sound liberal arts and science background as well as a good preparation in physical education. They were concerned also about the religious preference of the applicant. Professor Cobb did not quite understand their reasoning in this last matter, except that Mr. Slaughter, the athletic director, and one other male staff member were Catholic. The administration seemed to want to preserve a balance of Protestants over Catholics on the staff.

Mr. Slaughter, who was a keen judge of men, wished to obtain the best man possible under the circumstances. He was particularly concerned about the individual's ability to assist in varsity football and to coach another sport as well.

Professor Cobb agreed to a large extent with the others. He wanted to get a man with a broad philosophy of physical education. At the same time, he was anxious to find a person who would fit harmoniously into the staff picture. There was some unrest between the athletic department and the physical education department, and Cobb thought it was important to hire someone who would not wish to overemphasize one aspect of the program.

Professor Cobb wrote to the placement office of a long-established private institution in New England, about 400 miles away from Dixon College. This college had been one of the first to establish a teacher-training program for physical educators and had the reputation of turning out well-qualified men in professional physical education work. Because so many professional courses were included in a four-year curriculum, the liberal arts background of its graduates was a bit weak. The placement office sent Cobb the credentials of six graduating seniors. Professor Cobb, Mr. Slaughter, and other senior staff members carefully screened the credentials. One man, Arthur Donaldson, seemed to be qualified. In addition, he would be available for an interview at Dixon within the next two weeks, as he was planning to visit his father in a city only 150 miles away. Since the dean was quite anxious to save on travel money, they decided to invite him for an interview at that time.

Mr. Donaldson was twenty-six years old and had served in the Air Force for two years. He was five feet eleven inches tall and weighed 190 lbs. He was Catholic and had been married after his first year in college. There were no children, and his wife was anxious to seek employment wherever her husband worked. His major subject at college was physical education; his minor, recreation. During college he had participated in a variety of extracurricular activities, including football, basketball, wrestling, and tennis. During the summers he had been active at various camps as a waterfront director. His grades were above average, and he was anxious to start graduate work in the summers. Many references were included in his brochure, and they all added up to one conclusion—Arthur Donaldson had made an excellent record as a student and as an athlete in his college.

Mr. and Mrs. Donaldson came to Dixon College for the interview. They spent the afternoon looking around the campus and meeting members of the staff and the college administration. All seemed favorably impressed with the couple. Art was a rugged, personable fellow with a strong jaw and just about the right amount of aggressiveness. He had strong opinions about a number of the current problems in physical education, but he tried to be tactful. He was full of confidence and highly praised his college course. He spoke in glowing terms about his football coach, who had evidently been a real "slave-driver." The Donaldsons were an attractive, well-dressed, personable couple. The dean commented especially about Mrs. Donaldson's appearance and personality. The president didn't have much to say one way or the other.

The Donaldsons had dinner at the home of Professor and Mrs. Cobb, and about 9:00 P. M. made a pre-arranged visit to the home of Mr. and Mrs. Slaughter. Upon their return, they appeared impressed with the new home that Mr. Slaughter had just built. They mentioned the names of several influential people in town that the Slaughters had said they could introduce them to. Mrs. Cobb mentioned to her husband later that this couple would find it difficult to live on an instructor's salary. In the morning, the Donaldson's took their leave after thanking all profusely for their kindness. A few days later, Professor Cobb received the following letter from Mr. Donaldson:

Box 6, Lynwood College
Lynwood, CT.

Dr. Robert Cobb
Professor of Physical Education
Dixon College
Waterloo, Michigan

Dear Bob:

Thank you for your kindness during our visit of March 24th and 25th. I greatly appreciate the time and consideration you gave us.

We were deeply impressed by the College and all the fine people that we met. The physical education position that we discussed is definitely interesting to me, and I hope that I shall have the good fortune to become a member of such a congenial staff.

Please give your wife our very best wishes.

Sincerely,
Arthur Donaldson

Slaughter mentioned to Cobb that he also received a letter.

The second candidate asked to come to Dixon for an interview was George Nelson. Cobb had heard about George from Professor Farquharson of the Dixon physical education staff. Farquharson had a friend completing his degree at Greer State University. When this friend heard about the available position, he had suggested to Farquharson that George Nelson might be the man for the position. George was just completing his M. A. degree at Greer and had been serving as assistant wrestling coach. George had majored in physical education at a small midwestern college that was known in the athletic world for its outstanding wrestling teams. Farquharson asked the head coach of wrestling about George and received a fine recommendation. The coach pointed out that George was an excellent student, a fact that was substantiated by the department head at Greer. Upon Cobb's request, Farquharson asked Mr. and Mrs. Nelson to come to Dixon for an interview.

The Nelson interview followed the same pattern as that with the Donaldsons. They were shown the campus and the particular facilities that would be of most interest. Cobb liked Nelson instinctively, probably because he was personable, quiet, and yet calmly confident. Mrs. Nelson was not so attractive a person as Mrs. Donaldson. Mrs. Cobb liked her and described her as more of a "home-body" type. The dean for some reason liked the Donaldsons better. Professor Cobb arranged for the president to meet him and Mr. Nelson at the cafeteria for coffee. Mr. Nelson talked easily with the president and mentioned that he knew quite a few high school wrestlers who might be interested in coming to Dixon if they knew that he was going to coach wrestling. When Professor Cobb talked to the president later, the point arose that Mr. Nelson ought to have some plastic surgery performed on one of his ears that had been "cauliflowered" by wrestling competition. The president seemed to prefer Mr. Donaldson even though he was Catholic.

Later in the afternoon, Cobb had a long talk with Nelson about the position. Nelson was relatively inexperienced with football, a point that Mr.

Slaughter stressed later. In addition, Nelson felt that he couldn't afford to take the position under $45,000. He mentioned that this figure was the "going price" at which men with Master's degrees were leaving Greer. If he couldn't get this salary, he indicated that it might be better for him to proceed with his doctorate at Greer.

The Cobbs had the prospective candidate and his wife to their home for dinner, as they had done with the Donaldsons. Mr. Slaughter did not appear to be interested in having the Nelsons visit his home, as the Donaldsons had done. The evening was spent in pleasant fashion. Before the Nelsons left in the morning, Professor Cobb told Nelson that he would hear from him shortly after the third candidate had been interviewed.

Professor Cobb had met the third candidate at a national convention. This man, Roger Baldwin, was four or five years older than Donaldson or Nelson. Roger appeared to have an excellent background and was extremely personable. He had his doctorate with a joint major in physical education and history from Rockwell State University in the Far West. At present, he was director of physical education and instructor of history at a small midwestern college. Cobb asked Baldwin if he would be interested in a post at Dixon, and Baldwin said that he would be in the Dixon area within the next two weeks and would be glad to pay a visit. He also mentioned that he was interested in an assistant professorship and a salary of at least $50,000.

Two weeks later, Dr. Baldwin telephoned Dr. Cobb from a nearby city and said that he could visit Dixon the next day if convenient. Arrangements were made and Cobb met him at the railroad station. For some reason, although he was very anxious to like Baldwin because of his excellent qualifications, Cobb was not so impressed with him out of the convention atmosphere. Baldwin was well dressed, but his clothes were rather ill fitting because he was overweight. Cobb and Baldwin made a rather hasty trip around the campus and stopped briefly to see a number of the staff members. Baldwin impressed Slaughter with his knowledge of football as well as his willingness to coach wrestling, although he had been away from the latter since college.

Baldwin was very interested that Dixon College had made tentative plans to start graduate work in physical education. Cobb felt that another man with a doctorate would give increased stature to his staff. He reasoned also that other departments on the campus would look upon this man's background in history favorably. Baldwin had held a very responsible position in a private agency before taking his present college position. Cobb felt that this administrative background would be helpful at Dixon. Cobb took Baldwin to meet the dean and then the president. Both were favorably impressed, as was the head of the history department at another meeting. Cobb mentioned that perhaps he could make arrangements for Baldwin to teach one history course and thereby augment his salary a bit. Cobb talked to the president later about Roger Baldwin. The president mentioned that he didn't see how they could obtain the services of Dr. Baldwin at the rank of instructor with a salary of only $42,000. Cobb said that Baldwin would like a position as an assistant professor at $50,000. He stressed that Baldwin had a wife and two children. He asked the president if he would consider paying a bit more for a better-qualified man, if everyone agreed eventually that Dr. Baldwin should be offered the position. The president did not commit himself, but said that he would discuss it with the dean.

Professor Cobb took Dr. Baldwin home for dinner. He took him out to see the horses that he raised. Although Baldwin had expressed an interest in horses, he continued to talk about physical education and hardly looked at the animals that Cobb was trying to show to him. When they went into the house, Baldwin excused himself for a minute and came back with a bottle of rye whiskey that he had brought for a gift. He seemed anxious to have a drink before dinner, so Cobb mixed a drink for him and explained rather apologetically that he and Mrs. Cobb didn't drink. He suggested that Baldwin might as well take the remainder of the rye with him so that it wouldn't go to waste. Baldwin said he hoped that the Cobbs didn't mind the fact that he liked an occasional drink. They assured him that they certainly had no objections. Later in the evening, Baldwin had several more drinks.

Cobb and Baldwin talked enthusiastically about physical education during supper and after. Baldwin described his various undertakings at great length. Professor and Mrs. Cobb found his analysis of living conditions in his own state quite interesting. At one point in the conversation, Baldwin mentioned that a mutual friend had told him earlier that day that he (Baldwin) would be the best thing to ever happen to the Dixon physical education staff. Professor and Mrs. Cobb laughed about this later, because they thought that this remark was a little out of place, even if true. Dr. Baldwin thanked Professor Cobb for his courtesy the next morning with a cheery goodbye. He said he would be looking forward to hearing from Cobb when a decision had been made.

As Cobb thought about the various applicants, he didn't really know whom to recommend to the administration. He talked to the dean and the president, who said that it was up to him, Mr. Slaughter, and the staff members to make a recommendation. They didn't commit themselves about the salary requirements that would be necessary for the applicants with the higher degrees. They did appear quite anxious to conserve money and the dean made the point that the Donaldsons were "certainly a fine couple."

Mr. Slaughter seemed partial to Arthur Donaldson, although he was impressed with the qualifications of Dr. Baldwin. The fact that both could help in coaching football was important to him.

The staff members were divided in their opinions. Professor Farquharson was partial to Nelson, because the head coach of wrestling at Greer and the department head had recommended him so highly. Another staff member seemed concerned that Dr. Baldwin wanted an assistant professorship.

Professor Cobb liked them all, but he realized that the dean and the president wanted to conserve money. After meeting Donaldson, the president had said nothing more about the fact that he was Catholic. Cobb agreed with the dean that the Donaldsons were a fine couple, but he was impressed with Nelson's wrestling background. He thought also about the fact that Baldwin had his doctorate completed and would lend stature to the department. He wondered a bit how Baldwin's personality would "click" with the rest of the staff, but he reasoned that it wasn't fair to judge a man only on the basis of a casual visit. He remembered the president's comment about Nelson's cauliflower ear. He considered further that Donaldson had no teaching and coaching experience at all and held only a Bachelor's degree. Cobb was puzzled. Whom should he recommend for the position?

Suggested Questions for Discussion

1. What do you think of an arrangement whereby a physical education

staff member is used part-time by athletics?

2. Why do you suppose the dean and the president were concerned about the religious preference of the applicant?

3. When hiring a new staff member, which quality should you consider most important, if any?

4. How much difference does it make whether an applicant graduated from a "recognized" college or university?

5. Does the possession of a sound liberal arts and science background make a great deal of difference?

6. Who do you think should be responsible for screening the various sets of credentials that are received when a position is available? Should Professor Cobb have circulated more widely a notice about the opening?

7. Should an applicant or the school pay for his traveling expenses? Should an applicant ever be hired without a personal interview?

8. What do you think of Arthur Donaldson and his wife?

9. How did the Nelsons appeal to you? How much would you take into consideration that Farquharson's friend, the wrestling coach, and the department head at Greer all spoke highly of George Nelson?

10. Why do you suppose Mr. Slaughter did not encourage the Nelsons also to visit him at his home in the evening?

11. What do you think of Dr. Baldwin? Would his joint major in history be an important consideration?

12. Do you think the dean and the president might be willing to pay a little more for an instructor if necessary? Do you think they would consider offering a man like Dr. Baldwin an assistant professorship?

13. In what way, if any, did the dean and the president try to influence Professor Cobb?

14. What influence do you think Mr. Slaughter would have on the choice of a man?

15. Why was Farquharson partial to Nelson?

16. How much consideration should be given to candidates' differences in age, experience, and professional background?

17. Was the decision really up to Cobb? Whom would you select?

3. STATE UNIVERSITY
("Personnel Relationships")
(As reported by the dean of the school)

Taylor Washburn was an assistant professor in charge of the major program at State. His department was one of many which came under the jurisdiction of the School of Health, Physical Education, and Recreation. He had an excellent background for his position. In addition to a B. A. degree with a major in history, he also held a B.S. and an M.A. in health and physical education. He was thirty years old and a bachelor. He apparently had no intention of getting married.

Taylor's superior at State was Dean Carlson. He and Taylor got along together very well. No one kept any secrets from anyone else on the staff, and this applied especially to the relationship between Carlson and Washburn. All staff policy was discussed openly and freely at regular meetings. It should be mentioned that too well the rest of the staff did not like Washburn, because he fought hard for the rights and privileges of his own department. He often came out with strong statements at staff meetings, but Dean Carlson did not worry about this too much about this. He knew that he could generally reach an acceptable compromise with Professor Washburn. Carlson sensed also that Washburn was not too popular with the students, but he reasoned that students did not have to like an instructor so long as they respected him.

Washburn paid careful attention to the administrative details of his post. All who associated with him knew exactly where he stood on administrative matters. For example, the locker room supervisor thought highly of him, because he was thoughtful and yet businesslike in all his dealings. The other staff members who worked completely under his supervision did not get along with him very well. Dean Carlson reasoned, however, that certain differences of opinion that arose were not insuperable. Matters never appeared black and white, and Washburn seemed to be making a sincere effort to get along with his departmental staff.

The administrative officers of the university thought highly of Washburn, although it must be admitted that they knew relatively little about the specifics of his work. He dressed well, attended meetings regularly, spoke meticulous English, and in their opinion was a fine representative of the physical education field.

Professor Washburn's father and mother were quite old and their health was poor. They lived in a city about 400 miles away and were very attached to this locality. He visited them whenever possible. Because he was an only child and felt a strong responsibility to his parents, he had mentioned several times to Dean Carlson the possibility of taking a post at the high school level back in that city. In this way, he would be able to help them over some of life's rough spots late in life.

The State Director of Physical Education held Washburn in high regard and always asked about him when Dean Carlson visited the state office.

The entire staff of the School understood that the Ph.D. degree was considered necessary for promotion to the rank of associate professor. Except for this qualification, Professor Washburn could have reasonably expected to receive this rank shortly. For this reason, he had made tentative plans to complete his doctorate.

Professor Washburn was not too happy about the dictatorial habits demonstrated by the university president at meetings. Dean Carlson felt exactly the same way. Policies decided upon democratically by the staff of the school often received rather harsh treatment when they were brought before the Administrative Board, which the president chaired. As the president was fairly young and likely to hold his office for a considerable time, Washburn wondered if the school was going to continue to progress. He and Carlson had discussed this matter on occasion.

When Dean Carlson presented his budget for the forthcoming academic year, he said that he could not recommend a promotion to the rank of associate professor for Professor Washburn. Washburn understood that his lack of the advanced degree was Carlson's reason. Carlson did recommend, however, a sizeable salary increase, because he felt that Washburn was underpaid. The next morning the vice-president directly over Dean Carlson called to say that the Administrative Board was going to recommend the promotion in rank for Professor Washburn. Dean Carlson did not like to hold a person back, but he said that he could not agree wholeheartedly. He explained that several other staff members also should be promoted, if the matter of the Ph.D. degree was to be overlooked. The vice-president stated that the president felt that Washburn should have the promotion and that was the way it would have to be. Dean Carlson didn't know what to do.

No sooner had the telephone conversation concluded than one of the outstanding senior men students entered Dean Carlson's office. He asked the dean if he would come with him to one of the classrooms on the same floor to discuss an important matter. When they arrived, Dean Carlson found sixteen men students present. Bob Reynolds, the student who had come to get the Dean, explained that the group wanted to air some grievances about Professor Washburn. Dean Carlson was dumbfounded. He didn't know whether he should listen to what they had to say. Finally, he stated that he would listen, but that he wanted to get both sides of the story. Carlson wondered if he should have called Professor Washburn to the room, but he reasoned that such a meeting would be embarrassing to all concerned. The dean listened quietly as the students spoke. On several occasions he argued on behalf of Professor Washburn. On certain points he stated that he would look into the matter. Finally, Bob Reynolds presented Dean Carlson with a list of all the complaints. Dean Carlson promised to consider the matter carefully.

After Dean Carlson read over the list several times in the privacy of his office, he decided to discuss the matter immediately with Professor Washburn. He went to Professor Washburn's office and said, "Taylor, I don't know what to think of something that just happened, but I think I should discuss it with you right away." Washburn looked at him quizzically and said, "What's up?"~ Washburn could see that Carlson was very upset. In a kindly way, Carlson told him exactly what had happened and then showed him the list:

Physical Education Students' Complaints (by Men)

Prof. Taylor Washburn:

1. Teaching incompetence
    a. Washburn's organization of classes is poor.
    b. He cancels classes at will.
    c. He doesn't seem to care about students or their improvement.
    d. His grades are not computed objectively.
    e. Test papers are not graded adequately.

f. He taught us gymnastics for one-half year as part of our activity work but now says that the grades for this work won't count in our final averages.

g. He didn't cover the subject of Community Recreation but now he asks that we be responsible for this course inadequacy on the final examination.

h. In our course on Methods and Materials, all we got was information on materials.

i. As an instructor he has inadequacies, but he makes no apparent effort to improve his work.

j. In square dancing work this year, the students say they have learned nothing. Over half of the classes were cancelled. Now the students are being tested on last year's material. No theoretical examination was given at the end of the "course"— only a practical one.

k. One morning in place of teaching the regular class work, the group was read a fairy tale.

1. General Comments
   a. The reason there are only three men registered in the 2nd year of the major program is that the junior and senior men are telling younger students to take a minor instead of a major in the department.

   b. Students have lost their confidence in Mr. Washburn's ability, administration, and leadership.

   c. He has shown extreme favoritism with one junior student. The work and personality of other students have been discussed. d. Mr. Washburn, on a number of occasions, has interfered with the work of other instructors during class and has contradicted them in front of the group of students.

   d.

Washburn read this indictment slowly, without saying a word. Both Washburn and Carlson realized that the students had misinterpreted a number of the items. One question remained, as they both knew. Could Washburn continue in the face of this statement demonstrating the students' dislike and lack of confidence in him as a person? Both teachers sat quietly for a few moments. Then Taylor said, "Tom, maybe it's time for me to take that high school position near my folks." Carlson replied, "Taylor, the world isn't going to come to an end. Let's have lunch. It's my turn to buy."

Suggested Questions for Discussion

1. Because staff members and students did not seem to like Washburn, should Carlson have looked more carefully into this matter sooner? If the answer is "yes," how should he do it?

2. Everything considered, what opinion do you get of Washburn?

3. Do you believe that Washburn's dislike of the president and his anxiety for the welfare of his parents had anything to do with his work and conduct?

4. When Carlson learned that Washburn was going to be promoted despite the policy in effect, what should he have done?

5. Should Carlson have left the room when he discovered what the meeting with the students was about?

6. Should Carlson have discussed the matter with Washburn immediately?

7. What should Washburn do?

8. What should Carlson do, knowing that the promotion was to be approved the next day by the Board of Regents?

4. BENTON COLLEGE
("Office Management")
(As reported by a department head)

Benton College was a medium-sized, co-ed liberal arts college with a total enrollment of about 2,500 students. The physical education major program consisted of about 70 students rather evenly divided in number among the four years of the course. The staff members (seven full-time men and three full-time women) were considered full-time employees of the department, although all of them were "on loan" to intercollegiate athletics and received a share of their salaries from the athletic budget. The director of athletics was not listed as a faculty member on the physical education staff, and the department head received his salary completely from the departmental budget. The department head, however, did serve as track coach.

The physical education department was responsible for the one-year program required for freshmen as well as intramural athletics. All intercollegiate athletics were governed by the Athletic Board of Control, of which the director of athletics was an ex-officio member. At this time, the entire program moved into a new multiple-purpose building called Bartram Hall.

Just as the physical education office was being moved to Bartram Hall, the departmental secretary gave notice. The department head, Professor Roberts, told the rest of the staff about Miss Collins' resignation and asked them whether they knew of anyone who might be interested in the position. The Dean's Office was notified and a call was placed to the Dean of Men, who kept a file of positions available and received requests from applicants for jobs on the campus. At the moment, no applicant was available, and it appeared that it was going to be difficult to fill the position because of the low starting salary. Professor Roberts was concerned because it was important to keep the office functioning. He wanted to locate another young lady soon so that the retiring secretary could break the new girl in on the intricacies of office procedure.

Professor Roberts gave some thought to the qualifications that a new secretary should possess. Certainly she should be reasonably intelligent and personable. Age and maturity were rather important, because the individual would be meeting students all day long. Computer ability had to be considered, because she would be doing important work for the department such as keeping important records, greeting visitors, preparing notices, etc.. All this for the "going salary", less income tax, pension plan, and health insurance!

At lunch one day shortly thereafter, the Alumni Secretary, Mr. Rogers, mentioned that he had heard from a friend about an attractive and personable young lady who might be interested in the position. Her name was Ms. June Borden, and she had graduated several months previously from a nearby business school. An appointment for an interview was made. Miss Borden appeared right on time, and she made an excellent impression. When interviewed, she was an attractive, willowy blonde, exceptionally well dressed. Her personality traits were excellent and she appeared very interested in getting the position even after Professor Roberts explained about the starting salary. It seemed that she was living with her parents and could afford to work for that amount of money. She was 21 years old, had graduated from high school the previous year, and had been continuing in the business school to improve her computer capability. This last bit of information prompted Professor Roberts to forget about the idea of asking the applicant to demonstrate "secretarial proficiency." He thanked her for coming for the interview and promised to notify her shortly about the decision.

After talking over the appointment with the dean and the department members who had met Ms. Borden, Professor Roberts called her and informed her that her application had been accepted. It was generally agreed that it was not possible to locate an older person for the salary offered. In addition, Roberts thought it might be advisable to hire a younger person and train her gradually for the position.

Ms. Borden made a sincere effort to master the position. The previous secretary had been moody, but Miss Borden possessed an even disposition and treated all in a friendly manner. Her predecessor had not handled telephone conversations very well. She insisted on calling out for staff members by their first names and sometimes she would say, "I don't know where Jack is right now; he never tells me." Ms. Borden, on the other hand, handled telephone conversations very efficiently. The former secretary had shown a great affinity with members of the opposite sex and would leap from her desk to the counter to greet the young *men* who dropped in at the office for information. Ms. Borden was friendly, answered questions to the best of her ability, and returned to the work at hand. The other secretary had pounded over mistakes in her typing, but Miss Borden was very careful about took pride in the preparation of memoranda, reports, etc.

It was this latter point, however, that soon caused difficulty. Professor Roberts and the other staff members soon learned why Ms. Borden had stayed for a few extra months at the business school. She and the English language had never become "fully acquainted." This deficiency had not been apparent in her conversation, but it was obvious in her memoranda and other correspondence. Ms. Borden's inadequate vocabulary and poor knowledge of English grammar was to prove an outstanding problem, although she was always willing to re-do inadequate material that she had turned out. However, anything going out from the department had to be read carefully, and items could never be sent over the secretary's signature.

Another annoying problem developed. Ms. Borden was very careful about filing letters and their replies, and other material as well—in the wrong folder. Professor Roberts had hoped that Ms. Borden would be able to help with his own personal file. In a short time, he took a day off to straighten out his own filing system and relieved Ms. Borden from this extra duty.

A further problem arose in connection with the collection of a fee each year from student majors to help defray the expense of the variety of printed material that was given to them periodically. Ms. Borden left her desk drawers unlocked occasionally, and one morning noticed that sixty--eight dollars was missing.

Ms. Borden was very accommodating to staff and students alike, and students soon began to take advantage of her. Professor Roberts sometimes found her preparing short term papers and other items for students. To help her avoid these favors, it was suggested that she refer such requests to the department head. This problem had been relatively simple to solve, but another similar problem was somewhat more difficult. One of the senior professors outlined his class lectures in great detail and continually asked Ms. Borden to type out these notes. In a way this was department business; in another way it wasn't! Professor Roberts, who by nature of his administrative post made great demands on her time, was a bit fearful about discouraging this practice of the other professor, because he didn't wish to hurt his colleague's feelings. It did not seem part of the job of a departmental secretary, however. So he mentioned time and again at departmental meetings what a great help a knowledge of computer keyboarding was to a teacher. The professor concerned said that he "got the message" and said that he wished he knew how to use a computer. Eventually, this teacher, who was one of the top men on the staff, seemed to "ease off" on such requests.

A bulletin board in an office can be an asset or a cluttered-up affair that people rarely look at. Professor Roberts tried to keep it organized and suggested that Ms. Borden accept this as one of her responsibilities. Quite a large board was obtained, but even this was not large enough to hold all the items that appeared. Unfortunately, there was no additional wall space available for a second board. An effort was made to categorize the areas of the board according to positions available, timetables of the various years of the major program, the required program, certain intramural fixtures, daily notices regarding class changes, etc., current newspaper and magazine clippings, and newly published books. From time to time, the department head made an effort to tidy it up; Ms. Borden would occasionally agree that it "had become a mess again" and leave it at that.

The closing of the office during the lunch period caused a slight problem. Professor Roberts felt that the office should be locked when Ms. Borden went to lunch. Unfortunately, the door at the far end of the office, where the athletic director had his office, would be open at times and locked at others, depending on the presence of the director. Miss Borden put up a small notice on the office door at the physical education end that stated that office hours were from 9-12 A. M. and from 1-5 P. M. Thus, people would understand if the door were locked from 12 to 1. This was satisfactory, except that Ms. Borden did not always find it convenient to eat from twelve to one. The cafeteria was crowded at noon; at other times she asked if she might start her lunch hour a bit late so she could keep an appointment downtown.

Coffee breaks began at 10 A. M. sharp. All the secretaries went over to the cafeteria, roughly a quarter of a mile away. What started out to be a ten-minute break had a way of lengthening into half an hour. About three o'clock in the afternoon, this practice was repeated. As a result, the switchboard operators often found it difficult to get an answer when she called the departmental office.

Fortunately, Ms. Borden felt that most of the students were quite juvenile and did not have dates with any of them. The previous secretary had found many students interesting and would show her likes or dislikes, depending on whether a minor courtship was developing or had just been broken.

From time to time, other secretaries resigned from other departments in Bartram Hall and were replaced. Ms. Borden soon realized that new girls were starting at the same salary level as she, even though she had received small raises each year. Professor Roberts asked the dean of the school about this. He was told that the cost of living had been rising steadily, and it was necessary to pay more to obtain employees. The fact that Ms. Borden's seniority was involved to a degree did not seem to disturb him. Another disconcerting element was that Ms. Brown, the secretary for Intercollegiate Athletics, was making at least five thousand dollars more than any other secretary in the building. However, she had been working there for ten years.

Secretaries received one week of vacation for each year of service up to a maximum of three weeks. Miss Borden preferred to split her vacation in various ways, and she always asked about this well in advance and was careful to ask if this arrangement would cause any hardship. As there was no summer school in physical education, these "split" vacations did not create a problem in themselves. However, the Dean felt that much of the physical education department's secretarial service was unnecessary in the summer, and on several occasions asked to borrow Ms. Borden for other duties during this period. These absences, combined with Ms. Borden's "split" vacations, caused some inconvenience and hardship to Professor Roberts.

Car parking was a perennial problem. Although adequate space was provided behind the building, the athletic director insisted on parking in front of Bartram Hall very near his office. Other staff members resented this and gave the parking attendant a great deal of difficulty. Tickets were issued, but the rules could not be well enforced because the university property was private. Ms. Borden began to park her car out front on every occasion when the attendant might be in some other area on the campus. It was difficult to chastise her, since other people were also flouting the regulations.

The secretary in athletics often complained that she was too busy to work for various department members with duties in intercollegiate athletics related to that department. Some thought that she wasn't that busy and just didn't wish to be bothered. These requests for help then came to Ms. Borden, who did her best to keep up with them. At times her day became rather hectic, especially preceding athletic weekends in winter season.

A file of Alexander Bibliography Cards was kept in the physical education office, so that major students could check to see if certain books needed for reference were available in the main library. Individual staff members who lent them to students on occasion there had purchased many books not available. A system was devised whereby students could sign out for these books through Ms. Borden. This system worked fairly well until students became lazy. They began to borrow them from staff members' even though many of these books were actually in the main library.

At the end of the academic year, Professor Roberts noticed that eleven books were missing from his personal library. Miss Borden had no record of signing any of them out for use in the reading room close by. A similar system whereby films and other audio-visual aids were lent to local high school teachers and coaches was misused occasionally when staff members borrowed these items and did not make notations in the sign-out book provided. When Ms. Borden was not in the office, certain staff members would also lend departmental films and forget to notify her.

In a physical education office, decorum is often a delicate matter. Students should feel that the office is a friendly place, and that they are welcome. However, the Office is primarily a place of business. It was often necessary for Professor Roberts to come out of his own office and ask students and, at times, certain staff members to keep their conversations down to a "dull roar." Ms. Borden never complained since she enjoyed these "sessions," but naturally she did not accomplish much work at these times.

Miss Borden was helpful, however, with a problem that her predecessor had tended to ignore. This was the matter of the students' tendency to call staff members by their first names. She made an effort to refer always to staff members by their proper titles. This problem probably arises more often in physical education units than in other fields.

At the beginning of her fifth year, Ms. Borden's parents moved to another city. She found it necessary to rent an apartment and made an arrangement with one of the unmarried women staff members. She soon realized that her salary was not sufficient to cover rent, clothes, and the maintenance of her small car, as well as the many other necessary expenses. She spoke to Professor Roberts, who agreed that her salary was low. He said he would speak to the Dean about an increase, although he knew that this request would probably not be looked upon favorably. The Dean listened to the request, which was also given to him in writing at the same time. He promised to discuss it with the Academic Vice-President. Nothing more was heard back from him.

In the spring, a friend told Ms. Borden about an opening with a large airlines company. After a short training period at the company's expense in a nearby large city, she would return to the same community where Benton College was located. The position involved taking air reservations over the telephone. The starting salary was considerably higher than the College could pay, with regular increments as well. Ms. Borden asked Professor Roberts whether he thought she should apply. His opinion was that she should certainly look into the opportunity to see if the proposition appealed to her. One drawback to the job was that she would work from 7:00 A. M. to 3:00 P. M. one week and from 3:00 P. M. to 11:00 P. M. the next. In addition, she would have to work every other weekend. After several interviews, she was offered the position. She came to Professor Roberts again and asked for his advice about whether she should accept.

Professor Roberts was now in a quandary. He realized that he only had to apply a little bit of pressure, and it was quite possible that Miss Borden would stay. There were some disadvantages to the new position, but the salary was certainly more attractive. He thought of all the good points about Ms. Borden and her work (i.e., her loyalty, her willingness to undertake any assignment, her even disposition, her pleasant way of dealing with people over the counter, and the many other attributes that become apparent when an individual has given five years of service to an organization). On the other hand, he recalled that she still had difficulty with grammar and spelling and that her present position was indeed a dead-end job. He reasoned that it was her decision to make and that he, as an administrator, could not afford to lose sight of the welfare of individuals, despite the fact that her resignation would leave quite a gap for several years to come.

With these thoughts running through his mind, Professor Roberts told Ms. Borden that he didn't wish to influence her unduly and that it was truly her decision. This did not satisfy her, and she pressed for some further advice, because she insisted that "she really did not know what to do." Rather than offering any direct suggestion either way, Professor Roberts told her that they think it over some more. He promised to tell her what he thought would be best the next morning.

Suggested Questions for Discussion

1. What qualifications should a departmental secretary possess?

2. Do you think it advisable to give an applicant some dictation before hiring her?

3. Would it have been wiser to make a greater effort to locate an older, more experienced person?

4. When it was learned that Ms. Borden had difficulty with spelling and grammar, should she have been asked to find another position?

5. What should have been done when it was discovered that a petty thief had stolen twenty-eight dollars from Miss Borden's unlocked desk?

6. Should Professor Roberts have made it clear to the other professor that the typing of his class notes was not the sort of work that Ms. Borden should be doing?

7. Who should have been responsible for the maintenance of the bulletin board?

8. What arrangement should have been made for the lunch period when the office was left unstaffed?

9. What policy should be set about coffee breaks

10. Should employees be allowed to have dates with students?

11. What do you think of a situation in which new employees receive the same salaries as older staff members?

12. Should employees be allowed to take their vacations one week at a time?

13. Should Professor Roberts have insisted that Miss Borden comply with parking regulations?

14. What should have been done about the other secretary who refused, in

a sense, to do work that was rightfully hers?

15. Should a formal system have been devised whereby books and films were made available for loan?

16. How do you keep a physical education office from becoming a place for between-class social gatherings?

17. Should students ever call staff members by their first names?

18. Should Professor Roberts have forced the issue with the Dean about a raise for Ms. Borden?

19. Should Professor Roberts have refused to give Miss Borden any advice about her acceptance of the new position?

20. If he advised her, what should he have recommended?

5. BALDWIN UNIVERSITY

("Required Physical Education")
(As reported by Dr. Scott)

After the War, Baldwin University, a semiprivate university, retained a two-year requirement in physical education for men and women students. Dr. Johnson (M.D., Ph.D.), age 42, was chosen as the new President. Because of his experience as a college athlete, he showed a great interest in the affairs of the Department of Physical Education.

Upon the retirement of the Director of Physical Education, Mr. Jonas (age 38, no college degree), was appointed Director of Athletics. This was a newly created position, as intercollegiate athletics were previously under the Dept. of Physical Education. Upon the recommendation of the retiring Director, Mr. Robins (age 36, M.A.) was appointed head of the Department of Physical Education. Mr. Robins had just completed a successful military career as an army officer, where he had administered a large program.

At this time there were no indoor physical education facilities on the campus. The students used the local high schools and the Y. M.C. A. A new physical education building was planned for readiness in two years.

A general meeting was called by the president to discuss the physical education requirement. At this meeting, it was suggested by the president that to continue a requirement in physical education at the college level was unwise. There was a great deal of discussion about the subject. Miss Harcourt (age 36), the Director of Women's Physical Education, was very upset by the stand that the president took. Soon after, she resigned in protest, because she considered him to be a "most unreasonable man." To explain her action she wrote a strong letter and sent carbon copies to various influential people connected with the University, including the Board of Trustees. It was rumored that Mr. Robins had helped her to compose this letter, although this was never proved. Ms. Harcourt, because of her outstanding war record and many connections, soon located a top position in her field and has been very successful.

About this time, certain frictions were developing between Mr. Jonas, the football coach and director of athletics, and Mr. Robins. It became generally known around campus that Mr. Jonas and President Johnson were quite friendly both on and off the campus. It also became apparent that Mr. Robins and President Johnson were finding it difficult to agreement on a number of matters concerning the work of the Department of Physical Education. Their personalities seemed to clash. As a result, the Department was finding it difficult to operate with a sufficient degree of efficiency or effectiveness.

One of the staff members, Mr. Lawrence (B.S., age 23), was completing graduate study at the same institution where Robins was working on his doctoral degree. Lawrence was to return to Baldwin to take a post on the physical education staff. He would be teaching a variety of physical education classes and assist in the coaching of football and basketball. At the suggestion of Mr. Jonas and Dr. Johnson, Mr. Lawrence was charged with looking for a person at the same university where Robins was studying.—a person who would be qualified to take over the position of Director of Physical Education that was held by Robins!

Mr. Lawrence accidentally met Mr. Scott (M. A., age 28) on day during a summer session. They talked at length several times and Lawrence soon decided that Scott would be ideal for the "soon-to-be-open" position. Soon thereafter Scott was pleased to be offered a position as assistant professor with the understanding that he would be made a full professor and department head when his doctoral degree was awarded. Realizing that this situation looked promising for the future, Mr. Scott sought advice from one of his professors in graduate school. He was advised to ask Baldwin to hold the post open for a year. His professor reasoned that he would have his doctorate completed by that time, and that the problem with Mr. Robins and President Johnson might be resolved. This suggestion seemed ideal, and Mr. Scott accepted the appointment to begin in July of the following year when the new physical education building was actually completed.

Upon Mr. Scott's arrival on campus, Mr. Robins was still on the job. While at summer school, Mr. Robins had actually learned second hand that Dr. Scott was to take his place from the same graduate professor whom Robins had consulted (!), a person under whom they had both studied and in whom Scott had confided about his "new post." Hence, there was considerable strain in the relationship when Scott arrived on campus between himself and Robins. This was inevitable because of what both men knew was "going to happen". However, they treated each other fairly and developed a satisfactory working relationship. Because Scott served also as an football coach under Jonas, it must be admitted that the "presumably departing" Mr. Robins played a "lone hand" during that year.

In January of Dr. Scott's second year (his Ph.D. degree had been received shortly after is arrival on campus), he wrote the following letter to President Johnson:

Jan. 25, 19—

Dear Dr. Johnson,

I want to thank you for the time that you have spent discussing my situation and our department's development during the past few months. This past weekend, Mrs. Scott and I did practically nothing else but try to clarify our thinking about my position at Baldwin. When I learned that I wouldn't be able to see you until possibly Thursday or Friday, of this week I decided to write you this note. I hope you will understand my reason for writing instead of waiting to talk the entire matter over with you personally. I sincerely hope that you will be kind enough to take the matter up from this point and correct anything, which you think I have misstated.

I would like to say that the key factor in my decision to come to Baldwin was the telephone conversation that we had after I had called George (Jonas) about the other opportunity. At that time I understood you to say that if I came you would give me a full professorship when my degree was awarded. You stated also that I could be looking for someone to take Mr. Robins' place by this June.

Knowing that he would not be here after one year, I have made every effort to keep the entire situation peaceful. I'm sure that you realize what a problem this has been. The entire situation is one that cannot by the farthest stretch of the imagination be called professional. Many problems have come up that I never dreamed of, even after I had been here several months. I believe that I can help enormously a condition, which, at the moment, can be described only as sad.

Again in December, when you confirmed my earlier understanding about Mr. Robins, I continued to try to win friends for both departments, knowing that moving to a new building with a more harmonious "regime" would help to soothe troubled waters. At present, with many of the important matters coming up for next year, and Mr. Robins not giving the slightest indication of leaving, and your avoidance of the matter in our last talk, I cannot help wondering if he will indeed be gone.

If I do not succeed to this promised position, it is obvious that I have made a very grave mistake in coming to Baldwin. Giving up my previous position was a difficult decision to make, but I was confident that it was the right move. To date I have been completely happy about the move, confident that the promised position would materialize. I am very enthusiastic about the unusual opportunity for service to my field here.

I would appreciate it very much if you would clarify this matter for me, so that I can put my mind at ease. If we are to obtain further qualified help, we must start now. I sincerely hope that I will have the opportunity to be of service to Baldwin in a way that I feel qualified to do.

Cordially yours,
Roger J. Scott

In early February, certain pressures were brought to bear on Mr. Robins to encourage him to resign. It was rumored that he was guilty of some personal misconduct, but this was never brought out into the open. About this time the new physical education building was finally completed. In April, Mr. Robins resigned and Dr. Scott was appointed in his place. Dr. Scott and the rest of the staff (including Mr. Robins) moved into the new building. Mr. Robins was retained at full pay for six additional months to complete some research that he had started.

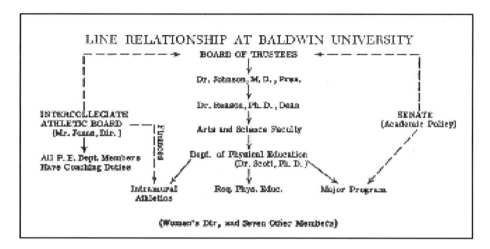

Dr. Johnson discussed his plan to reduce the physical education requirement to one year with Dr. Scott, who agreed that this amount of time for physical education should be sufficient at the university level. After getting the approval of other staff members, Dr. Scott recommended the one-year plan to the Faculty of Arts and Science. The Senate approved it.

Because the physical education staff felt that physical education was a very important subject for freshmen, a great deal of time was spent in planning for the program to be inaugurated. The staff decided that students could gain exemption from the various six-week sessions by passing proficiency tests in swimming, body mechanics and fitness, combatives (wrestling) for men, dance for the women, and leisure skills. The program appeared to be accepted as satisfactory. All staff members (including Dr. Scott) taught at least one section of this course. Students continued physical education activities in increasing numbers in their leisure during their remaining years at the University.

A physical education major program had been instituted at Baldwin two and one-half years before the new building opened. Seven years later it had the largest enrollment of any major program in the Arts and Science Division. With an increasing enrollment on the campus a need arose for more physical education staff members with a joint responsibility between the Department of Physical Education and the Department of Athletics. The budget of both departments continued to grow, as both programs expanded. Funds to operate the Department of Physical Education were provided completely by regular instructional funds. Athletics were supported by student fees, gate receipts, and some university money. When there was a deficit, the Board of Trustees had to vote an extra appropriation. During this period, television was increasingly making inroads on the gate receipts from football, a matter that caused great concern to the administration and some members of the Board of Trustees. Many rumors began to go around that certain athletes were receiving "under-the-table" help from Mr. Jonas, the athletic director. This rumor appeared to cause great embarrassment to the administration. Dr. Johnson told a member of the physical education staff one day that Mr. Jonas was to be asked to resign on the following day. This "resignation" did not take place, however, as Mr. Jonas threatened to call a press conference and bring to light from just what sources money had been obtained.

Four years after Scott's arrival, the Dean of Arts and Science became ill and retired suddenly. Dr. Reason (Ph. D. in English, age 48) was appointed in his place. Dr. Reason had been the commanding officer of the R.O.T.C. Unit at Baldwin during the War. He voiced opposition to the idea of *any* physical education requirement at the university level. Reason's predecessor had generally discussed departmental budgets with department heads before the budgets were finally approved by the Advisory Committee composed of the President, the Vice-President, the Business Officer, and the Dean. Last year, department heads had voiced considerable opposition to salary recommendations overall, which led to the abandonment of such discussions when Dr. Reason assumed office. The Advisory Committee evidently made this decision. A number of department heads expressed dissatisfaction with the decision. At this time, Dr. Scott composed the following letter to Dr. Reason, but for reasons of diplomacy it had not been sent:

Dear Dr. Reason:

Thank you very much for your letter containing information about our budget for next year. I know that all members of the department will be pleased to learn about their salary increases. We have appreciated the fact that for the past few years annual increments have been possible.

I know how many meetings you must have during the academic year. Because time was so short, I presume that you didn't have time to go over the budgets with us before they went to the Board. I thought this was a very fine practice. I would appreciate this opportunity in the future, if you deem it advisable and feasible.

I do sincerely appreciate the increase, which I have been given. I am sorry, however, that it was not possible to follow the 15% recommendation suggested by the Faculty Council [a group of all department heads formed to give them an avenue of approach to the President]. I mention this only because 1 feel that the differential between senior and junior staff members is not large enough. 1 do appreciate how difficult these matters must be.

Thank you again for this information. I sincerely hope that our department may continue to develop because of your increased support.

Cordially yours,
Roger J. Scott

The Faculty Council, a group ultimately responsible to the Faculty of the Arts and Science Division, had met only once or twice about inconsequential matters. It typically met at the call of the Dean, but for some reason was not convened in the second and third years of Reason's term of office.

During the spring, just after his appointment, Dr. Reason had said to Dr. Scott in a private meeting, "We don't like empire builders around here." On another occasion two years later, Dr. Reason had told his secretary, "It isn't that I dislike Dr. Scott, it's just that I don't like the place of his subject in the curriculum."

At this time, the Director of Physical Education and Athletics for women resigned for a variety of reasons. She was not happy with the situation in general. She got terribly annoyed several times at meetings of the Athletic Board, when Dr. Johnson appeared to be guiding the thinking of this group composed of students, faculty members, alumni, administration members, and some members of the Board of Trustees. Because one of her parents was seriously ill, she wished to be nearer her home. Her letter of resignation read as follows:

Dear Dr. Reason:

Please accept my resignation from the Department of Physical Education, and from Athletics, as of June 30, 1953.

Before leaving Baldwin I should like to say that the working relationship with Dr. Scott has been entirely satisfactory. He realizes that the staff has opinions, ideas, and ideals and gives them ample opportunity to express, explain, and justify them. He does his best to implement suggestions approved by the staff as a whole.

A sincere interest in the students and the course is of primary concern and I think the attitudes and atmosphere within the Department of Physical Education are good.

Yours sincerely,
Women's Director

Shortly before this, the following telephone conversation occurred between Dean Reason and Dr. Scott:

"Roger, this is John."

"Yes, Dr. Reason, how are you?"

"I'm very busy, Roger, but there are two matters which I must call to your attention. The first has to do with a report from Mr. X [the Business Officer] that young men are wandering around with their navels exposed when they go from the locker room to the special exercise room. Because our business offices are temporarily located on the lower floor of the physical education building, this has been embarrassing to some of the ladies in the office."

"I will speak to the locker room supervisor right away, Dr. Reason, to see if the men can be checked at the locker room door before leaving."

"The second matter has to do with one of your women staff members who was seen in her gymnasium costume holding hands with a young man in the hall. President Johnson reported this to me and it has got to be stopped."

"1 think I can explain this, Dr. Reason, she became engaged recently to a graduate student. I will speak to her about this."

"It's not only the holding of hands that bothers me, but these gymnasium costumes that the women are wearing are not appropriate outside of the gymnasium proper."

"I'll discuss this with the staff and give them your thinking on the matter. I'll feel sure they'll ...

"This is not a matter to discuss with them. The commanding officer [President Johnson] has spoken and it's our duty to obey."

"Dr. Reason, I have never been in the army. I'm not in the army now, and 1 don't believe I'll ever join the armed forces."

"Call my secretary and make an appointment to see me tomorrow morning" (Dr. Reason hung up).

Dr. Scott made the appointment for 11:00 A. M. the next morning and called a staff meeting for 10:30 A. M. A quick agreement was reached as to the approach to take in these two matters. To Dr. Scott's surprise, Dean Reason was very amiable. He congratulated Dr. Scott for causing him to lose his temper and hang up the phone. Dr. Scott said the staff was agreed on both matters and that staff members would do their best to prevent the occurrence of similar incidents.

During this spring, the Faculty appointed a committee to consider the workload of freshmen at the university. Dr. Scott was called in to explain the physical education program. Prior to start of the meeting, the physical education staff, in considering the best approach, had decided to submit a list of objectives for the required program, as well as a summary of the time length of the requirement at other universities in the state. The following is the list of objectives for the required program, which had been revised each year:

OBJECTIVES OF PHYSICAL EDUCATION 10

(Revised)

1. To develop physical recreational competence and to provide enjoyment.
2. a. Achieved by instruction and participation in leisure carry-over recreational activities such as golf, tennis, squash rackets, badminton, volleyball, etc.
3. To develop an understanding of, and interest in, the attainment of physical fitness.
   a. Achieved by the following program activities:
      i. Correction of remediable defects under supervision of physician.
      ii. Activities of a vigorous nature to bring the physically "illiterate" individual to a state of reasonable strength and motor ability.
      iii. Wrestling is included as an activity under this heading to increase strength and agility as well as to enable the individual to defend himself.
4. To develop the ability to swim (a physical recreational skill).
   a. Achieved by an instructional class twice a week until individual learns to pass beginner's test. It is felt that an individual should be able to save himself and possibly someone else in an emergency.
5. To develop desirable attitudes toward the field of physical, health, and recreation education and to foster an understanding and appreciation of its place in later life.
   a. Achieved by health lectures, healthful school environment, and an adequately planned activity program, which stresses the various benefits to be derived.
6. To foster the development of a desirable personality (cooperation, leadership, integrity, etc.) and to promote social efficiency.
   a. Achieved by participation in team, dual, and individual sports.

At the meeting, the matter was discussed fully and no recommendation was made to abolish the requirement. One member of the committee remarked to Dr. Scott as the meeting was breaking up that it was difficult to argue his department down on a point because it was always so well prepared. The chairman of the committee, a personal friend of Dr. Scott, told him later that some of the committee members were against the idea of a requirement, but that the committee as a whole decided that required physical education was at least as important as several other *service* courses demanded of freshmen.

The next spring, Dr. Scott gave an address on "administrative problem areas in physical education" at the state education convention. As the talk was to a group of physical education people, he asked several staff members to read it over first. They thought it was quite good and that it covered the problem areas thoroughly. When presented at the convention, the address was well received, but there was no further mention of it at the evening banquet.

The press, however, seized on certain statements taken out of some of the problem areas discussed. These points made headlines across the country. The newspaper in Dr. Scott's city, where the university was located, stressed his criticism of the state director's (of education) policy that removed gymnasia from a list of essential equipment for high schools. It was an election year; the newspapers in the convention city headlined on the first page Dr. Scott's point concerning under-the-table aid to athletes. The next day, the home newspaper highlighted the talk again, this time stressing the point that aid to athletes should not be "underhanded" but should be based on all-round ability and need. It evidently appeared to Dean Reason and others that Dr. Scott had given an address different from the one he had shown to some staff members, because the Dean sent the following telegram:

"PLEASE BE DISCREET IN YOUR PUBLIC UTTERANCES
AND
SEE ME MONDAY MORNING AT NINE!"

Because Dr. Scott received this telegram at a second convention being held a thousand miles away, he sent the following letter to Dr. Reason, airmail, special delivery:

April 12, 19-

Dear Dean Reason,

After seeing the headline in the Daily Journal, I wondered whether it might be advisable to continue westward. I can well appreciate your concern about ill-chosen headlines.

I have asked the State Convention Committee to mail the original copy of my talk for your perusal. Before giving this paper, I asked three colleagues to read it carefully for criticism. No one felt that it wasn't well organized and factual.

Naturally, we are very concerned with public relations in our field. Four high schools are planned in Parkhurst without gymnasia. In my opinion, this is a tragedy and we must speak out against it, if we would be true to our principles.

In like manner, our universities are faced continually with the problem of underhanded help to athletes. One of our students was offered two thousand dollars by a rival football coach to play for the other university next year. This must not continue.

My talk covered problems in our total field. There were fifteen general areas and these points were mentioned in passing under certain of these fifteen sub-headings. I'm sorry if it is considered wrong for me to state my principles on these matters to my associates.

Our National Association feels that we are usually talking and writing to each other, rather than to the public. It is recommended that we talk to the public at every opportunity. Quite inadvertently, I did just that. The headlines were unfortunate, but the thoughts expressed under those headlines should be the concern of all.

I hope this letter helps to clarify the situation.

Kindest personal regards.

Cordially yours,
Roger J. Scott

P.S. I am enclosing an extra copy of this letter for President Johnson, if you wish him to have one.

On Monday morning at 9:00 A. M., Dr. Scott appeared to discuss the matter of the newspapers' releases with Dr. Reason. The Dean appeared quite calm about the incident. He stated that he didn't see how Dr. Scott "could give so many public talks and write so many articles and still do his job." He stated further that he planned to recommend to the Faculty that the physical education major program be reviewed by a group of the faculty members. He said that he planned to recommend to the Faculty that the physical education requirement be dropped. He emphasized several times that there was no connection between these two recommendations and the "unfortunate publicity."

President Johnson asked Dr. Scott to see him about the newspaper publicity. Very quietly, he explained to Dr. Scott that this publicity might well cost the University a further grant of $500,000 from the State Department of Education. President Johnson had called the State Director personally to explain that this address did not represent the opinion of the University. Dr. Scott again expressed his regret for the unfortunate publicity. The further grant did eventually come to the University.

Just before Dr. Scott had attended the two conventions, he had written two letters to a local "Letters to the Editor" column, answering sharp criticisms of physical education in the schools. The second letter appeared in the newspaper shortly after Dr. Scott's return. Dr. Scott received this letter from Dean Reason:

PERSONAL AND CONFIDENTIAL

April 20, 19-

Dr. Roger J. Scott
Department of Physical Education

Dear Roger:

I have been informed that you are the author of several letters, which have appeared in the local newspaper over the signature of "University Professor." Of these, the only one that I have seen is that which appeared last night (April 19). From the

address and the internal evidence, I assume that this information
is correct.

I should like to point out that I strenuously object to the use of
a university rank as the signature for what is a personal
expression. I might as well admit that after our interview on
Monday morning the appearance of this letter startled me, as I
didn't think that you were anxious to rush into print again. It
may be, of course, that your letter was mailed to the editor before
you started on your travels.

Yours sincerely,

John J. Reason, Dean

Dr. Scott called Dean Reason and explained that he had actually
mailed the letter before he left for the convention. He stated that he had
asked the editor to leave out his name so that he might avoid personal
publicity. He mentioned also that he would not write to the newspaper
again.

From this time on, the Advisory Committee embarked upon a course
of action designed to eliminate the physical education requirement. When a
physical education staff member resigned, a replacement was not appointed
even though recommendations were made.

In June, Dr. Rogers, the University Health Service physician who had
joined the staff six years earlier, wrote a letter to Dean Reason stating that
he didn't think any freshman should be forced to take physical education.
He expressed particular concern about the number of injuries, which had
occurred in wrestling, one of the required areas for men who could not
demonstrate competency. This stand was prompted possibly by the fact
that Dr. Rogers was hired for only three hours a day, five days a week, and
did not have time to care for all the health problems. Dr. Rogers had gone
directly to the Dean once before with the complaint that the supervisor of
the men's required program was demanding written excuses for absences
when the student was obviously unable to take part.

> Note: The practice of written excuses had started
> several years before Dr. Rogers had assumed office. In
> his letter to the Dean, Dr. Rogers raised several other

minor objections to the required program. The Department of Physical Education met after this letter was read by Dean Reason at a total faculty meeting, and later informed the Dean that it was ready to accede to all recommendations.

Despite this concession by the Department, Dean Reason appeared determined to eliminate required physical education and asked the faculty to refer the matter to its Educational Policy Committee. Meetings were to be held during the summer months, and Dr. Scott was invited to attend one of these sessions. Almost all of the faculty members at this meeting appeared to have no strong convictions on the problem. A number of these people were personal friends of Dr. Scott and made a point to tell him privately that they favored the one-year physical education requirement, with possible exemption from certain areas upon demonstration of proven competency.

Dr. Reason seemed to be "spearheading" the idea of abolition of the one-year requirement at the meeting, which Dr. Scott attended. Dr. Scott suggested that he would like to outline the case for retention of the present arrangement. He said he felt that he should then withdraw so that the matter might be discussed freely. As he was not a member of the committee, this suggestion was accepted.

After a number of meetings during the summer at which many of the members were often not present, Dr. Reason informed Dr. Scott that the committee would recommend to the faculty in the fall that physical education should be elective, except for non-swimmers and serious corrective cases needing remedial exercise. He suggested further that the elective program should be instituted immediately to solve the staff shortage problem for the fall. Since no additional staff was to be made available, Dr. Scott concurred that this would be the better approach until the Faculty and Senate could decide. A few days later Dr. Scott sent the following letter to all his staff members:

August 5, 19-

Dear _____:

Dr. Reason called to my attention the other day that the Educational Policy Committee is recommending to the Faculty that Physical Education 10 be an elective subject henceforth, with the exception that non-swimmers should receive instruction, and that those requiring remedial corrective work should receive help, if possible, as recommended by Dr. Rogers and Dr. Mason [a specialist in Physical Medicine]. It was stressed further that students should be encouraged to participate in leisure skills on a voluntary basis.

Naturally, this will change our entire approach to this work, and it appears that we will have to decide quickly after Labor Day just what we are going to do, and how much staff it will take. The Advisory Committee has re-affirmed its decision not to replace Mr. Yost [the staff member who had resigned to take another position]. This leaves us two staff members short according to last year's workload. We will still have to offer beginning swimming at each hour left free for such election by Dr. Reason. We could probably offer one other leisure skill at that hour.

I had suggested that Mr. Ort (another staff member who had resigned in 1954 to take up medicine) might be approached to administer Intramural Athletics for men during the next few years, but I think that the Advisory Committee feels that we should be able to handle this within the department. At any rate, we should know early in September what workload seems to be required.

Dean Reason has suggested that we inaugurate the elective program immediately to help solve the staff shortage problem. He feels that the recommendation of the Educational Policy Committee will be approved by the Faculty and the Senate.

Dr. Reason is still anxious to have our major program reviewed. The feeling exists that we are working our students too hard in the laboratory phase of the curriculum.

I wish you would think about some of these matters. I'll be looking forward to seeing you in the early fall.

Kindest personal regards.

As ever,

Roger

All staff members of the Department of Physical Education were present at the fall faculty meeting where the recommendation of the Educational Policy Committee was presented by its chairperson. The chairperson was asked to give some reasons for the recommendation. He didn't appear able to do this and called for support from the other members of the committee. No one gave him much help; so Dean Reason had to speak for the committee. The Faculty then discussed the matter at considerable length. When it appeared that the recommendation would surely be defeated, a member of the committee moved that the matter be laid over to the next meeting of the Faculty. This motion passed.

At the next meeting of the Faculty, the chairman of the committee presented the case much more forcibly. Someone suggested that there appeared to be great haste to "push this matter through" the Faculty. Dr. Scott read a statement made by President Johnson several years before, challenging the field of physical education "to take its rightful place in general education, or else be cast aside as a branch in a swiftly flowing stream rounding a bend." Again there was considerable discussion of the matter. A science professor mentioned that he thought the committee had made an excellent point when it recommended that freshmen needing remedial work be required to take corrective exercise. Dr. Scott pointed out that not one freshman had been recommended this fall by the University Health Service for such rehabilitative work, although Dr. Rogers had known that this recommendation was supposed to take effect a month ago at the time when all university students received thorough medical examinations. After more discussion, Dr. Reason put the motion of the committee to a vote. Upon a show of hands he stated that, since the voting was quite evenly divided, those voting should stand and be counted. The motion was defeated by one vote.

Note: During the next week, Dr. Rogers called the professor in charge of women's physical education and blamed his secretary for forgetting to send the list of women's remedial cases to her. No list for the men was ever sent.

Matters appeared to quiet down. Dr. Scott was called in by Dean Reason to discuss certain questions. In a friendly atmosphere, Dr. Reason pointed out that he felt that Dr. Scott had, to all intents and purposes, called him a liar at the Faculty meeting when he disagreed with Dr. Reason's explanation about the necessity for temporarily inaugurating an "elective program" for this year only because of a staff shortage. Dr. Scott denied this and stated that he had said that Dean Reason "had unwittingly misinterpreted the facts a bit." The point was dropped. No guarantee was given by Dean Reason that there would be sufficient staff for the required program in the next year.

Several months later the rumor spread around the campus that Dr. Scott was considering an offer to take a responsible position at a nearby larger university.

Suggested Questions for Discussion

1. Might it be expected that President Johnson, a medical doctor, would have certain feelings about a program of required physical education including the opportunity for remedial corrective work?

2. Would President Johnson's previous experience as an athlete influence his thinking about required physical education?

3. Why do you suppose that two separate departments were created upon the retirement of the original Director of Physical Education?

4. What do you think of Miss Harcourt's action in writing a "strong letter" after resigning? Do you attach any significance to the fact that Miss Harcourt located a comparable position soon after, which she has held for ten years?

5. What is your reaction to the reported "friendliness" of Mr. Jonas and President Johnson? Why do you suppose Mr. Robins had difficulty getting along with both Mr. Jonas and President Johnson?

6. What do you think of the method whereby Mr. Robin's successor was located?

7. Do you think it was wise to have Mr. Robins and Dr. Scott on the same staff at the same time?

8. What insight into the situation does Dr. Scott's letter to President Johnson give you?

9. What implications come to mind when it is realized that Dr. Scott served for two years as asst. football coach under Mr. Jonas?

10. Why do you suppose that Mr. Robins left without "writing a letter" or giving his story to the newspapers?

11. Why do you think that Mr. Robins was allowed to stay on for six months to complete his research?

12. What do you think of the physical education staff's plan for a required program allowing exemption for proven proficiency in the various areas?

13. Do you attach any significance to the inauguration of a major program in physical education after President Johnson assumed his post?

14. Why do you suppose that the plan to force Mr. Jonas to "resign did not materialize?

15. Do you attach any significance to the letter that Dr. Scott wrote on April 24th to Dean Reason, but did not send? Do you believe that Dean Reason was responsible for the deviation from the previous policy of allowing department heads to see their budgets again after the Advisory Committee had made its recommendations?

16. What significance do you attach to the fact that the Faculty Council had not met for two and a half years?

17. Why do you suppose that Dean Reason made the statement

about "empire builders" to Dr. Scott so soon after taking office?

18. What might be gleaned from the letter of resignation written by the Women's Director on May 17th?

19. What do you make of the telephone conversation between Dean Reason and Dr. Scott? What do you think of Dean Reason for more or less apologizing the next day?

20. Why do you imagine that the Faculty had not decided to abolish the physical education requirement sooner?

21. How do you suppose that Dr. Scott learned about Dean Reason's remark to his secretary that "he didn't dislike Scott, just the place of his subject in the curriculum"? Do you believe Dean Reason?

22. What do you think of the "Objectives of Physical Education," as revised?

23. Do you think there was any connection with the decision of the administration to re-open the matter of required physical education after Dr. Scott's convention talk?

24. What do you think of the telegram? Of Dr. Scott's reply?

25. Do you think that Dean Reason felt that Dr. Scott wasn't carrying out his campus duties satisfactorily when he made the remark that Dr. Scott should write and talk less for public consumption?

26. Why do you think that Dr. Rogers, the University physician, wrote the letter to Dean Reason without discussing the matter first with Dr. Scott?

27. Do you think the department was right in acceding to all the suggestions made by Dr. Rogers?

28. What significance do you attach to the fact that the meetings of the Educational Policy Committee were held during the summer?

To the fact that Dean Reason appeared to be guiding the discussion when Dr. Scott was present? To the fact that the chairman of the committee appeared unable at first to defend the recommendation?

29. Why do you think the Faculty voted to retain the requirement? Do you think that Dr. Scott's quotation from the President swayed them in their thinking?

30. Do you feel anything significant is indicated by the fact that nine physical education department members (not all included in the case narration) had resigned?

31. Why do you suppose that Dr. Rogers, the University physician, had sent no list of students needing remedial corrective exercise to the department until after this matter had come up in the faculty meeting?

32. What do you think of Dr. Scott's answer to Dean Reason when the Dean said that he felt he was being called a liar?

33. Do you think Dr. Scott should resign his position?

6. OAKWOOD HIGH SCHOOL
("Interdepartmental Cooperation")
(As reported by the athletic director)

As in most large high schools, the administration at Oakwood is organized with the principal at the head of a line-relationship pattern. The various departments are supervised by department heads, who are responsible for the administration and supervision of matters pertaining to their own departments. All departments' practices are subject to the principal's approval on all matters affecting total school policy. Most departments are able to work in a cooperative and yet independent manner insofar as the curricular activities are concerned. When it comes to the matter of those activities traditionally conceived as extra-curricular, difficulties quite often arise over the use of facilities and personnel.

No matter how large or small the school may be, there seems to be a certain "core" (not clique) of students upon whom the success of these extra-curricular activities depends. Teachers look to these people (the "doers") as their source of personnel.

The varsity basketball team at Oakwood High was potentially the strongest in many years. Many felt that Oakwood stood a good chance to win the state championship. Pre-season training and practice schedules were arranged with this end in view. The coach and the athletic director scheduled two trips to preseason tournaments. The athletic director, Mr. Carlson, agreed with Mr. Leonard, the coach, that this tournament experience against good competition would payoff in later season results. When Mr. Leonard asked Mr. Carlson if the team might have new "dress" warm-up suits to build morale, Mr. Carlson agreed and arranged for their purchase.

The major project of Oakwood's music department each year is the production of a "Varsity Show." This typically includes a wide variety of acts ranging from slapstick and drama to fine musical numbers, all involving groups of various sizes. Ms Smythe, the head of the music department, organized this project. It is looked upon as the "school effort" of the year, a project in which all departments must co-operate to assure success.

One of the acts in the show, which is always a "howling success", is a boys' kick-line. Although this number falls in the slapstick category, the boys usually put much effort into it. They usually become adept at the various steps, and the audience seems to appreciate their skill as well as the comedy of the situation. Roger Jackson and Jim Blake, two of the outstanding performers on the basketball team, were chosen by Ms. Smythe for the line. They were both tall and their long "skinny" legs and fine co-ordination made them naturals for this act. Roger and Jim were flattered by their selection, as it gave them a different type of opportunity to earn the praise of their school friends. Mr. Carlson, the athletic director, was pleased about their selection, also. He reasoned that it gave some tangible evidence of the right type of co-operation between the athletic department and the music department.

Mr. Leonard, the team coach, took a different point of view. He could see that the necessary rehearsals were going to conflict with his practice sessions. The late hours that the players would have to keep on the three nights of the performances would interfere with the training routine that he had planned for the team. To make matters worse, the Varsity Show was scheduled to take place just one week before the regional tournament.

As it happened, the regular basketball schedule was arranged so that it would be completed two weeks prior to the regional tournament. The coach had figured that this would leave sufficient time to rest injuries, to recover from "staleness," and to drill on certain details of team play for the tournament. He had also made tentative arrangements to take his team to a neighboring city for a preparatory game as a final tune-up for the tournament. As it happened, this tune-up game was planned for the same week as the Varsity Show.

A third member of the basketball team, Ray Saunders, was an accomplished piano player. Earlier, Miss Smythe had asked him to accompany the boys' chorus in one of the acts. Because he was on the second team, Mr. Leonard had told Ray that he was free to take part if he was interested. When Ray had participated in the last year's show, a number of the other boys had kidded him and behind his back referred to him as a "sissy" and a "mamma's boy." He was sensitive to this criticism and had asked to be excused from the show.

He said that he feared his position on the team would be jeopardized by missing practices to rehearse for the show. To Miss Smythe, it became apparent that this was another non-co-operative gesture by the athletic department. She decided that matters had gone far enough and she spoke to Mr. Regan, principal of Oakwood High. She wanted support for her viewpoint. Mr. Regan decided to call a meeting of all the teachers concerned to discuss the problem.

Mr. Carlson asked Mr. Leonard to come to his office to talk over the matter before the general meeting. He hoped that they could reach an agreement between themselves.

Mr. Leonard had considered the problem very carefully. He reasoned that there were many other boys in the school who could perform as well in the kick-line as his star basketball players. Why not use some of the football players not engaged in a winter activity? If his basketball players didn't get involved in the show, his practice schedule could go on uninterrupted, as well as his pre-tournament game. Mr. Leonard did not think that any great value was attached to the "co-operative" view, although he had made a concession by offering the services of Ray Saunders, a player from the second team. In conclusion, he reasoned that he would be indirectly helping the show by playing his tune-up game in a neighboring city, leaving the student body free to attend the performance of the show that night.

Mr. Carlson, as athletic director, was quite concerned about this matter of co-operation with other departments. He felt that keeping the basketball players out of the Varsity Show would tend to split the school into factions and work to the detriment of all. He reasoned that no department is strong enough to stand by itself. He stated that Mr. Leonard's attitude would put the athletic department in a bad light, perhaps even in the minds of the athletes.

Mr. Carlson added that although he was anxious to see the team do well in the forthcoming tournaments, he feared Mr. Leonard's approach would make the team members seem a group of "pampered darlings" with special privileges.

Finally, however, Mr. Carlson agreed to back the coach on all but one point-the playing of the tune-up game the same night as one of the performances. To him, this was an open display of indifference to a total school project.

Suggested Questions for Discussion

1. How far should co-operation go between departments in a high school?

2. How far should the interests or the desires of Roger and Jim be allowed to enter into the final decision?

3 .Should anyone tell Miss Smythe the real reason why Ray didn't want to take part this year? If so, who?

4. What do you think of Miss Smythe's action in going to the Principal, Mr. Regan?

5. What do you think of Mr. Leonard's stand in his preliminary meeting with Mr. Carlson, the Athletic Director?

6. Is Mr. Carlson being disloyal to Mr. Leonard if he refuses to back him in the general meeting on any or all points?

7. Should either Mr. Leonard or Mr. Carlson speak to Miss Smythe before the general meeting?

8. Should Mr. Leonard present his arguments to Mr. Regan before the meeting, inasmuch as Miss Smythe has already spoken to Mr. Regan about the matter?

7. PRESTON DISTRICT HIGH SCHOOL
("Rural Football Problems")
(As reported by one of the brothers)

Preston was a small town with a population of about 2,500. Because the high school served an area within a 15-mile radius, a fairly extensive bus system was necessary to transport pupils. The buses picked up students starting at 7:30 A. M., and left for outlying areas at 3:45 P. M., promptly.

James Smith, the only male physical education teacher, was in his first year of teaching at Preston, although he had had experience elsewhere. He came to the school "brimming" with enthusiasm and new ideas. As football coach, he was keenly interested in the game. He spent many of his free hours discussing football and devoted a great deal of time to planning and organizing his team's schedule. Naturally, he desired to do as well as possible in his first year at Preston. Mr. Alexander, the principal, had made it clear that "football is your baby."

Football training began about one week after the opening of school. A general meeting was held with the coach and the prospective squad members. After much discussion and a vote, it was decided that practices would be held every afternoon from 4:00 to 5:30. Some of the rural boys opposed the "practice every night" idea, but voted for it when it was apparent that everyone else, including the coach, wanted it. The boys caught Coach Jim's enthusiasm and interest in the team was running high. Practices were very successful.

Preston's squad looked promising, as many of the boys were large and well coordinated. About 50 per cent were from rural areas. The outstanding players appeared to be two brother combinations. Doug and Murray Clifford were in their fourth and second years respectively, while Ken and Sam Brock were in their fourth and third years. The four boys occupied key positions on the first team. Since these boys had lived in the same district all their lives and had attended the same rural schools, their parents were good friends. Mr. Brock had heart trouble and was unable to do heavy farm work. The burden of the farm work fell on Ken and Sam. Ken, as the older of the two sons, had assumed the major responsibility for the management of the farm. This was his graduating year and he was finding it difficult to keep up with his studies.

All four of the boys had been attending practices regularly for two weeks. One week before the opening game with one of the strongest rivals in the league, the principal was surprised by a visit from Mr. Brock. He explained the reason for his visit:

"My boys leave home at 7:45 A. M. after helping with the chores. Following school they practice for about an hour and a half. It is too late for them to catch the bus and they have to hitchhike home. Some nights they don't get home until 7:00 p.m. We haven't enough money to hire help; so the boys must do the farm work after supper. Some nights it's 9:00 or 9:30 P. M. before they get back to the house. To get their schoolwork done they have to sit up until midnight. That wouldn't be so bad, if they didn't have to get up at 5:30 A. M. to help with the morning chores. I've always been interested in any of the activities of my boys, but football on this basis is just too demanding. I'm afraid they will have to drop off the team, as much as I would like to see them continue."

Conditions became worse when Mr. Clifford, the father of Doug and Murray, appeared later the same day with a similar argument against his boys' taking part in the sport. Although Mr. Alexander was an avid football fan and took great pride in winning teams, he realized also that the boys' scholastic work was suffering. He was forced to agree with the stand of the two fathers. Mr. Alexander had not called Jim Smith to his office when the fathers were present, but he notified him immediately about the visits and the decision. Smith, needless to say, was stunned by the decision and also was annoyed that he hadn't been consulted when the fathers appeared.

Practice was cancelled that afternoon. The principal and the coach met to discuss the problem. Both men realized that they had a potential winning team, but without the four boys there was little hope of finishing even fourth in the league standings. Jim, attempting to "salvage the situation," suggested a temporary solution. He had just purchased a second-hand car. As he was single, he had some free time. He suggested that the mid-day lunch period be shortened 15 minutes, so that practice could begin 15 minutes earlier. Furthermore, he would cut practice time to one hour. After practice, he would drive the four boys home and take two other boys who lived along the way. This plan would get them home by 5:30 P. M., at the latest. Mr. Alexander agreed to the idea, provided the arrangement was satisfactory to Mr. Brock and Mr. Clifford. That night, Jim visited both families, and all agreed to try the plan to see how it would work.

However, a new problem arose. The young coach found this taxi service quite expensive. He asked the principal if he would consider asking the Board of Education for gas money. The principal was wary of this idea, because the Board had already purchased fifteen new uniforms at considerable expense. Then there had been much discussion and divided opinion as to whether the expense of this equipment could be met. The Board had never reimbursed coaches for gas expenses under similar circumstances before, and there was always the danger of setting a precedent. For these reasons, Mr. Alexander did not wish to go to the Board with the matter. In an effort to help, however, he offered Jim the use of his own car to drive the boys home two nights a week.

A second problem developed. Those players who lived in the rural areas other than that of the six boys presently getting rides, felt that this arrangement was showing favoritism. Because of this feeling, dissension developed among members of the team. A delegation of players met with the coach. They expressed their opinions of the transportation system. They felt that it was unfair for some of the fellows to get rides home, while others had to borrow their father's cars or hitchhike. The coach didn't know what to say or do. He met with the principal again. In the end, practice sessions were reduced to two nights a week. Players were responsible for their own transportation home. The original six boys involved were quite annoyed at the others for opposing the original plan. It was occasionally necessary for Ken Brock to miss practice.

Jim Smith, the coach, lost most of his enthusiasm, but continued to coach for the rest of the season. Preston's team finished third in a six-team league.

Suggested Questions for Discussion

1. Was the coach justified in encouraging the boys to vote for a daily practice in a district high school where the buses left at 3:45 P. M.?

2. Should the principal have been consulted before the first meeting of the squad was held?

3. Were Mr. Brock and Mr. Clifford justified in their original approach to Mr. Alexander?

4. Should the principal have called the coach to the office when each of the fathers appeared?

5. Should the coach have suggested such a transportation arrangement in the first place?

6. What do you think of the "gas money" idea?

7. What do you think of Mr. Alexander's actions in the case?

8. As a player who hitchhiked home from practice, do you think you would have cause to complain because the coach was giving six other boys a ride home?

9. Do you think Smith and Alexander "gave up" on the problem too soon?

8. EASTERN HIGH SCHOOL
("Beginning Teachers' Problems)
(As narrated by a new teacher

In September, 2004, I walked into Eastern High as a greenhorn. My previous teaching experience consisted of some student teaching and a few weeks of supply teaching when the regular teacher at another school had fallen ill. The "acting" head of the boys' physical education department talked over the situation with me. His name was Lorne White, and he had been a successful teacher and coach for a number of years. His football teams had done exceptionally well.

In addition to a full teaching load of physical education, as well as some health instruction, English (for which I had no special preparation), and geography, I was expected to take over certain extra-curricular activities. These included being backfield coach of varsity football, coach of varsity volleyball, coach of varsity basketball, supervisor of intramural volleyball, and chairman of the publicity committee for the school variety show. Later I was asked also to supervise some of the school dances, and I volunteered to gradually develop varsity boxing.

Unfortunately, my youthful appearance was such as to discourage respect. I looked more like a high school student than some of the students themselves. The fact that I had a crew cut and usually wore sport clothes may have had something to do with the students' attitude toward me. In college, I was a welterweight boxing champion in our conference, and I also earned a varsity letter in football in my senior year. I had a good academic average that year and was elected president of our student professional group.

I learned indirectly that the normal line relationship in the physical education department existed only on the surface. The actual authority for the department was not really in the hands of the nominal department head, Mr. Laithwaite. He was about 60 years old and taught no physical education classes, coached no sports, never entered the gymnasium, and never even checked equipment. As far as I could see, his sole duty as head of the department, apart from signing requisitions, was to collect his pay.

At first, when questions arose, I went directly to Mr. Laithwaite. He gave me only vague, off-hand answers, or simply said that he did not know.

Gradually I turned for help to Lorne White, who, by reason of his long service, certainly seemed to be "acting" head of the department.

Having graduated from a well-equipped university, I was somewhat appalled by the situation in Eastern High School. The building was old-an "architect's nightmare." The gymnasium was short and narrow, poorly lighted, and badly ventilated. Since its seating capacity was about 200 at most, the spectators' legs often protruded annoyingly into the playing area. Many of the onlookers sat in a balcony that threatened constantly with loud creaks and groans to collapse. During games, the air became quite close in the room. To open windows, we were supplied with a battered length of steel pipe that was hardly designed to manipulate window handles 12 feet overhead. At each end of the gym, it was necessary to hang mats on the walls under the baskets because the distance from the baseline to the wall was only 18 inches.

During regularly scheduled physical education classes, the boys and girls used the gymnasium on alternate weeks. A similar system of alternate days was used for extra-curricular activities. The girls had the "facilities" on Monday and Wednesday afternoons; and the boys, on Tuesday and Thursday. Friday afternoons were split between the two groups. The group that did not have the gymnasium used a small, low-ceilinged "spare room." The only activities possible in this room were games of low organization, wrestling, boxing, and some gymnastics. High bar work was not possible because of the lack of room overhead. One day, the box horse collapsed. Two weeks later, the low bar "succumbed to old age" while a student was on it. Luckily, he was uninjured.

The dressing rooms were archaic. There were no lockers and pupils merely hung their clothes on hooks along the walls. This resulted in a great deal of petty thievery. To avoid the taking of soiled gymnasium clothes into classrooms, we were forced to dismiss classes a bit early so that students could store their gymnasium costumes in their hall lockers. This resulted in noise in the halls and complaints from other teachers that their classes were being disrupted. At one teachers' meeting early in the fall term, I heard that three different teachers had complained. This didn't help the relationship among departments.

Shower facilities were poor and inconvenient. The shower room was equipped with five nozzles controlled by a master valve in the office. To take a shower, pupils had to walk down a narrow corridor past two urinals and one flush toilet. Because lunchroom trash facilities were inadequate, the urinals sometimes became plugged with lunch bags. The resultant overflow caused puddles through which students had to tiptoe on their way to the showers. When I asked Mr. White about the possibility of improved facilities, he pointed out the Eastern High was in the center of a city that was expanding rapidly. He did not believe that anything would be done to the building until such time as it might be condemned.

On one occasion, when the high school supervisor was being shown through the school, the group came to the spare room. The supervisor's comment, after being introduced to me, was, "Quite satisfactory for apparatus work, isn't it?" Before I could reply, he had started to leave. I called after him, "Yes, but you can't use a high bar here and it will never take the place of a decent gymnasium!"

As a coach, some of my problems arose mainly because I was inexperienced and because my looks belied my age and position. One night, after attending a teachers' meeting, I came a bit late to the practice football field. The varsity squad was going through its warm-up calisthenics, which I usually led. The field was in the middle of a residential block and was used also by the varsity and junior varsity teams of another high school. As I came through the gate on the opposite side of the field, a raucous voice hailed me from the ranks, "Where the hell have you been, you little ---!" This was followed by a wave of laughter at my expense. The field was very muddy, and I was not dressed to walk through such a mess. So I ignored the shout and went into the dressing room to change into my football clothes. I knew who had made the remark, but by the time I got out on the field the opportune moment for a reprimand had passed. I took the boy aside later and spoke to him about the incident, but he just shrugged it off. I wondered if this lack of respect might have been caused by the fact that the head football coach, Lorne White, encouraged the boys to call him by his first name. Naturally, they all started right in to call me by my first name also.

When the basketball season rolled around, I took the reins as head coach of the team. Most of the boys who played football played basketball as well. The previous coach had been a very mild person. While I had been a student teacher, I had thought of him as a bit slipshod in his ways. He had encouraged first-name calling, and it had been my impression that he had been "manipulated" by the team, rather than controlling it in the right way. The members of the team had played together as a unit for three years. Although many of the individual boys were quite good basketball players, the team had won only 3 out of 12 games in the past season.

After the first few practices, I observed that the best players were all members of the football team. They treated me with a combination of good-natured condescension and a "hail-fellow-well-met" attitude. The center, John, was a big, well-coordinated boy with an indifferent, joking manner. He did not mind losing. When things went against him, he tended to treat it as a joke. I think he was protecting his feelings by pretending not to care.

Tom, the boy who had made the remark on the football field, was the ringleader of this clique. He had a very sarcastic tongue, a cocky attitude, and a show-off manner that tended to disrupt practices. He was an excellent performer, but thought practices were merely fun. To him a joke was good only if you laughed at someone.

Art, the boy later elected captain, was of a different ethnic origin than the large majority of the students. One night after practice he confided to me that he never went to dances. He said this in a sort of "sour-grapes" manner. He was somewhat quieter than the others, although he would join in and approve of any horseplay that the others might initiate.

A fourth player, Joe, was what might be called a "follower." He could be led one way or another. Like the rest of the clique, he was very resentful when criticism was offered. One day at football practice, he had walked away swearing after I had told him that he hadn't been trying his hardest.

I was concerned that this clique existed on the team. I wondered how it got started. I discovered that these four boys were what might be called the "tail end" of a series of fine athletes that had attended Eastern High. They had been on the squads of teams that had won football titles year in and year out and occasional basketball championships. I wondered how this winning streak might have affected their attitudes, especially since Eastern had slipped down a notch from this position of athletic supremacy.

With these four boys forming the nucleus of the team, the basketball season started with a game in a nearby town. On the bus going to the game, the varsity players made the illogical request that they would like to go downtown while the junior varsity game was being played. I refused adamantly. Upon our arrival at the host school, the varsity players quickly brought their equipment into the dressing room and promptly disappeared. With one minute left in the junior varsity game, they finally showed up at the gymnasium. I had sent the manager after them, and he had found them eating in a downtown restaurant. I was angry and spoke to them sharply about eating just before a game. During my 'lecture" given in the dressing room, Art (the captain) got up and went to the lavatory. We lost the game.

Two weeks later I learned from Mr. White that some of the players had started an informal "jam session" after practice one night during the past week. They had gone to the band room and damaged $40 worth of equipment.

We lost three subsequent games, all of which were played chiefly by this clique. Fortunately for our record, these were not all league games. There was no doubt that these four boys had superior ability in comparison to the other members of the varsity team.

What disturbed me most was that in two games Tom had been ejected for talking back to the referee and for unsportsmanlike conduct. In one game, he cost us 6 points on technical fouls. In addition, practices were difficult to run because he was constantly engaged in horseplay, either bouncing the ball into the hoop from the ceiling or throwing fake football cross-body blocks.

One night in a fast break drill, he acted particularly stupid. I said to him, "You can stop showing off now, little boy, everyone knows you are here." After this criticism I heard him say, "Let's run it once more and get it right this time." The practice was over too soon after the reprimand to ascertain whether it had any effect. Several days later I spoke to him in the shower and asked him when he was going to get down to business. He replied half-jokingly, "Oh, you're always picking on me. Besides, a guy's gotta have a little fun."

I must admit that I seriously considered that perhaps the time had come to cut Tom and maybe one other clique member from the team to see if it would improve matters. I reasoned, however, that they had nothing else to lean on except basketball, and that perhaps I could help them somehow through allowing them to share in a good team experience. Of course, I had to consider also that they were my best players.

After we lost our fourth game, I informed the team that I would now use a two-platoon system and each unit would play equal amounts of time. I split up the regular starting team between the two units. We won the next game by 20 points. After the game, I walked into the dressing room and was met by a "wall of silence." Backs were turned on me; questions were answered in monosyllables; and a number of players just walked away from me. I decided to stick to the newly inaugurated system for the next game, and we won that one also.

The next contest we lost to a team, which used a zone defense. This seemed to baffle my players completely. They made all the mistakes typical of a team playing against a zone for the first time. I gave them instructions during the time-outs, but I couldn't seem to get my thoughts through to them. At half time in the dressing room, I spoke to the captain about the possibility of shooting long shots in an effort to break up the effectiveness of the other team's defense. Although this is a standard offensive practice, Art only cursed in reply.

The following game, against the second place team, was important. Obviously a two-platoon system wouldn't work, because the opposition would simply outclass some of the team personnel. With the first team in, Art scored 20 points and played most of the game, which, incidentally, we won. When I replaced him in the fourth quarter, he walked to bench muttering and shaking his head. After the game, however, I noticed that his attitude seemed improved and he chatted quite pleasantly.

The team continued to play well. On the morning of the day that we were to play in Southport, a nearby town, we learned that Eastern had just missed being invited to the state invitational tournament. The second place team, whom we had beaten the night Art scored 20 points, received an invitation. We beat Southport that night.

After the game, I went back to the lunchroom where our team dressed to make a final check for stray pieces of equipment. Of course, I never thought to look at the ceiling. You can imagine my surprise when I learned the next day that members of my team had punched nineteen holes through a new ceiling in the lunchroom by standing on the tables and using a couple of broom handles. The matter was to be reported to the Southport School Board. I gave the team a stiff "dressing down" after this display of vandalism.

I began to recall some of the other troubles of the season, which was now over. I remembered the dispute with John, my center, on the question of the players' transportation to the games. He didn't like the school policy of taking players on trips only in authorized cars or buses. He wanted to ride in a private car. When I refused, he countered that the private car was insured. If he were to pay the driver, he said, it would be just the same as a taxi. I couldn't seem to get it through his head that the school could be sued if an accident occurred while he was traveling in a car with an unlicensed chauffeur. Finally, by speaking rather harshly, I managed to get him to drop the subject.

Joe, the fourth boy described earlier, did improve somewhat in his attitude. However, I recalled that in one game we had to play without our second-string center, I had asked Joe to sit beside me and stand by. John, our regular center, had four personal fouls on him already. Joe was a forward, but I told him that I wanted him to substitute for John if he fouled out. About two minutes later I heard him yell, "Come on John; foul out!" I turned to him quickly and asked him which team he wanted to win. He answered, "I just want to get in there." I was so angry that I rasped back "Don't be so selfish." The next time he yelled he cheered for John, who had just scored a goal.

On the whole, I was quite discouraged about the season. One week after our last game, I went to see a district play-off game that involved some of our earlier opponents. At the half time, Lorne White came over to me and said that the four boys of "my clique" were half-drunk down at the other end of the gym. The next day Lorne told the principal, who contacted their parents.

Three days later, the following article appeared in the local newspaper:

WIN COSTLY FOR EASTERN QUINTET

Exuberance over their team's victory over Southport's Varsity Mustangs will cost a group of Eastern High School basketball players at least $185.00 because of a move made last night by the Southport High School Board.

This sum will be the approximate cost of repairing 19 holes punched in the ceiling of the boys' lunchroom in the Southport school following the basketball game.

Deciding against permitting the boys to repair the damage themselves, the board agreed the work would be done by contractor and the bill forwarded to the principal of Eastern High School. From there it is assumed the students responsible will be assessed the cost.

None of the boys were identified.

In a way I was pleased that the names of the boys hadn't been listed in the newspaper. The Southport School Board would have been surprised to learn that the damage had been done before the victory. As I thought about the entire season and the many problems, I wondered whether I had acted wisely. I wasn't very enthusiastic about coaching basketball in the coming year.

Suggested Questions for Discussion

1. What do you think of the workload assigned to Bill? Do you think he should have volunteered to take over boxing?

2. Do you feel that Bill's appearance might have encouraged disrespect?

3. How might the "acting" department head situation affect Bill's reaction to his new position?

4. What attitude should Bill have taken toward the poor facilities for physical education at Eastern High School?

5. What should Bill have done when someone shouted at him in such a manner as he reported for football practice?

6. What should Bill have done, if anything, when he realized that a clique existed on his basketball team?

7. What do you think of Bill's analyses of the four players in the clique?

8. What should Bill have done about the boys' request to go downtown during the junior varsity game?

9. When Bill learned about the episode with the band instruments, should he have said anything to the boys or taken any action?

10. Why do you suppose there was so much horseplay during practices? Should Bill have cut Tom from the squad?

11. What do you think about the idea of splitting up the first team in order to try a two-platoon system? Even after they won the game, why do you suppose the players were antagonistic to Bill?

12. Why do you imagine the boys punched the holes in the ceiling at Southport before the game? Should any action have been taken as soon as Bill learned about the incident?

13. What do you think of Bill's remark to Joe, when Joe wanted John to foul out of the game?

14. Do you think the basketball experience helped the personalities of the four boys?

15. What can we learn about Bill from reading his self-written case?

16. What should have been done about the four boys appearing at the play-off game half-drunk? Do you think it would have helped to speak to their parents?

17. Had Bill acted wisely? Should he feel discouraged? Should Bill try to get another position at a different school with a better class of boys and newer facilities

9. BAKER HIGH SCHOOL
("Special Physical Education")
(As reported by a new teacher)

My name is Gerald Scanlon. I'm a physical education teacher at Baker High School in Porterfield. I've been teaching here for two years and I like my work. They keep me busy, but I expected that. I'm in charge of all the boys' physical education work and I teach two classes in history. After hours I coach the three major sports at this high school-football, basketball, and track.

I've had a good education. I came from a school where they had a superior physical activity education course-one that is recognized in the profession. In addition to a quite good arts background, I had all the necessary foundation work in science. Our courses in professional physical activity education and professional education were well taught. By the time I graduated, I realized more fully that there was a great deal to be done in our field. In addition to physical activity education, I acquired some knowledge about school health education, school recreation, and safety education. I thought at times that there was too much crowded into our curriculum, but at least my eyes have been opened to the many areas for which we may be responsible.

Most of my responsibilities I can handle. I do have one problem that has me licked. What can I, or should I, do about those boys in my classes who need corrective or adapted work. Oh, I know it's not supposed to be called "correctives" any more. From my course in the history of physical education, I know that it used to be called "remedial gymnastics." Now it goes under an assortment of names. Some call it the adaptive program; others like the term "adapted program." One thing I know: whether it's called correctives, adapted physical education, individual physical education, adaptive physical education, special exercise, or special physical education, I still don't know what to do about it!

In my undergraduate course, I studied general biology, mammalian anatomy and physiology, human anatomy and physiology, kinesiology, physiology of exercise, adapted physical education, and care and prevention of athletic injuries. I feel that I have a good background in these areas, but now I find myself stymied when it comes to dealing with individual problems.

Porterfield is like a lot of other towns. We have one high school with one gymnasium. Fortunately, there are folding doors in the gym, so that Miss Collins, the girls' physical education teacher, and I have two teaching stations. But our schedule is so arranged that we don't have time to deal with individual cases. Even if we did have time, there is no special equipment for corrective work.

Day after day we see kids that need special help. One youngster has marked lordosis; another has overcarriage. Kyphosis, lordosis, scoliosis, overcarriage, ankle pronation-you name it, we see it every day. One boy returns after an abdominal operation; another has had a broken arm. John Ford, the halfback on my football team, had the cartilage removed from his knee. The physicians release them, and the public or private insurance may or may not cover rehabilitation including physiotherapy. What should we do with these cases? Fortunately, nature helps in many cases, but it takes so long and much valuable class time is missed.

Most cases are not so bad. But then there is the case of Peter Sabo, a fine-looking, rugged lad with one withered arm as a result of a birth injury. Pete has all the attributes to make a successful athlete-except two good arms. He wants to be one of the boys and take part in everything, but it's difficult. Several weeks ago, I noticed that Pete was doing some things with his bad arm. I questioned him about the arm and learned that he hadn't been to a doctor about it since the fifth grade. I gave him a few simple tests to see if he could flex, extend, supinate, etc. I was surprised to discover that a number of the muscles seemed to be working. Then I suggested that Pete see Dr. Rawson, Porterfield's only orthopedic surgeon. I told Pete that the examination would be at his own expense. Pete made the appointment, and I talked the matter over with Dr. Rawson. Do you know what I found out? Pete should have been doing exercises for that arm all through his childhood days! Dr. Rawson said that there might have been a chance for seventy or eighty percent efficiency. Fortunately, he could still improve somewhat, but not very much. I promised to help him, but I knew that there wouldn't be much time.

Who should be handling cases like this and similar ones? Should local doctors be referring youngsters to *us* for specific exercises? Should there be someone on staff in the elementary school, junior high school, and high school to help these boys and girls? Or should children get special care only if their parents have the knowledge and money to do something about these problem?

I could go on and tell you about other youngsters whom we come across in our classes: Bill, who is overweight-obese actually-and miserable; Jack, who wants to gain weight so I'll consider him as a football lineman possibility; Ken, who wants to do something because he thinks he's a 98-lb. weakling; and so on down the line.

These are the kids that haunt me whenever I think about my position and all that I have to do. Where do I look for help? Should this be part of our job? I wish I knew.

Suggested Questions for Discussion

1. What do you think of Gerald's undergraduate course?

2. Why do you think there are so many different names for this type of physical education work?

3. Is a specially equipped room absolutely necessary for adapted work?

4. Do you believe the average physical activity educator is qualified to work in this area?

5. What should Mr. Scanlon do about Peter Sabo?

6. Should a relationship exist between the school physician, or family doctors, and the physical activity education teachers whereby specific exercise programs are recommended for school children?

7. Should Mr. Scanlon ask for help?

10. FABER COLLEGE
("Training Rules")
(As reported by a student)

During a practice session in January, Mr. Lawton, the coach of the Faber College swimming team, called the team members together for a brief meeting. Mr. Lawton was well liked and respected by the team. He had the reputation among the swimmers of being a strict conditioner with a good knowledge of coaching techniques. Prior to becoming head coach, he had worked three years as an associate coach at Faber. Within the physical activity education department, matters were decided by majority vote if general agreement concerning a policy could not be reached. Mr. Lawton had told the department head many times that he was not in complete agreement with such a democratic approach. He felt that the administrator of a group of individuals might have to overrule them on occasion if he knew he was right, especially since he was responsible to higher-ups for the total operation.

Mr. Lawton was short and slight. He had not been a competitive swimmer, although he understood the mechanics of swimming quite well. On occasion, he had a sharp tongue and was regarded as quite a "kidder." He was very helpful to the department head and was an exceptionally loyal staff member, even though he often disagreed violently with majority opinion in staff meetings.

When the swimmers gathered on this particular day, Mr. Lawton told them that, after the last swimming meet, he had observed one of them smoking, which constituted a violation of the training rules laid down by him in October. Rather than name the offender, he requested that the person involved make an appointment to see him. He stated further that the offender would not swim in the next meet; and if the person did not come to see him at all, he would not swim in any more meets that season.

This action created quite a problem for the team members, because there were five of them who were smoking at the time! By a process of elimination, the boys came to the conclusion that Ron, the team's outstanding middle distance swimmer, was the only person whom the coach could have seen smoking. Ron had shown great promise as a swimmer before he came to this school. There had been some pressure on Ron to choose several other schools with far greater reputations in the swimming field. Since coming to this school, Ron had not attained the quality of his previous efforts. This was probably because not so much emphasis was placed on swimming at this school, and the schedule was shorter and with mediocre teams. Ron was a quiet lad with a mind of his own, but he was very enthusiastic about swimming, his only sport. Without him the team would probably lose every meet that year. He did not wish to miss a meet, but at the same time he did not wish to give up smoking. The next day, Ron made an appointment to see the coach.

In the meantime, Mr. Lawton discussed the matter with the athletic director and also with the head of his department. Because he was so concerned about the problem, Mr. Lawton presented it in a general sort of a way to the members of his senior class. Although he mentioned no names, the students knew about whom he was talking, and a lively class discussion ensued. In private conversation with the former head coach, both he and Mr. Lawton agreed that something should be done. No definite action was suggested by the department head.

Before he went to see Mr. Lawton, Ron got together with the other smoking members of the team. With some encouragement from Ron, and because of a rather strong feeling of guilt among them, they all decided to go with Ron to the appointment. When five team members appeared, Mr. Lawton was greatly surprised. He talked the problem over with them for two hours and finally asked what they thought he should do. They told him that he should not allow any of them to swim in the next meet. Mr. Lawton was not convinced of the wisdom of this suggestion, because he wouldn't have much of a team left to swim against the next opponent He again emphasized the bad effects of smoking on an individual's performance and on the morale of the team. Finally, he said that he would let them swim, despite the infraction of the training rule. When the team members left his office, they promised that they would stop smoking until the season was over.

At practice that night, the coach told the other members of the team what had happened, and that he had decided to let the offenders swim in view of their promise to stop smoking for the remainder of the season. Then he asked the team if they knew who the one swimmer was that he had seen smoking in the cafeteria. They said that they knew; so Mr. Lawton said that he would like them to vote secretly to decide whether that one person should swim in the next meet. The squad voted to let Ron swim. The feeling of the team was that Mr. Lawton had used bad judgment. In defense of Mr. Lawton, it should be mentioned that the former head coach had told him that he had used the voting idea three years before when a valuable team member had missed many practices for no apparent reason. At that time the team members had voted in favor of suspending the offender for one meet.

One week later, Ron and another team member were seen smoking by the coach in the school's cafeteria.

Suggested Questions for Discussion

1. Should a coach lay down strict training rules for a team at the high school level? At the college level?

2. Do you think that Mr. Lawton should have suspended the offender immediately and then told the team about it at practice?

3. What should Mr. Lawton have done when five young men appeared at his office?

4. What do you think of Mr. Lawton's discussing the matter with the athletic director and the department head? With the senior class in a general way?

5. What do you think of the idea of asking the team members to take a vote in a matter of this nature?

6. Did Mr. Lawton use bad judgment in this matter?

7. What should Mr. Lawton have done when he saw Ron and the other team member smoking again?

11. MARLTON HIGH SCHOOL
("A Male Coach for a Girls' Team")
(As reported by a woman student practice teaching...)

Marlton High School had about 500 students and a staff of 11 teachers. The school had one small gymnasium in which it was impossible to hold more than one class at a time. There was no other room for a physical education class. The auditorium was already being used as a regular classroom. As a result of these conditions, physical activity education was forced to take a back seat to academic courses. The community of Marlton, however, was extremely sports conscious, and there was considerable interest in school athletics.

One year, the situation arose in which no woman teacher on the staff had the knowledge or experience to coach the girls' basketball team. Because of the lack of facilities, a qualified physical education teacher was not employed for the girls. Instead, the teacher with the lightest workload was to be given the responsibility for the program. Who should coach the girls' basketball team?

Mr. Barton, the principal, liked to win. It was all or nothing with him. One year, the school's top track and field athletes went to the regional meet but did not win. The next year, even though Marlton won its district meet, no one was allowed to enter the regional meet. Thus, the person chosen to coach the basketball team would be under pressure to win.

The woman in charge of the women's physical education program was conscientious and willing to learn the game. She had never played herself and didn't understand many of the terms and skills. Two girls in the school who had attended the leadership training camp in the summer were ready to help. Ten girls from the previous year's team were back, so she had an experienced team on hand. The principal decided, however, to appoint Mr. Allan as coach. Mr. Allan was a history teacher who taught a few boys' physical education classes.

The other schools in the league were taken aback at the thought of a man coaching a girls' basketball team. At the coaches' meeting, there was a heated discussion, but no action was taken. Mr. Allen did not want the assignment. He had refused to help coach the backfield of the boys' football team on the grounds that he had too big a workload already. It was rumored that he and the football coach didn't get along. He had no idea of the girls' game of basketball and would have to learn it. As a result, he was none too pleased with his new position.

Another thing he had to learn was that girls were a lot different to handle than boys. One girl went home crying when he yelled at her. He couldn't stand their shrill talk and giggles when he was driving them somewhere. He couldn't understand their greater excitability and smaller endurance powers. He was newly married and his wife didn't like him coaching girls or spending the extra time away from home.

Immediately, Marlton got the reputation for being a rough team. It was the team to beat, the team to get. The games became rough shambles, lost all pretense of friendly competition, and became earnest battles. There was great emotional stress on the players. No friendships were made between Marlton team members and members of other teams, although the other teams still remained friendly to each other. At lunches after the games, the Marlton team sat in a group alone.

The coach himself had many difficulties. He couldn't very well take his team into the dressing room at half time. He couldn't understand the girls' lack of interest in the games. Other male teachers were constantly ridiculing him. The women coaches couldn't make up their minds how to treat him. Above all, his wife didn't like him coaching.

Despite these difficulties, Marlton managed to win the district championship. They were easily eliminated from the regional semifinals, however. The next year, a woman physical education teacher coached the girls' team, because Mr. Allan had moved to another school.

Suggested Questions for Discussion

1. Was the district championship worth the emotional stress on the players?

2. In your opinion, would the woman teacher with interest but no knowledge of the game be better for the team than Mr. Allan with knowledge but no interest?

3. What are the advantages and disadvantages of a man coaching a girls' team?

4. What is the significance of Mr. Allan's personal life on his coaching?

5. Could Mr. Allan have coached and still have maintained friendly relations with the other schools?

6. What is the significance of Mr. Allan's refusing to coach the football team but accepting the coaching of the girls' basketball team?

7. What is the significance of the principal's decision to leave Mr. Allan as coach despite protests of coaches from other schools?

8. What would be the community's reactions to the situation?

9. Should use have been made of the student leaders?

12. LEWIS COLLEGE
("Student Managers")
(As reported by a team member and the coach)

Jay Proctor reported to body-building workouts before the regular swimming sessions started. The coach soon saw that Jay might have difficulty in making the team because of his physical condition and his lack of co-ordination.

A good deal of kidding took place at these sessions among the returning lettermen and some of the newcomers. Jay liked to enter the bantering back and forth, but he seemed to get upset when some pointed remarks were directed particularly at him. One day before the land drill, he mentioned to Coach Walters that he really had come out only for the experience, because he probably wasn't a good enough swimmer to make the varsity. Actually, he didn't seem qualified to make the junior varsity team, but the practice was to cut no swimmer who was willing to work.

When the coach realized that last year's assistant manager would not be able to assume the post of manager, there was some discussion at practice as to who should be manager. Proctor announced that he would like to take over the responsibility. This would give him an opportunity to take the trips, which he probably wouldn't get otherwise. Several of the returning lettermen pointedly suggested other possible candidates. But Coach Walters, anxious to secure the help that a manager would provide, missed the intent of their suggestions. When no one else appeared to be interested in the job, the coach announced that Proctor would be the manager.

Even then, certain team members suggested that perhaps last year's manager would be available after Christmas vacation. For a week, they discussed with Proctor that perhaps it would be better for him to serve as an assistant manager for a year, if last year's manager could serve again. Finally, last year's manager told the coach that he just could not spare the time because of his poor academic record. Proctor hadn't been too enthusiastic about this idea anyhow, but he had been willing to accept it.

This swimming team was a closely-knit group containing a small clique. This clique was composed of students who were fraternity brothers and former teammates; some had worked together in the summer. The general atmosphere involved much kidding of a personal nature. The kidding sometimes went to extremes among the members of the clique.

Coach Walters prepared an outline of the manager's duties and discussed it at length with Proctor. Because the manager's post involved so many duties, they agreed that Proctor could not handle everything. The coach offered to do those items that Proctor, because of his inexperience, did not appear capable of handling.

The first few weeks of practice slipped by and Jay did very little. Some squad members felt that he should have kept accurate records of membership attendance. After the Christmas vacation, the team buckled down to harder workouts. Proctor did not appear to be improving on his poor start. Managers usually take a lot of kidding, and Jay didn't get into the spirit of the idea at all. He missed practices with rather lame excuses. When he did appear, he usually had to leave early. Actually, there wasn't too much for him to do at practice sessions, and he certainly didn't look for things to do. He installed the lanes when he arrived on time, and he took them out when he was still present at the end of the sessions. He asked if he might continue to swim with the inexperienced swimmers for practice. This request was granted, because it was pointless for him to stand around for a certain length of time each day. On Thursdays, when time trials were taken, he was expected to help in several ways, mainly as a recorder. Several times when he didn't know a freshman's name, he called "Hey, kid," which didn't seem to go over so well with the freshmen.

Before the first meet, which was scheduled at home, he reported to the coach and a division of duties was discussed. Everything would have been fine, except that he was late and almost all the details had already been handled by the coach and several other swimmers. He chatted with the visiting team members, while the coach and others scurried around making last-minute preparations. Finally the coach said, "Jay, I'm doing what you agreed to do and you're doing what I generally do." Jay readily saw the point and rushed to attend to the installation of the rope lanes, a task that another swimmer had begun.

Jay did a capable job of announcing (considering it was his first effort), but immediately after the last relay he said that he wanted to get away in a hurry because someone was waiting for him. He asked the swimmers to return their own suits and robes to the locker room attendant. They let him know in no uncertain terms that this was his job, but he left anyhow, telling them that they were being unreasonable. Several of the veteran swimmers were irked over this incident.

On Thursday, time trials for the first away meet were held. Proctor was timing the races and neglected to take split times. Barry Campbell, a veteran swimmer and a member of the clique, asked him, "Proctor, you lazy crumb, why aren't you taking split times? How are they supposed to learn pacing if you don't bother getting the splits? Here, give me the watch and I'll do it!" Proctor retorted, "Here you are, Big Noise." Proctor appeared to relish his new name for Barry. He used it and other "terms" whenever he saw him. Barry was a small fellow and Jay didn't hesitate to "hand it back" to him.

On the first trip away from home, the veteran swimmers did not care to travel in the same taxi with him. Finally, the coach asked him to travel with the first cab, because one swimmer was late and Coach Walters figured it would be better to wait himself with the second cab. Lewis won the meet handily and started back home. Proctor got "car-sick" and seemed quite ill. This was a huge joke to most of the other swimmers in the cab. The next week, Jay informed Coach Walters that he would not be able to make the second trip away. In addition, he missed several more practices. One of the swimmers volunteered to assume Proctor's duties for the second away trip and did a fine job. Lewis won their third straight meet and team spirit was high.

On Monday, evidently after some discussion with other veterans, the team captain, Jerry Thomas, spoke to Jay and suggested that he improve his efforts. Everyone respected Jerry, including Jay, and he said he would try to do better.

On Tuesday afternoon, Jay came to the pool in a pair of grey flannel trousers. He got rather close to the edge of the pool and was "accidentally" splashed by Barry Campbell. The dripping manager ran around the deck of the pool crying, "Come out and fight like a man, you coward!" Barry simply remained in the center of the pool, laughing so hard he could barely stay afloat. Jay became enraged, tore off his clothes, and jumped in after Barry, who evaded him with ridiculous ease. Jay floundered around for a few minutes, became discouraged, and went to the dressing room for a towel. He left his trousers behind, and another swimmer hid them on top of the 3-meter diving board. When Jay returned and couldn't find them, he was so furious that he was shaking all over. He attempted to start a fight with Barry, but all were laughing so uproariously that it simply couldn't materialize. Frustrated, Jay strode from the pool area, having lost the last vestige of any dignity.

At this point, Coach Walters was passing through the locker room on his way to the regular workout after the warm-up period. He greeted Jay, but got no reply. Jay didn't seem to see or hear him. Upon entering the pool area, Coach Walters found the swimmers still in a state of uproar.

The next afternoon before practice, Proctor appeared at Coach Walter's office, still quite disturbed about the whole affair. He was determined to quit the managerial post. The coach, who knew Jay's mother slightly, had called her earlier in the morning to discuss the matter. He learned from her and a teacher at Jay's high school that Jay had experienced difficulty in personal relationships before this time. He decided to make an effort to get Proctor to continue, because he felt that this might be an opportunity to help him. Coach Walters knew that he could get the other team members to "lay off" Jay somewhat. (Before offering a careful report of the discussion that took place, it should be explained that Coach Walters was interested in non-directive counseling as recommended by Carl Rogers of the University of Chicago.)

Proctor: I suppose you heard about what happened in the pool yesterday before you arrived for the regular session?

Walters: Yes, I was sorry that I did not arrive sooner.

P: I hate to say this because you have been so nice to me, coach, but I have decided to throw in the towel.

W: You feel that you want to quit because of this incident?

P: Definitely, I don't want to continue, because some of those fellows aren't gentlemen.

W: You feel that they treated you badly?

P: They certainly did. How would you feel if they soaked your best trousers?

W: I would probably be quite upset also. You don't think you deserved such treatment?

P: Well, hardly, I merely walked into the pool and started to put in the lanes when Campbell splashed me.

W: You feel that he shouldn't have done such a thing?

P: Oh, I know he doesn't like me, but he certainly didn't have to interfere with me when 1 was trying to do my job.

W: He doesn't like you?

P: He rides me all the time. I guess he feels that I am not doing the various "joe" jobs that he thinks a manager is supposed to do.

W: He doesn't think you're a good manager?

P: I'm sure of that and, for that matter, neither does Porter [another varsity swimmer]. Most of the other fellows are gentlemen, but these two, and I don't like to talk about them, are on me all the time.
W: Those two are giving you the most trouble.

P: Yes, that's why I decided to quit, although I didn't want to let you down. I suppose I haven't been a very satisfactory manager.

W: You don't think you've done very well as a manager?

P: In some ways, yes, but in a number of other ways, no. I haven't had the time to do all the jobs that a manager is supposed to do, according to the list of duties you talked over with me.

W: You haven't had time to carry out all the duties?

P: No, you see it's very important that I do well with my studies, because my mother is working to help put me and my brother Bob through school.

W: You figured that you had a responsibility to your mother to do well with your studies and that everything else is secondary?

P: That's true, although I realize that I shouldn't have accepted the job if I didn't intend to carry it out in the best possible way. I did want to continue. I think it's important to face up to these clashes of personality that arise; yet, in this case, I just don't think it's worth it.

W: It isn't worth the trouble to convince the squad members that you can take such incidents in your stride and still carry on?

P: I suppose I could have belted him one, if I could have caught him. But fighting never accomplishes anything, at least it never has for me.

W: I think you're right. From the way you say that, I gather that you have had some previous scuffles.

P: Yes, someone was always beating me up in high school. I think I've outgrown that now.

W: How does your mother feel about this problem?

P: She's quite concerned, but she feels that the decision is mine to make.

W: It is your decision.

P: I want to do the right thing, but I don't want to put up with that sort of nonsense any more. Furthermore, I think the team's sympathies are mostly with Campbell.

W: You feel that, in the main, they are siding with Campbell?

P: Not the large majority, but quite a few, I guess. I imagine that most of the fellows are neutral in the matter. I suppose if he doesn't stop riding me, the others will sympathize with me a bit if I control myself and show Campbell that he can't get my goat.

W: You feel that maybe you should try to keep calm and ride it out? P: At least then I would prove that Campbell and Porter can't chase me away that easily. Maybe I will take another crack at the job and try to do better. Hey, I had pretty well decided to quit when I came here to see you. I better think it over some more.

W: Well, it is your decision, Jay, but why don't you prove that you can stick it out and do a better job?

P: I think I will. Thanks, Coach.

Proctor did not show up for practice the next day. Coach Walters did not know whether he would be back. Barry, who was quite a "card," said with a smile, "I'll really miss him. I'm sorry he quit because of a little thing like that. If he would only apologize, I'm sure we could get along."

Suggested Questions for Discussion

1. Do you think Coach Walters should have appointed Jay Proctor to the position of manager in the first place?

2. Should a coach try to control kidding of the type that took place on this team?

3. Should a coach try to break up a clique on a squad?

4. Why do you imagine Proctor was such a poor manager?

5. Do you blame Barry Campbell for beginning to ride Proctor?

6. Do you think the captain of the team should have spoken to Proctor about improving his effort?

7. What is your reaction to the "wet trousers" incident?

8. Should Coach Walters have allowed Jay to resign from his post without attempting to convince him to continue?

9. Should Coach Walters say anything to Campbell and Porter about this incident?

10. Do you think Proctor will carry on with the job?

13. MILLER UNIVERSITY
(Coach-Player Relations"
(As reported by two students)

Miller University was a small, semi-private university with a very good football team that had won the conference championship 7 of the last 10 years. This year the team was favored to repeat as league champion. The first two games were with non-conference teams. Miller won the first contest by a narrow margin, but lost the second decisively. The third and fourth games were with regular league rivals. Although Miller was favored in both contests, they managed to salvage only a tie against what was supposed to be the weakest team in the league. The next game was against Riverside College, whose stock had risen sharply after the sudden acquisition of a good quarterback. Riverside now appeared to be the team to beat.

Miller's coach, Frank Howard, was rated highly by his opponents and many of the men on his team. As the captain of the club expressed it, "He was rough and gruff on the outside, but underneath it all he was soft-hearted and sentimental. Coach Howard's success is due to his ability in handling players and in bringing out the best in people, rather than to coaching ability in the mechanical sense of the word."

This particular season, Coach Howard had an unusual number of player problems. Early in the season, a promising sophomore had become disgruntled and quit. Another player, Bill Sulyak, a key man in the backfield, had quit when the coach scrapped his formation and had asked his backfield assistant to tell Sulyak that from that time on he wanted him to play at the wingback spot. Then Jim McLeod, an end, became angry when he wasn't used in the first game and told Coach Howard that he was playing "favorites." He stated further that some of his friends felt they also were getting a "raw deal."

The team had an unusually large number of sophomores and juniors; however, they were starting to work well together. There was a great deal of kidding and "riding" on the team, and nearly everyone seemed to get on well with the coach. Some, of course, knew the coach better than others. They all laughed at his humorous antics, but to outsiders they presented a solid front in regard to their individual opinions of their leader. There was an unwritten rule on the team that each man was to put the team ahead of his own personal desires.

Peter Rodin, a regular lineman, came from a small town in the next county. His parents were from Central Europe. He was serious minded, a diligent student, and friendly. He had difficulty with his class work, but studied so hard that he seemed certain to get his degree. This was Peter's senior year, and he had been on the varsity team since the last few games of his sophomore year. He had earned letters in track and wrestling, also. The wrestling coach had found him hard working, personable, and anxious to excel. The team captain said that Peter bore the brunt of many jokes, but that he seemed to enjoy the relationship with the other members of the team. He added that Peter took almost everything seriously and tended to underestimate his own worth as a football player.

During the summer, Rodin had agreed to be an usher at a friend's wedding that was to take place on October 15th, the day of the game with Riverside. On Monday, October 10th, he told Coach Howard of his plans for the following Saturday. On hearing this, Howard lost his temper and gave Rodin a rough time. The coach was worried about the personnel changes that he would have to make if Rodin didn't play in the important game with Riverside. As time went on, Howard's anger subsided but he was still upset.

On Tuesday, Howard talked to Rodin and told him that he was letting the rest of the team down. Rodin thought this point over and decided to call his friend to see if he could locate another usher. His friend wasn't home, so Peter talked to his friend's parents. The conversation was carried on in their native tongue, but Peter had difficulty explaining the situation to them over the phone. To make matters worse, the long distance connection wasn't too good. In despair, Peter told them to forget his call and that he would see them on Saturday.

On Thursday, Rodin told Coach Howard that he had decided to go to the wedding. Howard became angry once again and said, "If you're not on the train Friday, hand in your equipment!" On Friday, the train pulled out without Rodin.

(Up to this point the case has been reported mostly by another member of the varsity team. From this point, the narrative is reported directly by Peter Rodin.)

"I have been asked by Dr. Carl Dorland, Chairman of the Department of Physical Education at Miller University, an NCAA Division 3 institution, to tell just how my participation in intercollegiate athletics at Miller came to an abrupt end.

I came to Miller and registered in the physical education course. I liked football and other sports very much, but I was really anxious to get a sound education. I went out for the freshman football team, enjoyed this experience very much, and soon became a regular guard on the team. When I came to college, I thought I knew something about football. However, when I got in the thick of things, I realized just how little I really did know. I could see that I had a lot to learn, especially if I hoped to make the varsity club the next year. I learned my basic football under the freshman coaches and I appreciated their help a great deal.

In the fall of my second year, I tried out for the varsity team and was doing reasonably well. Toward the end of the season, two other sophomores and I got a break. One regular lineman was injured, and two other senior halfbacks had to attend a wedding on the day of the next game. All three of us did quite well, and stayed up with the first and second teams in preparation for the final game that would decide the league championship. We won that championship game on a brilliant touchdown pass in the last few seconds of play. To me, it was the thrill of a lifetime to have something like that happen to me so early in my athletic career.

In our conference, the track and field championships were held in the fall. I was the team's only entrant in the shot-put event and earned a fourth place in the championship meet. This meant that I had earned two varsity letters in my second year. My pleasure was lessened a bit by the fact that my studies had not gone well during this fall season.

In the winter season at Miller, basketball, wrestling, and swimming dominated the athletic picture. Not having any previous experience with any of these sports, I decided to spend more time on my studies. My grades seemed to pick up somewhat during the period from the end of football to Christmas vacation.

In our physical education classes, we were given fundamental instructions in wrestling, and I became increasingly interested in this sport. I was tempted to tryout for the wrestling team, but at the time I decided to stay with "the books" instead.

After the Christmas vacation, I was approached by the wrestling coach, who asked me to come out for the vacant 191 lb. position on the junior varsity. I learned the sport of wrestling and enjoyed the keen competition and conditioning that it offered. I wrestled for the junior varsity all season and again got another break when a fellow wrestler was injured. I managed to earn the varsity spot to represent Miller in the conference championship. I won only one bout out of three, but our team tied Branford University, a school with five times our enrollment, for the title. To sum it all up, this year was a success for me athletically, but I failed one of my subjects and the rest of my grades weren't too high.

My junior year went quite well. I played regularly on the defensive team. I did not go out for track and field, because I felt that my schoolwork couldn't stand it. I decided to skip wrestling for the same reason, but after Christmas I just couldn't stay away from wrestling. I made the varsity at 177 lbs., but separated my shoulder at the beginning of my first match in the championships. I figured that my athletic career was over, but a surgeon decided not to operate and the shoulder healed very well. At the end of the year, I had passed all my subjects, although there was still room for improvement.

In June, I was asked by a close friend in my hometown to be an usher at his wedding on October 15. He knew that I played football and asked me at the time whether the wedding would conflict with a big game. I accepted his invitation and told him that I didn't think the coach would mind, as it wouldn't be too difficult to replace me for that one game. I expected, as all the sports writers were predicting, that Miller would be as strong as usual. I remembered, too, that a couple of other players were permitted to attend a wedding two years previously. From this, I concluded that I would have no trouble getting a leave of absence for one game early in the season. My good friend and I ordered our tuxedos together for the big day.

The first game of the season was a non-conference game. On that day, we were minus a veteran interior lineman and an end, who both of whom were acting as ushers at the wedding of a former teammate.

Two weeks later, we played our first conference game with Branford University. Our new "1'" offense was a flop. The tailback was blamed by the fans and the sportswriters for the loss. I didn't blame him, because I felt that the line had bogged down in their protection. You might wonder why I'm writing about the tailback, but his subsequent resignation from the team, I feel, led to the turn of events in my case.

The following week our offense was changed radically. The tailback quit after the backfield coach told him that Coach Howard wanted him to shift to the wingback spot, which was almost the same as playing running guard. As Coach Howard put it, "Bill Sulyak has decided to quit football, so he can spend more time on his studies." In the second conference game, we walked all over our opponent, but for some reason we couldn't score. We were lucky to get a tie. This meant that it was "do or die" on October 15th against Riverside!

When should I tell the coach that I couldn't play the next Saturday? I hadn't wanted to tell him earlier, because I didn't want to bother him. I had thought of telling him before the second conference game, but had decided to tell him after the victory. However, that game ended in a tie!

I talked the matter over with a couple of my friends on the way home and they gave me the devil for not telling him sooner. I began thinking about it, slowly realizing that I should have told him sooner. Bill still thought that there would be no trouble in grooming another guard to take my place for one game. There were a number of good men trying out for my position; surely for one game they wouldn't miss me.

On Monday afternoon, October 10th, I went to see the coach in his dressing room at the stadium. The conversation went something like this:

"Hello Coach, I don't think I'll be able to play this weekend."

"Why? What's the matter?"

"I have to go to a wedding this Saturday."

"Come on, Rod, not this weekend! We've got a big game!" There was a pause. I just stood there bewildered. He sat down in his chair. Without looking at me he said, "Who's getting married?"

"One of my good friends back home asked me to be an usher at his wedding."

There was a deep silence in the room. He didn't yell or shout. However, there was a certain degree of anger in his quiet manner. We both remained silent. Seeing an anger in his face that I hadn't seen before, I walked out of the dressing room without saying another word. I went into the players' dressing room thinking that he would get over it soon. I was a little disgusted with myself and with his reaction to the matter. Maybe it was the way I just came out and told him. I certainly didn't feel like practicing.

I finally went out to the practice field, a little late, just as the coach was walking out too. He gave me a disgusted look, but said nothing. Many of the players knew about it by this time and began ribbing me, but in general they didn't think it was a serious blow to the team. The other guard began running the plays, and I substituted with him. I understood the change and accepted it because I wouldn't be playing that Saturday.

At Tuesday's practice, the coach asked me in a disgusted tone, "Still weddying?" I was running down to some other players who were doing warm-up exercises. "Yep," I replied, and kept on going.

On Wednesday morning, while I was walking through the corridor in the physical education building the freshman line coach happened to see me and asked me to drop into his office.

"I hear some rumors that you're going to a wedding instead of the game on Saturday."

"Yes, that's right."

"I'd like to know more about it, if you don't mind. I was talking to the coach this morning and he mentioned something about it. He didn't ask me to do anything like this, but I'd like to know why you're going and why you told him so late."

He asked me a few questions about the wedding and asked how close a friend I was to the groom. He told me of the seriousness of "taking off" whenever one feels like it, and stressed that this would only add to the disharmony on the club. The spirit of the team wasn't just what it should be, plus the fact that we were struggling with a new offense. He told me that the club was weak in the guard spot, especially for this game.

He went on to tell me that if this were his team, he wouldn't hesitate to drop me from the club for pulling such a trick. He didn't know what Coach Howard was going to do, but the way he painted the whole picture made me feel like two cents. I told him that I didn't think it was as serious as this. He seemed to understand my predicament and told me of a similar incident, which involved him a few years back. I felt terrible, so I decided to get in touch with the groom and tell him I couldn't come.

I placed a call to the place where the groom worked, but they couldn't seem to locate him. I decided then to call my hometown that night and talk to his mother. I thought of a friend of ours who could take my place and wear my tuxedo.

Before practice that night, I had another talk with the coach and apologized to him because I had not let him know sooner. He mentioned again that I would be letting the team down if I went. I told him that I was going to phone home that night in an attempt to get out of the wedding.

In the dressing room before practice, I asked a couple of the other players, who both agreed that it was a ticklish situation. They went on to say, however, that they saw no reason why I shouldn't attend the wedding. But after the conversations with the coaches, my mind was made up. At practice, the coach used me in the plays as if nothing had happened.

I wondered if the people at home would understand the situation.

After our nightly chalk talk, I used the coaches' phone to place the call. I got my friend's mother on the phone and told her that I probably would not be able to make the wedding on Saturday, but that I would get our mutual friend to take my place. I then called the friend, but he wasn't home. I was even more "twisted up." I told the coach on the way out that I hadn't yet achieved my purpose, but that I would call home again in the morning.

I couldn't sleep that night because I had made such a mess of things. No matter what decision I made, I would be letting good friends down. In the morning, I talked to some more friends, who were divided in their opinions. I placed the call to the intended "substitute," and he said he couldn't make it. I then phoned the groom at his place of employment and explained the whole situation to him. I just didn't know what to say, but I finally did say, "Don't worry, I'll be there."

Now I had to tell the coach of my decision. I was so nervous that I broke out in a sweat as I approached his office. I went in and said, "Coach, I won't be able to play because I'm going to the wedding." No words were spoken for a moment. Then I explained about all the phone calls and my inability to get a replacement. "Well," he said, "it's your decision." He had nothing else to say to me, so I walked slowly out of the office.

I went out to practice that night, but I felt out of place. After a few minutes I went to Coach Howard and said, "Coach, where do I stand?" 'What do you think?" he said. With a nod, I answered quietly, "Yeah, I guess I'm through then." He replied, "How do you think the boys feel?" I nodded my head again and said, "Can I play with the junior varsity next week?" "No," he replied, "I don't think you should be allowed to play any more football here." I walked off slowly and went to the dressing room. As I took off my uniform, I realized for the first time that I was through with football at Miller.

The team lost the game that Saturday, although our line play was terrific. No one except the tackle who played next to me knew about my dismissal until the following Monday. Many of the players told me they were sorry I was through. They said that they hadn't thought I would be dropped. What a mess a simple little incident had become! That was my last experience in athletics at Miller.

Suggested Questions for Discussion

1. What do you think of the captain's appraisal of Coach Howard?

2. What is your general impression of Peter Rodin?

3. The details of the events of the "fateful" week for Peter seem to differ in the two accounts. Whose story do you believe?

4. Should Peter have declined the invitation to be an usher at the

time when his friend asked him in June?

5. What do you think of Coach Howard's treatment of the affair?

6. Was it right for any of the assistant coaches to have tried to influence Peter?

7. Why do you imagine Peter didn't tell Coach Howard about his friend's wedding sooner?

8. Do you think Peter should have made the effort to locate a substitute?

9. Should Coach Howard have denied Peter the opportunity to play with the Junior Varsity?
10. Do you think the other players were truly sorry that Peter had been dropped from the team?

11. What lesson, if any, can we learn from this incident?

14. MEADOWBROOK HIGH SCHOOL A
("Equipment Purchasing")
(As reported by a Bob Change)

Meadowbrook High School just after the turn of the century. Three years later, Bob Change was hired by the Board of Education to teach physical education. During the next three years, the school enrollment more than doubled, with a corresponding increase in the number of staff members.

The principal, Mr. Lord, was a man much worried over details. As a result he had to take part of a year off with ulcer trouble. He was regarded as an efficient administrator, but Bob had the feeling that he did not regard physical education as a subject on a par with the other curriculum offerings. He, along with many other members of the staff, appeared to be much more interested in the marks and scholastic ability of students than in anything connected with physical education. Mr. Lord liked to consider the staff as one big happy family of which he was the father. To Bob he appeared to be very helpful, honest, and sincere, although sometimes a bit naive.

Because of the increase in staff, the Board of Education decided that it was time to appoint heads of departments. Bob was appointed head of the boys' physical education department, which gave him an extra $2000 a year on his salary. Bob began his new duties with great anticipation. One of his new responsibilities was the selection and purchasing of physical education supplies. As the equipment on hand was of poor quality, he made out his requisitions only after much shopping around for good merchandise at the most reasonable prices. On each requisition, he stated model numbers plainly. If unable to give the number, he wrote out a careful description of the equipment desired. In most cases, he listed the names of the companies where excellent equipment was available at the lowest prices.

When the first few orders were delivered, Bob noticed that everything had been bought from a local man, Mr. Dobson, who ran a sporting goods store in the suburbs. Mr. Dobson was known to Bob as a loud, fast-talking, high-pressure salesman. He was active in several of the service clubs in Meadowbrook of which many of the Board members were members. In this first shipment, Bob discovered that many items were missing and that very few of the pieces of equipment were of the quality specified. As Bob needed the supplies to carryon his program, he accepted many of the items reluctantly. He returned some of the equipment, although not having it available inconvenienced him a great deal.

This situation put Bob on his guard. The next time he had to make a large order, he prepared his requisitions in even greater detail and specified all the model numbers. He was careful also to recommend the names of the sporting goods companies whose prices were lowest for the quality of merchandise required. Once again all equipment was purchased from Mr. Dobson, and once again a number of items were missing and a great deal of the equipment was inferior. Bob decided that he bad no other choice but to seek aid and advice from the principal, Mr. Lord. Bob made a list of the reasons why the present method of purchasing equipment was unsatisfactory and showed it to Mr. Lord. It was decided that Bob should go to the next Board meeting and present his case.

The Board agreed with Bob that the head of a department knew best how to spend the money allotted for the purchase of equipment. According to Bob, "This meeting with the Board resulted in the ideal situation for the purchasing of physical education equipment and supplies." From that time, Bob was to have a free hand in this matter.

At the next meeting of the Board late in the fall, one member mentioned the fact that there had been a large number of injuries during the past football season. A recommendation was made to the principal, Mr. Lord, that Bob be told that the football team should be better equipped to avoid any public criticism of the school's effort.

In the spring, Bob prepared his budget for the coming year. Keeping in mind the strong recommendation of the Board, Bob asked for enough money to equip the football team properly. As soon as his recommendations were approved by the Board, Bob did a great deal of shopping for suitable equipment and invited a number of sporting goods representatives to the school to display their stock. He finally decided to place the order with a reliable company that offered a 40% discount, along with other convenient services such as economical repairing and cleaning. This firm was new in this particular line and anxious to get some good customers. Bob placed the order verbally, and then sent the requisitions in shortly thereafter. This procedure had become commonplace in order to get equipment approximately when needed. The requisition, which usually took two weeks to get to the Board, was more or less a written confirmation of the verbal order.

Mr. Dobson, who had provided the equipment in the past, quickly heard about Bob's action. He began to speak to various members of the Board and went so far as to contact the manufacturers of the equipment, asking them to place pressure on the firm from which Bob had ordered. Mr. Dobson felt that the manufacturers should not allow this sporting goods supplier to undersell him. As a result of this controversy, the Board asked that at least three tenders be made on the total order.

Bob was embarrassed about this turn in events. He had already placed the order verbally and had expected the Board to approve his requisition the very night that they decided to ask for tenders on the order. At any rate, he got the three tenders. The supplier with whom Bob had placed the order was still the lowest bidder on the same equipment.

A special meeting of the Board was called on May 5th. Despite the fact that the equipment was already being manufactured, one member of the Board suggested that the whole order should be given to Mr. Dobson, whose prices were at least twenty-five per cent higher. After a great deal of heated discussion, it was finally decided that the Board was obligated to stand behind Bob.

Following this problem, the Board quickly invoked a new policy that any order up to $50 could be purchased by the head of the department with the confirmation of the principal. Purchases from $50 to $200 must be confirmed by the Board's business administrator, Mr. Ross. Any order over $200 must have at least three written tenders submitted, and then the Board would decide where the purchase should be made.

At this time, Bob heard that Mr. Ross and Mr. Dobson were very good friends. According to Bob, Mr. Ross was one of the "hail fellow-well-met" types, who practiced much patting on the back, but who evidently did a lot of talking behind people's backs. He exerted a strong influence on the Board and was very close with two or three of its members. The Board had in the past often taken his suggestions about physical education equipment, because he had once been a teacher in that line. The rumor began to go around that the business administrator had been getting a kickback from Mr. Dobson for a number of years.

In September, the vice-principal suggested to Bob that perhaps some of the business could be given to Mr. Dobson in order to restore harmony. Upon making inquiry, Bob learned that Mr. Dobson was a friend of the vice-principal also.

During this same month, Bob discussed the matter with Miss Giles, the head of the girls' physical education department. Miss Giles, an older woman who had previously worked as a supervisor in the State Department of Education, told Bob that she had been having the same trouble in purchasing sports equipment for the girls' program. She had not been greatly concerned because only a relatively small amount of money was involved in running the girls' program. Although Bob had placed the orders for her also, she felt that she was only indirectly involved. Previously, the Board had ordered her equipment with the help of Mr. Ross.

In March of the next year, when it was time to place an order for spring equipment, the Board's recommendation was carried out. Several dealers were invited to bring their equipment to the gymnasium for display. Mr. Dobson, however, brought his equipment to the Boardroom while the business administrator was present. The outcome was that two or three small orders for softballs, bats, and bases were given to Mr. Dobson. When his order arrived, two bats and two softballs were missing. The bases were of inferior quality, but a high price was charged. Bob simply did not know what to do.

Suggested Questions for Discussion

1. Should Bob have gone to Mr. lord, the principal, as soon as he saw that first order had not been filled properly?

2. When the Board originally recommended that Bob should be given a free hand in the purchasing of equipment, should he have questioned this freedom?

3. Do you think that Mr. lord should have taken Bob to the meeting of the Board of Education to present the list of grievances that Bob had prepared?

4. Should Bob have placed a large part of his order verbally in the spring after being given a "free hand" by the Board?

5. When the Board invoked the new three-part policy about the purchasing of equipment in May, what should Bob have done?

6. Is it wise to order equipment by means of tenders? What are the advantages and disadvantages in this method?

7. What influence might the vice-principal's suggestion about giving some of the business to Mr. Dobson have had on Bob?

8. Does the fact that Miss Giles faces the same problem influence the situation?

9. Should Bob have examined Mr. Dobson's equipment in the room where the Board meets?

10. When some of the business was given to Mr. Dobson and certain items were again missing in March, should Bob have gone to Mr. Lord? To Mr. Ross? To the Chairman of the Board? To Mr. Dobson? To the police?

11. If you were Bob, would you resign as of the end of June? Or would you ask the Board to replace you as department head but remain on the staff?

15. MEADOWBROOK HIGH SCHOOL B
("Planning Facilities")
(As reported by a high school teacher)

Bob Change was appointed head of the boys' physical education department at Meadowbrook High School. Three years later, the school enrollment had increased to such an extent that the school plant was inadequate. The Board of Education commissioned an architect to draw up plans for an addition, including eight classrooms and a second gymnasium. Subsequently, the Board approved the plans for the additional classrooms, but turned down the proposal for the second gymnasium. It was rejected because the state director of education had ruled that his department would no longer give grants toward the cost of "frills" such as gymnasiums, auditoriums, music rooms, and home economics rooms.

The fact that Meadowbrook would have to pay the complete cost of a second gymnasium undoubtedly influenced the Board's thinking. The architect was asked to devise a plan whereby the present regulation gymnasium could be divided with temporary doors. When the Town Council heard about the Board's plan, a resolution was passed that the Council was willing to provide the necessary funds for the total cost of the second gymnasium. The Board, however, wanted to go ahead with the substitute plan.

Bob and one of the other teachers in his department, Doug Bray, became quite concerned about the turn of events. They started a strong program of public relations through the students and the parent-teacher association to encourage the Board to change its recommendation. So many letters and phone calls were made to various members of the Board that the question was re-opened. At this meeting, the Board finally approved the plan for another gymnasium.

While all this discussion was going on, the principal, Mr. Lord, had asked Bob and Miss Giles, the head of the girls' physical education department, to write a list of all possible reasons why there should be additional physical education facilities. These were never called for by the Board, nor were Bob or Miss Giles allowed to speak at any time during the Board meetings. Bob became discouraged and actually mentioned to Mr. Lord that perhaps someone else should be appointed head of the department. He would continue simply as a department member.

As the plans were being drawn up for the new gymnasium, the Board requested through Mr. Lord that Bob and Miss Giles should submit suggestions concerning the amount of storage space, extra locker rooms, and shower facilities that were necessary. With a great deal of apprehension, Bob discussed the matter with Miss Giles. Then he and Doug Bray drafted their plan for the new gymnasium. Again the presence of the heads of the departments was requested at the Board meeting, but for a second time they were not consulted or asked to present their suggestions. The architect presented his plans. When Bob spoke to him after the meeting about their suggestions, the architect was perturbed that Bob should think that he could have any influence on the matter.

When the construction work was finished, there was insufficient storage space, poor shower facilities, and not enough locker room area. To make matters worse, there were innumerable other inconveniences. Bob was completely discouraged. He felt that he was no longer interested in the administration of the department because his opinions had not been considered. Again he spoke to Mr. Lord, and this time he stated definitely that he would like to resign as department head. He said that he would like to continue as a teacher and coach. Just before leaving the interview with Mr. Lord, Bob asked him if he could suggest some means to relieve him of the administrative responsibility in a way that would seem acceptable to all concerned.

Suggested Questions for Discussion

1. Do you think the State Director's ruling that there would be no more grants for the construction of "frills" had some influence on the Board's attitude toward suggestions from the heads of the physical education departments?

2. Should Bob and Miss Giles have accepted the Board's recommendation that the existent gymnasium should be divided with temporary doors?

3. Did Bob and Doug Bray go about their "public relations" campaign in the right way?

4. Why do you imagine that Mr. Lord asked Bob and Miss Giles

to list reasons why the new physical education facilities were necessary?

5. When the Board asked Bob and Miss Giles for suggestions concerning storage space etc., should Bob have gone ahead and

6. Why do you suppose that, after their presence was requested for a second time at the meeting of the Board, they still weren't given a chance to speak?

7. Why do you think the architect was perturbed about their ideas?

8. Do you think Bob was right when he requested to resign and department head and continue as a teacher and coach only?

16. RAND HIGH SCHOOL
("New Department Head"
(As reported by a department head)

On April 16th, Mr. Cox called Mr. Ludlow, who had been appointed principal of Rand High School two years before, about the available position as head of the boys' physical education department. Mr. Ludlow expressed interest in Mr. Cox' application and made an appointment to discuss the matter on April 20th. As Mr. Cox thought about the time for the meeting, he reasoned that Mr. Ludlow would have sufficient time to inquire about his qualifications for the position because they were both in Newport, a city of about 100,000.

At their first meeting, it was immediately apparent to Mr. Cox that Mr. Ludlow had not made any detailed inquiry about him. Mr. Ludlow did mention that he had read about Mr. Cox on the sports page of the *Newport Record*. In this first interview, Mr. Cox was assured that he would have a "free hand" to experiment with the physical education program if he became head. Mr. Ludlow mentioned also that Mr. Cox would be permitted to teach another subject in the curriculum, a point that was interesting to Mr. Cox because of his broad educational background.

As Mr. Cox thought about the new situation, he felt that here might be a chance to get out of the "rut" that he had been in for the past fourteen years. During this time, he had taught physical education in two situations under widely differing personalities as department heads. He felt that there had been many frustrations and many overly heavy workloads. As a possible deterrent to the acceptance of this position, Mr. Cox realized that these fourteen years might have left him with a little less of his original zeal and initiative for physical education work.

In early May, Mr. Cox was notified that he was the first choice for the position. He accepted. Soon after, Mr. Cox made two requests of his new principal. First, he asked for the opportunity to visit Rand High to observe the program. Second, as there was another position open on the department staff, he asked if he might speak to possible applicants at a forthcoming convention. Mr. Ludlow thought that a visit by Mr. Cox was a fine idea, and he asked the retiring department head to arrange for this tour. (Mr. Cox said later that he was taken on a "breathtaking round" of the school. Many door keys did not seem readily available. When doors were finally opened, the rooms were dingy and ill kept. It was necessary for Mr. Cox to return for two days during the summer vacation to re-trace his steps. At this time, of course, he could not observe the existing class routine.

Mr. Ludlow did not agree to the second request. He did not see the need for Mr. Cox to be involved in the appointment of the second teacher in the boys' physical education department. He explained that he had advertised in various newspapers, and that the applications received gave promise that a good candidate would be among them. Mr. Cox asked if Mr. Ludlow would have the other new teacher contact him after the appointment had been made. When the second teacher signed his contract in the office of the Superintendent, Mr. Cox was only two blocks away. Four months later, Mr. Cox and the other teacher finally met after several letters and a motor trip by each one. In the meantime, Mr. Cox had discovered that a fine prospect with two years' experience had been interested in this second position. This person had not applied because of "the lack of the personal touch" that Mr. Cox felt he could have given to the search for a co-worker.

When Mr. Cox reported to his new position in the latter part of August, the first problem was the purchase of new equipment and the repairing of the equipment on hand. This had to be done within the grants of the Board of Education. Certain items for extra-curricular activities were within the budget of the Student Athletic Association. Mr. Ludlow gave Cox the figures available for gymnasium equipment and repair. Since these amounts had to be shared with the girls' physical education department, Mr. Cox spoke to Ms. Larson, head of this department. She said, "That is the first time in my eight years at this school that I have heard those figures." The buying she had done had not been extensive, but she had no idea how the items fitted into the total budget picture.

Mr. Cox learned that a significant amount of the money granted by the Board had been turned back. He noticed that some of the equipment on hand was of good quality, while other material did not seem up to standard. Miss Larson appeared to appreciate the honest approach that Mr. Cox had made to her about this matter. Mr. Cox asked her to let him know if the requirements of her department amounted to less than half of the total budgetary allotment. His plan was to build up the stock on hand for both departments with any surplus that became available. However, as

Mr. Cox related it, "Her years of going to the 'boss' for every little item had become established as a behavior pattern that will tend to keep the department from full co-operation within."

The procedure to be followed in purchasing equipment for the extra-curricular activities was more complex. Mr. Cox was referred to Mr. Root, the vice-principal, who had charge of Student Affairs, and was responsible for the Student Athletic Association. Another staff member, responsible to Mr. Root, looked after the financial accounts of the Association. When Mr. Cox approached Mr. Root about the purchase of some needed athletic equipment, he was told that Rand High was not a "rich" school. Having been thus warned, Mr. Cox proceeded with caution in buying any items. Mr. Root had mentioned further that Mr. Cox should "call on the experience of Mr. Lawson, the equipment manager." Mr. Cox learned that Mr. Lawson had formerly been head of the boys' physical education department. In the five months Mr. Cox had been in his new position, he had asked a number of times for an "accounting of the Association balances." Mr. Root told Mr. Cox that "things are going well."

Another staff member was treasurer of the Athletic Association, taking receipts from admissions charged at the athletic contests. When cash was needed, the treasurer gave Mr. Cox and Ms. Larson the money requested. Orders for any substantial list of items were initialed by Mr. Cox and co-signed by Mr. Root. Already, two incidents had occurred with sporting equipment suppliers. One storeowner, "who keeps notoriously bad books," was certain that Rand High owed him $100 but had no proof. The other supplier had recently presented two invoices for small purchases that still had not been paid. Mr. Cox had stated that these matters had been embarrassing to him.

There appeared to be no direct connection between the equipment manager and the boys' department. Mr. Cox and Mr. Lawson, the equipment manager, had discussed buying certain items of sports, equipment, but as matters stood both Mr. Cox and Mr. Lawson had purchased equipment without first consulting the other. Up to now, they had not bought items for the same purpose, but this possibility existed. Mr. Cox had always told Mr. Lawson what purchases he had made, but Mr. Lawson had not reciprocated. Mr. Cox had had to learn incidentally from suppliers what Mr. Lawson had purchased.

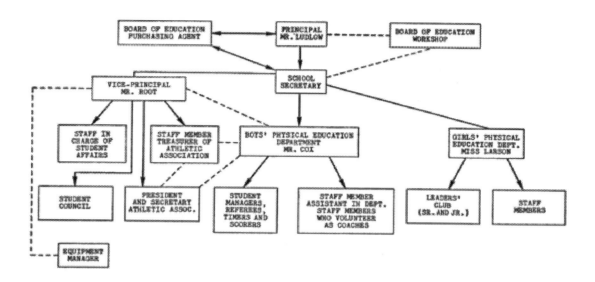

In drawing the diagram for this case, Mr. Cox listed the Student Athletic Association in dotted lines. He reported that "heretofore students elected to office in the Association have been considered to be holding honorary positions." In the fall, the students prior to the election of officers conducted an enthusiastic campaign. When the voting was over, Mr. Cox asked Mr. Root when the meetings of the Association were usually held. Mr. Root explained that there were no meetings. If student assistance was needed, Mr. Root simply called in the president and the secretary and told them that there was a job to be done. Mr. Cox had discovered that a volunteer set-up of managers, timers, and water boys was in effect. Mr. Cox felt that it was a credit to the students that they "see their duty" to Rand High and to the department, and carry on without an organized Student Athletic Association.

Suggested Questions for Discussion

1. Do you attach any significance to the lack of knowledge that Mr. Ludlow seemed to have concerning Mr. Cox at the time of their first meeting?

2. What effect did Mr. Cox's "frame of mind" have on his approach to this new position as department head?

3. Why do you suppose Mr. Ludlow did not allow Mr. Cox to have anything to do with the hiring of his departmental co-worker?

4. What insight into this case do you get from Mr. Cox's inspection of the physical facilities, from Mr. Cox's discussion concerning the budget with Miss Larson, and from Mr. Cox's observation that the quality of the various equipment items on hand varied from excellent to poor?

5. What do you think of the plan concerning the use of surplus money that Mr. Cox suggested to Miss Larson?

6. Why do you suppose that the Student Athletic Association never held meetings? How might it have happened that students were even elected to office?

7. Why do you think that Mr. Root didn't appear inclined to give Mr. Cox an accounting of the finances of the Athletic Association?

8. How do you suppose that the position of equipment manager was created?

9. Why do you suppose the "two incidents" with the sporting goods suppliers had developed?

10. What significance do you attach to the fact that Mr. Lawson did not tell Mr. Cox what equipment he had purchased?

11. Why was Mr. Cox disturbed about the fact that the student officers were called in and told when there was work to be done?

12. What should Mr. Cox have done? Should he have discussed the problem with the equipment manager? With Miss Larson? With Mr. Root? With the student officers? With Mr. Ludlow?

17. SASKAN HIGH SCHOOL
("Staff Relationships")
(As reported by a physical education teacher)

In February, the Saskan Board of Education passed a motion that Mr. Tower's contract would not be renewed for the following year. Mr. Tower was the senior (in length of service) male physical education teacher on the high school staff. This action came as the climax of a series of events after a student reported that Mr. Tower had struck him. To fully understand the situation, it is necessary to review the events that led up to the dismissal.

Mr. Tower had been employed at Saskan High for six years. He had graduated from Eastern University with a major in physical education and a minor in social sciences. For three summers prior to this incident, he had attended summer school and expected to earn his Master's degree shortly. Since his arrival at Saskan, he had coached the senior basketball team to four league championships, and this year his team was again leading the league. He was well liked by all members of the team. When asked about Mr. Tower, Bob McTavish, the team captain, stated, "There isn't anything that we wouldn't do for Mr. Tower. He has always been on the level with us and treated each team member fairly." Jim Stokes, a sophomore who took physical education classes with Mr. Tower, said, "Mr. Tower is a good instructor and is well-liked by his classes."

Mr. Tower was head of the boys' physical education department, but all physical education work came under the supervision of Miss Robson, a long-time staff member. The other two men in the boys' physical education department had great respect for Mr. Tower. Each had worked with him for four years and there was an excellent spirit and fine morale among the three teachers.

Ms. Robson was a teacher in her late forties. She was very efficient and was well liked by the girls. Her philosophy of physical education differed considerably from that of Mr. Tower. She thought inter-scholastic athletics had a place, but that place had been greatly over-emphasized. With this and other differences in philosophy and certain personality conflicts, Mr. Tower and his associates conducted their program with a minimum amount of contact with Ms. Robson.

On several occasions when there had been a clash because of a ruling laid down by Ms. Robson, Mr. Tower and his associates had taken their case to Mr. Waldon, the principal. Once Mr. Tower and the other two teachers had threatened to resign as a group, but Mr. Waldon guaranteed them that he would do all in his power to allow them to run their program with a minimum amount of contact with Ms. Robson. Evidently there had been some discussion about making Mr. Tower the head of both departments, but Mr. Waldon could not persuade the Board that Ms. Robson should be relieved after so many years of excellent service.

The particular incident that led to the Board's decision not to renew Mr. Tower's contract occurred at the end of the basketball season. The boys were preparing for the play-offs. They had the gymnasium during the season on Monday and Wednesday afternoons, while the girls used it Tuesdays and Thursdays. The girls had been eliminated from further play; so Mr. Tower approached Ms. Robson for permission to use the gymnasium at least three and possibly four afternoons for the next week just prior the tournament. Ms. Robson refused to give up the time, because she had planned to use the gymnasium on those afternoons to teach badminton. Four girls had already signed up for each afternoon.

Thursday afternoon before the game, Mr. Tower called a shooting practice for his team. He put a rope across the center of the gymnasium. Miss Robson protested violently that this action "crowded her four girls into one-half of the gymnasium." The senior team had a shooting practice even though she grew angrier as time went by.

It so happened that Bill Thorn was to meet his aunt, Ms. Robson, at the school after her activity was over. Bill was a Grade 11 student who was intelligent but did not apply himself to his schoolwork. He often broke school rules and spent considerable time in the detention room. On this Thursday afternoon, he appeared early and joined in the shooting practice immediately. He was not a member of the team, and he wore street shoes on the gym floor, a definite infraction of school rules. Mr. Tower noticed him and asked him to leave. As soon as Mr. Tower's attention was elsewhere, Bill returned to the floor and began shooting baskets again. This time Mr. Tower showed him to the door and, as he was escorting him there, cuffed him. Miss Robson saw this incident.

When Mr. Tower entered his office the next morning, there was a note on his desk asking him to come to the principal's office. When he arrived at Mr. Waldon's office, Ms. Robson and her nephew were describing the incident to Mr. Waldon. Bill said that Mr. Tower had hit him on the head, thrown him out of the gymnasium, and kicked him as he went through the door. Miss Robson agreed with Bill's description. Mr. Tower told his side of the story and called his team captain to the office to corroborate it. Bob McTavish agreed with Mr. Tower and added, "Bill deserved what he got. He was making a nuisance of himself. Mr. Tower had asked him to leave once and then the second time helped him to the door. He didn't hit him hard enough to crack an egg."

At the next meeting of the Board of Education, the incident was reviewed again. The Board concluded that Mr. Tower had used the gymnasium without his superior's consent and had struck a student. Under these circumstances, they had no choice but to refuse to renew his contract. When this motion was passed, Mr. Tower's two associates got up and handed in their written resignations.

At this point, Mr. Waldon jumped to his feet and protested that this was no solution. He said that these three men had given Saskan High School a fine physical education program and that this loss was far too drastic. He asked the Board to reconsider the matter. The chairman of the Board asked for a motion to re-open the matter. When this motion was approved, one of Mr. Tower's two associates, Mr. Nagel, stood up and said in a quiet voice that they would stay only if Miss Robson were relieved of the headship and if one of the men were given this responsibility in her place.

Suggested Questions for Discussion

1. Do you feel that Mr. Tower was justified in insisting that his team be allowed to practice on one half of the gymnasium floor the day before the game?

2. What should Mr. Tower have done when Bill Thorn went on the gymnasium floor with his street shoes on for the second time?

3. Do you believe that this matter should have been referred to the Board of Education?

4. Do you think that Mr. Tower and his associates had acted wisely in the past when they took matters of difficulty to Mr. Waldon? Should Mr. Waldon have discussed with these teachers the possibility of relieving Ms. Robson from her post as head of both departments?

5. Was the Board of Education justified in passing the motion that Mr. Tower's contract should not be renewed?

6. Was Mr. Nagel, Mr. Tower's associate, wise in presenting such an ultimatum to the Board?

7. Could Mr. Waldon have taken any action which would have prevented the Board from being placed in such a difficult situation?

18. OAKWOOD HIGH SCHOOL (B)
("Excuses from the Required Program")
(As reported by a woman physical education teacher)

Mr. Robert Cramden was a successful young businessman, who lived on a large farm about 10 miles from Newport, a city of about 100,000. He was manager of the local branch of a large business machine corporation, a position that he had held successfully for 10 years.

Bob was interested in athletics and often served on a volunteer basis as a timekeeper at the University football games. On other occasions, he could be seen as a swimming or track official. He seemed to get a great deal of satisfaction from these public appearances. In addition, he always had the inside story (or thought he did) as to why the local team or a certain individual won or lost. He seemed to like this association with athletes and coaches. Sometimes during the year, for example, he would wander into the physical education office to pass the time of day. He often did a little needling, and he seemed to enjoy it when he got a lively discussion on athletics going. During the last war, Bob had been a physical training instructor in the armed forces. One day he offered a fine pair of instructor's trousers to the physical education department head at the university, because he didn't think they would ever fit him around the middle again.

Bob had a daughter called Carol, who was 12 years old and a fairly proficient swimmer. She swam for the local Y.W.C.A. team, and Bob was always present at the home swimming meets. When the team traveled, he drove his car to help out whenever he could. Carol was a freshman at Oakwood High School.

In March, Ms. Maxine Lanning, one of the two women physical education teachers at Oakwood, received a short, terse note from Mr. Cramden demanding that his child be excused from physical education. He stated in the note that no tumbling should be done without harnesses. Until such time, he wanted his child withdrawn from "all and any tumbling routines and any other nonsensical physical contortions from which she may wish to be excused."

Ms. Lanning was annoyed by the note and the way it was worded. She had been teaching the girls some very simple routines, including a forward and backward roll. The class was under her supervision at all times, and she herself served as spotter when any of the girls seemed to be having difficulty. No girl was forced to try any skill of which she was afraid. Ms. Lanning knew also that the program was compulsory, and that a student could be excused only by a written excuse from a physician.

Ms. Lanning learned from Carol that she had told her father of an injury to another girl in the class. In a note to Mr. Cramden, she explained how this occurred and informed him that the injury was very slight. She said that advanced routines were attempted only on a voluntary basis. She mentioned that it was not customary to use a harness for such simple stunts. In conclusion, she pointed out that a medical certificate would be necessary if Carol were to be excused from further participation in physical education.

Mr. Regan, the principal, had been shown Bob Cramden's original note and also the reply. He told Ms. Lanning that Carol should continue with her physical education classes. If she heard anything more from Cramden, he should be referred to the principal.

In the meantime, Bob Cramden had gone to see one of the members of the Board of Education, a Mr. Bovard. Mr. Bovard listened sympathetically to the story about the injury and the need for harnesses. Mr. Cramden told him that he was experienced in such affairs, and that he simply did not trust his daughter in the hands of such a "green" woman teacher. Mr. Bovard reminded Mr. Cramden that the subject was a compulsory one right through high school. He said that Ms. Lanning had been well recommended to the Board. He suggested that this matter was rightfully a subject to discuss frankly with Mr. Regan and Ms. Lanning.

Having gone this far, and evidently not wishing to back down on his original stand, Mr. Cramden appeared unannounced at Oakwood High School on March 28th. He went to the principal's office and repeated his demand that his daughter be excused from this sort of "nonsensical physical contortions" unless harnesses were used at all times. Mr. Regan was polite but adamant. He sent word to Ms. Lanning that Carol's father was in the office to talk over the matter. As she walked to the principal's office, Miss Lanning wondered what to say.

Suggested Questions for Discussion

1. What do you think of Mr. Cramden?

2. Should Miss Lanning have been annoyed at receiving such a note?

3. Did Miss Lanning follow the correct procedure in this situation by sending a note in reply?

4. Should Mr. Bovard have been present at any meeting that was held?

5. What should Miss Lanning use as an argument against a man who she knew was very interested in athletics?

19. PINEVILLE HIGH SCHOOL
("Forming a New Conference")
(As reported by Gilbert Lawrence)

In March, Gilbert Lawrence, a senior physical education major at Northwood Teachers College, met Mr. Steadman, the principal of Pineville High School, for an interview for a job as boys' physical education teacher. Mr. Steadman was accompanied by two of his education board members, Mr. Kye and Mr. Patten. These gentlemen said little, leaving the progress of the interview mostly to Mr. Steadman.

This interview was the third in three days for Gil. It was soon evident that this one would be quite different from the two others. Mr. Steadman had the job responsibilities completely written out, with a sample timetable attached. The position included teaching all of the boys' physical and health education classes. There seemed to be no room for misunderstanding and Gill was impressed. Several days later, Mr. Steadman phoned Gil and offered him the position, which he accepted.

During the latter part of August, Gil went to Pineville in order to have plenty of time to get oriented before school began. Pineville was a town with a population of approximately 4,000. The school, which was a district high school, had an enrollment of 425 students. Thirty per cent of these boys and girls came from the town, the remainder coming from the outlying areas by bus. The physical education facilities were for the most part not more than 5 years old. It appeared to be a very acceptable situation for a first year of teaching.

Although Mr. Steadman had mentioned the different sports in which Pineville fielded teams, there had been no discussion of any league that the school played in. As it turned out, there were no formally organized leagues. Some time before a particular sport season was to start, one school (whichever was the most "eager") called a meeting for all interested schools. (The previous year, Soonerville Tech had not been invited, because they had been "too rough for the league.") At this meeting, a schedule was drawn up and sent to the District Athletic Association office. There was little or no continuity to the inter-school program, and it was extremely difficult to plan very far in advance.

During the latter part of January, Gil began to think about his second year. The District Athletic Association had a ruling by which schools with a student population of over 450 were classified as "A," and schools under 450 were classified as "B." He knew from a conversation with Mr. Steadman that Pineville would be an "A" school next year. The conference had, however, allowed Inco and Soonerville Tech to remain "B" in order not to upset the existing "1eagues." From conversations with the Inco coaches, Gil learned that Mr. Boston, their principal, was determined not to have Inco move into the stiffer competition, particularly against Waring, the perennial champion of the Tri-County League.

After another conversation with Mr. Steadman, Gill decided to talk with the District Athletic Association's general secretary, Mr. Lorenz. Gil was anxious to get a more permanent league, even though he and Mr. Lorenz realized that some schools might suffer temporarily. Mr. Lorenz suggested that if Gil called a meeting of all the schools involved, he would be glad to attend and give any help possible.

About the first of March, an invitation was sent to all of the schools explaining the purpose of the proposed meeting. Several charts and diagrams were enclosed with the invitation, and the representatives were urged to familiarize themselves with these to facilitate discussion.

During the meeting with Mr. Lorenz, three points of interest were brought to light. First, West Point High could be accommodated easily in another league composed of schools of similar size; this would involve less traveling. Second, Seaton High was unhappy about the distances that had to be traveled in the Tri-County League, but no other more suitable "A" league was available. Third, a notice of motion was to come up at the spring meeting of the District Athletic Association that would force schools with an enrollment of 450 or more to move into "A" competition. These points helped Gil, who had given a lot of thought to the entire situation.

The meeting of all the schools was held on the last Wednesday of March. West Point, Seaton, Poland, and Branden did not attend. The principal at Poland sent his regrets by mail, but expressed his interest in the undertaking. After thanking those present for attending and pointing out that what he was going to say was mainly a means of giving some basis for discussion, Gil outlined a proposal. He pointed out what Mr. Lorenz had told him, and then suggested the formation of an "A" league and a "B" league. Although Gil felt that the proposed leagues would operate independently, he suggested that there should be a joint committee to discuss matters of concern to both. Such an approach would, he felt, provide a continuity to the athletic programs and would aid "B" teams that might be close to entry into the "A" category. Then Gil, as the chairperson, threw the meeting open for discussion.

There was a great deal of discussion and progress was slight. Each group felt that it had to protect its own interests. The Tri-County League felt that it could not make a move without Seaton's approval. This league did, however, invite the teams moving into the "A" category to join them the following year. This would be close to the plan proposed. Mr. Boston, the principal of Inco, stated that he did not think the notice of motion before the District Athletic Association would pass. Furthermore, he wanted Inco to remain "B" for another year. It was finally agreed that Mr. Lorenz should try to make arrangements for West Point in the other grouping in its locality, and that all else would remain similar for the coming year.

The annual meeting of the District Athletic Association was held in the middle of May. Each school was entitled to one vote on all motions. After some heated discussion led by Mr. Boston, the proposal was put to a vote. A large majority, including Gil for Pineville, voted that all schools must play in "A" competition when their school enrollments reached 450.

A week after the District Association meeting, Mr. Boston phoned Mr. Steadman of Pineville and asked him to bring his coaches over to draw up new schedules. The meeting was held and the only change was that Inco replaced West Point in the western group's basketball schedule. The "A" and the "B" were still to play together, but each category would declare a winner and advance to its respective play-offs.

Gil was not happy with the situation, but at least he could plan for the coming year. He wondered if Mr. Steadman couldn't have given him a little more active support, because he didn't feel right about "crossing swords" with Principal Boston all the time. Mr. Steadman did tell Gil that he would like to see something similar to Gil's proposal in effect, but he didn't want to do anything that might hurt Mr. Boston's feelings. This was the way the situation stood when school opened in September.

There were no significant developments until May of Gil's second year. The sports were run off as scheduled. During the year Gil talked to the other coaches, and they all agreed that a more permanent organization was desirable. They felt that any change would have to go through unanimously.

During the second week of May, Gil received a call from Dick Leonard, the coach at Waring, who had learned that Seaton had entered a league in its own district. He wanted to know if Gil could come to a meeting of all the "A" schools on the following Wednesday evening.

All the coaches were present, including those from Inco. A temporary constitution was drafted and a schedule was planned for the coming year. It was agreed that copies of the minutes of the meeting should be forwarded to all principals and Mr. Lorenz. If there were any objections, the principals were asked to phone Mr. McKenzie, the principal at Tyre, within a week. If no objections were forthcoming, the plan would be considered final.

Gil came away from the meeting feeling that the coaches had accomplished something that would have beneficial results in interschool sports in that area for many years to come. Mr. Steadman also seemed pleased when he read the minutes. A week before school closed, a letter came from Tyre stating that there had been no objections. Everything would begin as planned in September, and there would be a meeting on the second day of school.

Satisfied that he could plan a fine program for the following year, Gil left Pineville to attend summer school. On July 26, he returned to Pineville for a visit. He visited Mr. Steadman and found him quite disturbed about the new plan. He had been talking with Mr. Boston, who was not happy about the new organization. He did not see how a new league could be formed without a meeting of all the principals. He felt that the coaches had stepped out of line, and he was considering Inco's withdrawal from the league. Evidently the wishes of his coaches did not carry much weight with him.

Gil returned to summer school quite disturbed. Should he try to contact the coaches by mail? Should he write to Mr. Steadman? He wondered if Mr. Boston's remarks were "the last gasp of a tornado." He shuddered a bit when he thought of the forthcoming meeting in September with Mr. Boston present.

Suggested Questions for Discussion

1. Do you think it advisable for a group to rule another school out of an informal league?

2. Do you think a school should be forced to move into another category?

3. Should Gil, as a new teacher, have taken the initiative by going to Mr. Lorenz with the problem?

4. Should Gil have chaired the meeting and offered his proposal before asking for discussion from the floor?

5. Why do you suppose Mr. Boston wanted Inco to remain a "B" school in athletic competition?

6. Do you think Mr. Steadman should have taken a more active role in helping Gil to effect the change?

7. Do you think Mr. Boston was invited to the meeting where a new constitution was drafted?

8. Should his coaches have discussed the proposal with him either before or after the meeting?

9. Why do you imagine that Mr. Boston had voiced no objection to the plan within the allotted time of one week?

10. Should Gil take any action during the summer, or should he wait until September?

20. CENTRAL HIGH SCHOOL
("Professional Ethics")
(As reported by a physical education teacher)

Charles Carson came to Central High as a physical education teacher and head coach in the first year of the school's operation. From the first, he was popular with the student body and most of the faculty. The principal soon discovered, however, that Mr. Carson could create problems.

Since Central was a new school, many policies had to be established. Carson caused some embarrassment by refusing to do anything that was not to his liking. He skipped faculty meetings, since he considered football practice more important. He didn't bother to initial a sign-in sheet system that had been started. He never showed up at P. T. A. meetings.

Carson had definite ideas about the importance of football and sports in general in the school curriculum. He was very outspoken on the matter. His philosophy was that anything worth doing was worth doing well. He didn't feel that he should be given any other extra-curricular assignments in addition to football. He wanted to devote all his time to the development of a top-flight football team. He neglected his duties as a class sponsor, a dance chaperone, and cafeteria supervisor. A clash between him and Principal Twombly was inevitable.

Twombly called Carson to his office many times regarding his dereliction of duty. The principal was an experienced administrator, but he was somewhat baffled by Carson's good-natured refusal to live up to what Twombly considered his duties. Twombly often had been called a fine "academic" man by his associates. It was generally recognized that he merely tolerated athletics.

Mr. Dixon, the assistant principal, was a man who delighted in accepting responsibilities and then "hanging on to them for dear life." He was also athletic director, director of school recreation, senior counselor, and golf coach. As a result, he forgot appointments and found that his duties often conflicted. Many of his mistakes were overlooked because of his pleasing personality, but he was obviously carrying too many activities at once.

The next year, Dixon intimated to Carson that he would be the man considered for the post of athletic director when he relinquished the post in a year or two. No changes were made by the end of Carson's fourth year. As a matter of fact, the superintendent had quoted Dixon as saying that he did not feel Carson was qualified to be athletic director, as he would probably emphasize football at the expense of other aspects of the athletic program.

Superintendent Blosdell was an understanding man who supported any reasonable request made by the athletic department at the high school. In the spring, Carson went in to talk to him about his future. He mentioned that he did not believe in "staying put" when he was not satisfied. Since there seemed to be no immediate possibility of the athletic director's position being available, he said that he would like to try to get into college coaching. The superintendent encouraged Carson to look for such a post and thanked him for having discussed the problem with him.

Carson began to look around for a college position. Although he was interviewed for several positions, he said nothing about this to either Twombly or Dixon. He did not sign his Central contract, intending to let it go as he had done several times before. On these occasions he had signed it late in the fall. This year the office staff had been more efficient in getting out contracts and having them turned in. Since Mr. Carson had heard nothing definite about a new position, he signed his contract, with the intention of breaking it if his college post came through.

During the first week of July, someone called the Central High School office and reported that Carson had been hired by Sommerville College as head football coach. Superintendent Blosdell checked with Mr. Dixon, who appeared to be quite upset, since he had not even heard that Carson was considering another position. When Carson heard about this turmoil, he contacted the superintendent immediately and told him that he still planned to return to Central. Mr. Blosdell thanked him for calling and said that he knew Carson would not leave Central in such an embarrassing position.

On July 18th, Carson was notified that he had been hired by Sommerville College. The story broke on the local sports page. Later that same day Mr. Blosdell received a note from Carson indicating that he intended to break his contract. He said that he was sorry, but that he couldn't afford to let this opportunity go by.

(See sample contract forms below.)

Suggested Questions for Discussion

1. What should be done about a teacher who doesn't live up to his responsibilities?

2. What do you think of Carson's philosophy as expressed to his associates?

3. As assistant principal and athletic director, should Mr. Dixon have disciplined Mr. Carson to some degree?

4. Should Superintendent Blosdell have mentioned to someone that Dixon didn't think Carson would make a good athletic director?

5. Why do you think Carson went to Blosdell in the spring of his fourth year?

6. How could it happen that someone might not sign a contract before late fall?

7. Should Mr. Carson have signed his contract if he intended to break it?

8. Do you think Carson was doing the right thing by taking the college post so late in July?

9. Do you agree with Carson's reasoning: "I simply couldn't afford to let such an opportunity go by"?

TEACHERS CONTINUING CONTRACT

CENTRAL PUBLIC SCHOOLS

THIS CONTINUING CONTRACT made the _____ day of _____ 19 _____.

BETWEEN THE CENTRAL PUBLIC SCHOOLS Board of Education (hereinafter called the Board) and _____ _____ (hereinafter called the Teacher).

WITNESSETH: Said teacher being the holder of a permanent, or life certificate and having been employed at least two (2) consecutive years by said Board, hereby contracts with said Board for the school year of _____ school months, commencing the _____ day of _____ 19 _____ and said Board hereby contracts to hire said Teacher to teach in the Central Public Schools. Such appointment to continue in full force and effect until the said Teacher resigns, elects to retire, is retired, or is dismissed for a reasonable and just cause after a fair hearing before the Board. For and in consideration of such services for the school year 19 _____-19 _____ the said Board will pay to said Teacher the sum of

_____ dollars, payable in equal installments every two weeks during the said school year.

Said Teacher shall annually, hereafter, so long as employed by said Board, receive a supplementary contract stating the salary and leave of absence for the ensuing school year to which said Teacher is entitled under rules of said Board. Said Teacher shall be subject to assignment and transfer at the discretion of the Superintendent of Schools or the said Board. The services of said Teacher shall consist of teaching the Public Schools of the school district administered by said Board and the Teacher shall not be required to perform any other services not connected with the Public Schools.

IN WITNESS WHEREOF the parties hereto have respectively set their hands and seals this day and year above written.

Central Public Schools

For the Board of Education:

By _____   _____
        President   Signature of Teacher

By _____
        Secretary

By _____
        Treasurer

TEACHERS CONTRACT

CENTRAL PUBLIC SCHOOL DISTRICT

THIS CONTRACT made between the Central Public School District, Rawlins Township, Welland County, State of Michigan, hereinafter called the School District, and _____
_____, hereinafter called the Teacher.

WITNESSETH: Said Teacher being certificated to teach in the Public School in said County and State hereby contracts with said School District for the school year of _____ months commencing the _____ day of _____ 19 _____ with vacation periods as the Board of Education of said School District shall designate, and said School District hereby contracts to hire said Teacher to teach as herein set forth, in consideration for which said School District will pay to said Teacher the sum of

_____ dollars payable in equal installments every two weeks during the said school year.

The services of the Teachers shall consist of teaching in the Public Schools of said School District, and the performance of such duties as the Superintendent and Board of Education of said School District shall designate. However, the Teacher shall not be required to perform services other than those connected with the Public Schools.

The Teacher is subject to assignment and transfer at the discretion of the Superintendent of Schools.

In case of illness the Teacher is entitled to one day of absence with full pay for each month of service performed, and such unused days shall be cumulated to a maximum of sixty days.

IN WITNESS WHEREOF the parties hereto have hereunto set their hands and seals this _____ day of _____
19 _____.

_____   _____
        Teacher   Superintendent of Schools

21. NORTOWN HIGH SCHOOL
("Student Teaching")
(As reported by a student teacher)

Nortown High School is a Class C training school for Adams Teachers College. The college has an enrollment of about 3,000 full-time students. Nortown is located 5 miles from the college campus and holds classes from grade 1 to grade 12. The students at Nortown might be considered typical public school children, although it has been said that they are a "tougher group" than the average. The parents of most of the students are farmers, factory workers, or white-collar workers.

In rather direct contrast to Nortown, the college has another training school, South High, situated on the campus. South High is also a Class C school, but the students are screened before admission. South High gets the "cream of the crop," as far as social and economic standings go. Most of college faculty members send their children there, as well as the families in the higher income brackets.

Nortown and South are both in the same athletic conference, and there is a strong rivalry. The fact that South uses the College's fine new athletic facilities adds greatly to this keen competitive feeling.

The teachers at these two training schools are considered to be on the staff of the college. They must have a master's degree to be employed, because they act as critics to the student teachers under them. The high school staff members all have a common goal: advance to the college-staff level and a full professorship.

All college students majoring in education are required to teach one semester at each training school in their senior year, one semester in his major field, the other in his minor field.

John Mank was a senior student majoring in physical education. His first assignment was to teach seventh-grade physical education at Nortown. John had won varsity letters in both football and baseball at Adams, and he felt that this background would help him with his student teaching. His minor subjects were English and business, but he dreaded the thought of having to teach either.

John's first day at Nortown was unfortunate. He had just been introduced to Mr. Blane, his critic teacher, when Mr. Blane started to criticize his clothes. Mr. Blane advised him to get in the habit of wearing a suit, dress shirt, and tie. John was offended, but he found out later that previous student teachers had made Mr. Blane rather sensitive about this matter. Mr. Blane was athletic director and head football and track coach.

For the first few days, John just took the shower check in order to get acquainted with the students in the class that he was to take over. The class consisted of 60 boys, and the gymnasium was much too small for a varied program. Mr. Blane ran the class by himself for the first three days. It soon became evident to John that the boys had no concept of discipline. Mr. Blane imposed no penalties for misbehavior and remained composed at all times. John felt that he was pleading with the boys instead of putting his foot down. John concluded he was going to have a difficult time.

When John took over the class, things were rough at first. He found out that Mr. Blane was insistent about a student teacher's using lesson plans and units. John was unhappy about the extra time that he had to spend on these lesson plans, but he could see that well-planned activities were essential to a successful physical education program.

As time went on, John felt that he was getting along fine with his class and with Mr. Blane, although the five-mile daily bus ride from the college was quite a chore. John disagreed with Mr. Blane over various methods, but he never expressed his feelings openly. What Mr. Blane wanted done, he did. He was not allowed to try any of his own ideas. The shirt and tie regulation was a nuisance and seemed pointless, because he changed into his gym suit immediately after he entered the school and never ate lunch there.

One of Mr. Blane's ideas was that the teacher should be dressed in the same outfit that the class was required to wear, shorts and a white T-shirt. Blane felt that this put the instructor on the same level with the students. It was a major task to get the students to wear this uniform, as some of the boys could not afford it.

Finally, there was just one week to go. Up to this time, John and Mr. Blane had only one "critic" meeting. Mr. Blane was always very formal with John and he never had a "heart-to-heart" talk with John about his teaching techniques. John felt that he was doing a good job, but would have welcomed an encouraging word from his mentor. John prepared the final exam, administered it, and then corrected some brief papers. He gave Mr. Blane some suggested grades, but radical changes were made by the critic even though John had taught every class after the first three days. John was disappointed about this, but he didn't want to make a big issue of it.

The second semester started, and it meant that John would be assigned to teach one of his minor subjects at South. He dreaded having to teach English or business. Much to his surprise, he was assigned to teach ninth-grade physical education. He approached this situation with confidence, for he felt that if he had survived a semester at Nortown, he would certainly do well at South. His critic teacher at South was Mr. Walk, who was head of boys' physical education as well as athletic director and football coach. Mr. Walk had his affairs carefully organized. He had been at South High for 20 years.

The conditions at South High were excellent, and John was pleased. There were only 20 boys in his class, and they were all in correct uniform. They addressed him politely. There was no discipline problem, as Mr. Walk knew these boys from their first day at school. What he said, the boys did. If any boy made trouble consistently, his parents would be asked to take him out of the school. There wasn't even any trouble with dirty uniforms, as this meant a certain number of demerits.

Mr. Walk had his good points as well as his bad points. He had a critic meeting every week. He would have an informal talk with John and the other student teachers about their progress and various teaching methods, always offering valuable constructive criticism. He didn't even require a shirt and tie.
Classes were easy to handle. Mr. Walk never mentioned lesson plans or units. He had everything in his mind. When it was time for the class to start a new unit, Mr. Walk took them for the first day. After he had set things up properly, John followed with the subsequent classes by imitating his pattern. John found himself taking things easy and not so seriously. He enjoyed this experience, but he wondered if this were the ideal type of experience for a student teacher to have. When it came time for the final exams, Mr. Walk simply referred John to his files. All John had to do was check the paper and record the score.

When the year was over, John wondered which situation had been most beneficial? He wondered also if it made any difference that he hadn't been asked to teach at all in a classroom situation?

Suggested Questions for Discussion

1. Do you feel it is advisable to give student teachers two different types of situations?

2. Could anything be done to improve the "bitter rivalry" between the two high schools?

3. Why do you imagine John dreaded having to teach English or business?

4. Is it necessary for student teachers to dress as other teachers do?

5. What do you think of Mr. Blane's class discipline?

6. Do you feel that lesson plans and units are advisable?

7. Should Mr. Blane have accepted John's rating of the students?

8. Why do you think there was no discipline problem at South?

9. What do you think of Mr. Walk's method of guiding student teachers?

10.   Which situation had been most beneficial to John? Why?

22. SUTTER ELEMENTARY SCHOOL

("Class Discipline:)
(As reported by a physical education teacher)

Sutter Elementary School, with an enrollment of over 1,000 students, was one of the largest elementary schools in Metropole. The school was located in an underprivileged neighborhood, which had been slowly deteriorating for the past 15 years. Each year, Sutter had a large turnover of teaching personnel.

In general, the students at Sutter were very un-cooperative, and a great deal of the teacher's effort was directed toward trying to maintain discipline. The teaching of subject matter was considered by many of the teachers to be a secondary objective of the program because of the discipline problem.

Principal Boggs was 60 years old. He had been at Sutter for 15 years, and this year he was going to retire. It was generally recognized (by the men) that he was more sociable toward the women teachers and seemed to get along better with them. Some of the teachers, including some women, mentioned that Mr. Boggs talked to them as if they were children.

It was said that a certain amount of the poor school discipline was caused by Mr. Boggs' very lenient attitude toward students who caused problems. Often when a student was sent to the office for misconduct, Mr. Boggs evidently acted as if he didn't believe the teacher's statement concerning the incident. He would often send students back to class without taking any action. Mr. Boggs took a fatherly attitude toward the children and wanted to avoid any unpleasantness either with them or with their parents.

The physical education department at Sutter consisted of four men, two of whom were Negroes. Every other elementary staff in the city had at least one woman in physical education.

Floyd Miller, a Black, was the director of physical education. He was 30 years old and possessed a Master's degree and 5 years of elementary teaching experience. Floyd had been sent to Sutter by the district supervisor to straighten out the "awful mess" in the department. When Floyd arrived, in 19-, there were two women physical education teachers, one of whom had a habit of drinking during working hours. Both of them resigned at the end of this year. Floyd was ambitious and hoped to become an assistant principal.

In September of the next year, John Brooks joined the physical education staff. He was 30 years old and had one year of teaching experience at another elementary school in the city. John had asked for a transfer from the other school because the facilities had been old and inadequate. He did not know he was coming to Sutter until the beginning of September.

One of the other male physical education teachers had been on the staff for 2 years, while the other was a young man who had just graduated from college.

During the first few weeks of school, Mr. Miller mentioned to the staff that Mr. Boggs had not agreed with his administration of the department on many occasions. In one instance, Mr. Boggs objected to the fact that Mr. Miller had disciplined a disorderly class by having them sit for an entire class period on the gymnasium floor. Mr. Boggs had said that if he would offer an interesting program, the classes would not be disorderly.

During the third week of school, Mr. Boggs called John Brooks to the office for a get-acquainted talk. He had a standard story that he told to all of his new physical education teachers concerning a former physical education teacher who had used force to maintain discipline. It was obvious that he didn't agree with this approach, but he did not suggest any alternative methods.

During the next 6 months of school, John had a great deal of trouble maintaining class discipline, as did the rest of the physical education staff. He did, however, manage to achieve a certain amount of teaching success. One class was unusually difficult, so that one day John made the entire class stand for 30 minutes. The next day, one of the parents phoned and complained to Mr. Boggs.

Mr. Boggs called Mr. Brooks and Mr. Miller in for a conference. He was upset about the matter and said that such punishment was too much of a physical hardship on the children. He pointed out that he personally would find it very difficult to stand that long.

John explained the situation as best he could, but Mr. Miller did not give him any support. Mr. Miller did ask if it would be permissible to have them sit on such an occasion. Mr. Boggs agreed to this suggestion. Mr. Boggs concluded the conference by advising John to consult with either Mr. Miller or himself for advice in all future disciplinary problems before taking any such drastic action.

John began sending students who were serious disciplinary problems to Mr. Boggs' office. After a few weeks, Mr. Miller came down to the gymnasium and told John that the assistant principal wanted John to take care of his own discipline problems.

Suggested Questions for Discussion

1. What do you think of Mr. Boggs' attitude toward the children?

2. Do you think John was right when he made the class stand for 30 minutes?

3. How would you discipline these children?

4. Should Mr. Miller have given John more support when they were called to the office?

5. What is accomplished by sending an unruly student to the principal's office?

6. Do you believe in corporal punishment for unruly students?

7. Why do children from underprivileged communities seem to present more disciplinary problems?

8. Should John ask for another transfer?

23. SUMNER HIGH SCHOOL
("Personnel Policies")
(As reported by a physical education teacher)

Sumner High School operated with a full staff that was well integrated and professionally minded. Consequently, some physical education staff members were soon quite disturbed with the teaching and coaching "attitude" of Mr. O'Brien, a first-year teacher 28 years of age. Superintendent Short was an old friend of O'Brien 's family and had hired him in the fall to teach science and boys' physical education in the junior high school, as well as some mathematics in the senior high school. His coaching responsibilities included junior high basketball and senior high track and field.

Other members of the physical education staff were Ray Bethwell, 29 years old with 5 years of experience, and Frank Carlstrom, 26 years old with 3 years of experience. Mr. Bethwell taught chemistry, physics, and boys' physical education in the senior high school. In addition, he coached varsity football, basketball, and baseball. He was assisted in all three sports by Mr. Carlstrom.

Halfway through the semester, several reports were made to Mr. Short by student committees, the supervisor, and board members that Mr. O'Brien's attitude was unsatisfactory. When confronted with these charges by the superintendent before the Teachers' Advisory Committee chaired by Carlstrom, Mr. O'Brien admitted his lack of interest in the fields he was teaching. He maintained that: "as a physical education major, his knowledge and skills were being wasted."

This attitude was evidently affecting the student body, especially in athletics. One day, Coach Bethwell was unable to attend a football scrimmage against East High and asked Mr. O'Brien to help Mr. Carlstrom. During the first part of the practice, O'Brien was still occupied teaching a class. The scrimmage was going fine for Sumner until O'Brien reported to the field. He began at once to shout and criticize each boy by name. Several members of Sumner's teaching staff observed the players' embarrassment and subsequent loss of spirit. They commented on this later to Mr. Carlstrom.

One day as Mr. Carlstrom was about to enter the coaches' office before basketball practice, he overheard O'Brien say to Bethwell that he resented the fact that Carlstrom, a physical education minor, had a "more responsible position in the athletic department" than he did.

Not long after this incident, Mr. Carlstrom was assigned the bus duty of driving Mr. O'Brien and his junior high basketball team to South High for the annual invitational tournament. Thirty minutes after the departure time, O'Brien had not yet reported. Superintendent Short told Carlstrom to leave with the team and asked him to supervise warm-up drills. In the meantime, he would try to locate O'Brien. When game-time arrived and O'Brien had not yet come, Carlstrom went ahead with the responsibility of coaching as best he could. Sumner lost by a big margin. The boys were very upset that their coach had not been there. Just after the game ended, O'Brien appeared and said that he had forgotten about the game and had been asleep at home.

At the close of the basketball season, Mr. Bethwell submitted his resignation to become effective at the end of the school year. He listed health and a desire to enter the business world as his reasons. He strongly recommended Mr. O'Brien as the man to take his position.

Superintendent Short asked Carlstrom his opinion about Mr. Bethwell's surprisingly strong recommendation of O'Brien for the post. Carlstrom gave an evasive answer, but Mr. Short pressed him. He wanted to know if Carlstrom would or could work together with O'Brien. Carlstrom finally admitted that he felt his philosophy was so different from O'Brien's that difficulties were bound to arise. O'Brien 's class work had not improved, and only 16 boys had turned out for his track and field team.

When contract time arrived, Superintendent Short consulted the Teachers' Advisory Committee and the supervisor regarding O'Brien's unfavorable recommendation from the principal. As a result of these meetings, Mr. O'Brien was not offered a contract for the coming year.

In the assignment talks that preceded the issuing of contracts, Carlstrom was offered the position of department head and varsity coach in three sports. Commenting on his "lack of full qualifications," Carlstrom refused Mr. Short's offer with thanks and signed a similar contract to the one he had held in the previous year. Later, he was approached on two different occasions by two influential board members with the same offer that Mr. Short had made. Interestingly, Carlstrom refused again because of his lack of experience as a basketball coach and other deficiencies in his qualifications.

During the summer, Carlstrom went to summer school to start work on a Master's degree. Toward the end of the session, he received a telephone call from Mr. Short asking him to be prepared to return to school as soon as possible. A new department head had not been secured and "someone had to start early football drills." On August 10th, Carlstrom returned to Sumner and began to prepare for football practice.

About a week before school opened, Mr. Short drove out to the football field and asked Carlstrom to drop into his office after practice. Upon his arrival, Mr. Short came right to the point. No man had been hired to fill Mr. Bethwell's position, although a considerable effort had been made. Mr. Short had learned that O'Brien was still not under contract to teach anywhere. Mr. Short then asked Carlstrom if the situation had changed, or did he still feel that he would have difficulty working with O'Brien—that is, if O'Brien were willing to accept the position. Carlstrom replied that he still did not like O'Brien personally, but that "for the good of the school he would do his very best to work with anyone that the superintendent placed in the vacant position."

Suggested Questions for Discussion

1. Do you think O'Brien was justified in having an "unsatisfactory attitude" because his "knowledge and skills were being wasted?"

2. Why do you imagine that Mr. Bethwell recommended O'Brien to take his place?

3. Why do you suppose that O'Brien resented the fact that Carlstrom held a "more responsible position" in the athletic department?

4. Should Superintendent Short have asked Carlstrom if he would be willing to work under O'Brien as a head coach?

5. Should O'Brien have been offered another contract at the end of the school year?

6. Should Carlstrom have refused Bethwell's position?

7. Do you feel that Short's final action was a "desperation" measure, or that he had planned to hire O'Brien all along?

24. AVON ELEMENTARY SCHOOLS
("Supervision")
(As reported by Bob Jones)

After graduation from Sumpter College, Bob Jones took a position as football coach in a small Pennsylvania high school. Several years later, he moved to a large secondary institution in Baltimore. Although he enjoyed athletics and had considerable success with winning teams, he left public school teaching when he was offered better money in an industrial school.

Heartened subsequently by the higher salaries teachers were receiving, however, Bob took a job as a fifth grade teacher in Avon. The field of elementary education seemed to offer a good opportunity for an ambitious person. The principal and the superintendent knew about Bob's previous experience. When he made several suggestions that might improve the physical education curriculum, the superintendent offered him the post of elementary physical education supervisor for the second year.

Mr. Smith, the superintendent, retired at the end of that year, however, and was replaced by Mr. Calvin Brown. Mr. Brown was a much younger man who had entirely different ideas about the administrative set-up of the fast-growing Avon School District. One of the first acts of the new superintendent was to eliminate Bob's new title on the basis that he was teaching classes.

Then, as a reward for 9 years of successful coaching at Avon High School (Bob was told), Bill Robb was made athletic director. To Mr. Brown, athletics and physical education were one and the same thing. For this reason, he put them under the same department in the system.

Bob was irked about losing his title of supervisor and $1000 additional salary that went with it. He didn't seem to have any choice in the matter, so he decided that he had to go along with the change. His feelings were helped by an $2000 salary raise that had been received by all teachers. In addition, he had received a supplemental contract as recreation director for the 2 summer months that gave him 2 months of extra pay. Then, in addition, Mr. Johnson, the assistant superintendent in charge of elementary education, told Bob that he would no longer have to worry about purchasing equipment and arranging for transportation. This helped because these responsibilities had forced Bob to put much overtime into his job.

What bothered Bob most was that other teachers constantly stressed the point that Bill Robb looked upon physical education only as a means of developing winning athletic teams. Bob had built his program with the idea that every boy in the fourth, fifth, and sixth grades was entitled to be on some team regardless of his present ability.

The Avon School District included eight schools where classes were conducted for these age groupings. One of the first directives that Mr. Robb gave to Bob was that there would be a league with regularly scheduled games, and that the best boys should play on these teams. Bob thought that elementary athletics should be on more of an intramural basis; so he spoke to Mr. Johnson about Bill Robb's directive. Apparently Bill had already spoken to Mr. Johnson, because Bob was told by Johnson that he thought it was a fine idea. He had agreed to find the money in the budget to pay for team trophies.

Bob reminded Mr. Johnson that in a conference at the end of the last school year, they had agreed to include the third grade in this program also. Because of this inclusion, Bob was no longer to have the responsibility of monitoring the study hall in the high school. This problem was soon settled by a directive from Mr. Brown stating that Mr. Beal, the high school principal, would need Bob as a study hall monitor for 2 hours each morning.

Although disillusioned over the turn in events, Bob thought the best thing was to simply work out the best schedule possible under the circumstances. His task was to teach physical education to the boys and girls of grades 4, 5, and 6 in the eight elementary schools. He talked over the problem of working out a schedule with Mr. Johnson, who had charge of elementary education. However, Bill Robb inserted himself into the picture at the time that he called a meeting of the athletic department. Just after the meeting, he mentioned to Bob that the two of them would have to get together to work out a schedule for Bob. Bob, of course, already had a schedule worked out, but he couldn't catch up with Bill Robb to discuss it until the first day of school.

On this Monday morning, Bill said he was too busy to go into it at the moment. He told Bob to go out to Whitmire School and start classes, and they could discuss the schedule later in the day. Bob was in a quandary; he knew by experience that to start classes without notifying the principal and the teachers beforehand was to invite trouble. The physical education schedule had to be co-ordinated with schedules for other special subjects. After vainly trying to explain this to Bill Robb, Bob went out to Whitmire, hoping all the while that he wouldn't run into Mr. Thompson, the principal.

Having been on good terms with the teachers in the past, Bob got by for a few periods by explaining the situation to the various teachers as best he could. Everything went quite smoothly until he went to Miss Crandall's sixth grade class. When Bob appeared, she went right to Mr. Thompson. He was very upset about Bob's unexpected appearance and told him that he wouldn't stand for his "barging in" whenever he felt like it. Bob tried to explain, but he left Whitmire School feeling a complete fool.

Bob returned to the office of the athletic director and told him what happened. He was hoping that Robb would let him use his own schedule. Bill, however, only called Thompson "an old goat" and told Bob to meet him after lunch to work out the schedule. At that time, Bill made it clear that he was now in charge of Bob's program, and that he was going to devote some of his free time to teaching elementary physical education. Bob figured that at last his load was going to be lightened a bit, as Bill had only two class assignments.

Once again Bob was wrong. In fact, as the schedule evolved, it was even worse. Not only did Bill assign Bob to all the eight schools, but in some cases he told him to teach the third-grade students as well.

Bob ran into another problem. The previous spring he had ordered ample equipment for the entire elementary program. As it turned out, however, there had been a great turnover of teachers in grades 7 through 12. Many of the departing teachers had failed to order equipment for the fall term. When the equipment that Bob had ordered came in, it was put in the supply room. Under a new policy instituted by Mr. Brown, Bob would have to get a requisition countersigned by Bill Robb in order to check things out for his classes. When he went to Bill, he was told that much of this equipment would have to be used by the junior and senior high schools because of the laxity of the departing teachers. Hence, Bob had to run his program with the bare essentials and found that no further equipment was forthcoming.

In the spring, Bob began to plan for the annual elementary school field day, which had always been one of the highlights of his program. Bob reminded Bill about this event in March and asked him if he should go ahead with the arrangements. It was a complicated affair, as a preliminary meet was held at each school to determine the finalists for the big day. Bill told him to run the preliminary meets, and that he would take care of the arrangements for the field day itself. A week before the final day, Bob happened to meet the bus foreman and asked him if he were all set for the big occasion. The foreman was quite surprised and said that this was the first thing he had heard about it.

Meeting with Bill the next day to discuss the plans, Bill told him they would have to decide on what events were to be run off. Bob was staggered, because he had already conducted most of the trials at the various schools in the same events that had been used the previous year. Bill changed most of the distances, lengthening them to the point where they violated the recommendations of the state high school athletic association.

Despite Bob's fears, the meet was run off successfully. Bill phoned the results to the newspaper. When the story appeared, it stated that the meet was conducted by the athletic director with assistance from an elementary physical education instructor.

When the school year ended, Bob was quite discouraged. Should he go to the superintendent and tell him what a farce the program had been, or should he simply look for another job?

Suggested Questions for Discussion

1. Should Bob Jones have protested to the superintendent immediately after he learned that his title of supervisor had been dropped?

2. Should an elementary school physical education program be under the guidance of the athletic director of the system?

3. Should Bob have refused to go to a school before the principal

was notified by Mr. Robb?

4. Should Bob have asked Bill which classes he was going to teach?

5. Could anything have been done by Bob about the division of the equipment that he had ordered?

6. How could Bob have clarified the division of responsibility in planning for the field day?

7. What should Bob do to improve his situation for the coming year?

25. JENSEN JUNIOR HIGH SCHOOL
("Intramural Athletics")
(As reported by Roberta Martin}

Two years after it was built, Jensen Junior High was overcrowded with an enrollment of 2,100 students. To accommodate this number of students, another junior high school was being constructed to be ready in 18 months. At present, however, the seventh and eighth graders were attending school on half-day sessions, while the ninth grade students went to school for the entire day. About 90 per cent of the students commuted by bus.

Because of difficulties in scheduling, only the eighth and ninth graders were offered regular physical education. Intramural activities were conducted in both the girls' and boys' departments. Inter-school basketball and track were offered to all grades, while inter-school baseball was available to the ninth grade boys only. There were two men and two women on the physical education staff. Three other faculty members helped the regular male physical education staff members with the athletic coaching, for which they received extra compensation.

The gymnasium was regulation size, but it was necessary to divide it with a folding door. The outdoor facilities were adequate.

The working relationship between the girls' department head, Miss Martin, and the boys' department head, Mr. Wilson, had been extremely good. Prior to the basketball season, Miss Martin and Mr. Wilson had a meeting to decide what times each would need the gymnasium after school hours for either varsity coaching or intramural athletics. Since both halves of the gym were needed to run a practice successfully, or to accommodate the large number of girls who would be participating in intramurals, it was decided that Miss Martin would use the entire gym once a week. The three boys' basketball teams would practice the other days. Miss Martin would have liked to have the use of the facilities two nights a week, but she realized how difficult it was for Mr. Wilson to find practice time for three different teams. Because of this arrangement, it was impossible to schedule basketball on an intramural basis for the rest of the boys until the varsity season was over. By this time, a good bit of the enthusiasm had been dissipated.

During the spring, Mr. Wilson decided that something had to be dropped. There simply were not enough facilities to offer a program for all the students. Since intramural basketball involved approximately 300 boys and girls, he decided that the facilities should be used for this group rather than the 45 boys on the three varsity basketball squads. A memorandum went out to the rest of the faculty that recommended the elimination of varsity basketball because of the lack of facilities. A meeting was called so that all interested parties could discuss the matter and possibly present a further recommendation to the principal.

The meeting was attended by the principal, the two assistant principals, the three teachers hired to help with the coaching, and the two men and the two women of the physical education staff. Mr. Benson, a classroom teacher who coached the seventh grade basketball team, was strongly opposed to the recommendation by Mr. Wilson. If "something had to go," he felt it should be the intramural program, as he believed that there was little value in it. He stressed that the boys who participated in varsity sports achieved a much greater satisfaction, as well as a finer educational experience. He pointed to his own case, as he had been a varsity track man in high school and college.

Miss Martin tried to point out to Mr. Benson that the first responsibility is to the larger number of students. She used the analogy of the physical education triangle, or pyramid, to explain her point. She stressed that the base of the triangle is formed by all the students learning basic skills and knowledges in required physical education classes. The middle section consists of intramural athletics, where the majority of the students should have an opportunity for a competitive experience at their level of ability. She agreed that the more highly skilled should have the chance to compete at their level too, but in this case it seemed impossible. If something had to be eliminated, she said that they, as educators, had a responsibility to work from the bottom of the triangle to the top.

Mr. Wilson spoke and said that it was a very difficult recommendation for him to make, because he believed strongly in varsity sports. He reasoned that perhaps the needs of all the boys could be met through intramural competition, because these boys were not yet highly skilled. They had no elementary physical education program behind them, and they had a backlog of skills to make up before they could compete on even terms with other junior high schools in the area.

Principal Glander stated that he wanted to let those faculty members concerned with this problem make their own decision. He could see both sides of the question; but he couldn't see an answer. The two assistant principals nodded their heads. Mr. Glander concluded by mentioning that he had received a phone call from Mr. Jackson, the high school basketball coach. Mr. Jackson was upset that the staff was considering the dropping of varsity basketball. He said that he was having a hard enough time as it was developing a good high school basketball team. Jackson was afraid that his position would soon be in jeopardy because of this proposed move.

Mr. Haggerty, the other male physical education teacher, pointed out that inter-school competition for junior high school students was a controversial subject anyhow. The American Association for Health, Physical Education, and Recreation had gone on record as being opposed to competitive athletics at this level, as had other educational groups.

Mr. Wilson, who was chairing the meeting, asked if anyone couldn't think of a solution whereby all interests would be satisfied. If not, he suggested that the group take a vote on the subject. He could see that there was going to be some bitterness over the issue, and he wanted to keep peace in what had been a "happy family."

Suggested Questions for Discussion

1. What influence should the construction of a second junior high school have on this problem, if any?

2. Should required physical education be made available to the seventh grade students also?

3. Should faculty members receive extra compensation for coaching duties?

4. Why should the girls be restricted to only one afternoon a week for use of the gymnasium?

5. Should the principal and the assistant principals be involved in the final decision?

6. What do you think of Miss Martin's argument as opposed to that of Mr. Benson?

7. Are inter-school athletics desirable at the junior high level?

8. Can you think of a solution to this problem?

26. FOREST LANES SCHOOL
("Evaluation and Grading")
(As reported by Ms. Newland)

When Miss Newland went to the Forest Lanes School for her first job, she was impressed by the school and the community. Everyone was friendly and helpful.

The girls' physical education program, which had been established 15 years before, consisted of two high school classes; a ninth grade class; a combined seventh and eighth grade class; and fourth, fifth, and sixth grade classes, which met on alternate days. The classes were small, and Miss Newland liked the variety offered by the combined elementary, junior high, and high school program.

When she started teaching, Miss Newland was told that she was expected to grade the junior and senior high school students each marking period. The elementary students received no grade for physical education. As the year progressed, she found that the boys were not graded at all. They received only a credit or noncredit rating at the end of the semester. When she inquired about this, she was told that the grades would help with discipline and other problems that came up in the girls' classes. She learned also that the girls had always been graded since their program had been established.

Two years after Miss Newland arrived, the boys' instructor started to give the junior high boys a letter grade at the end of the semester, instead of a credit mark. In this year, a new man was added to the boys' staff, and he graded either credit or non-credit for his ninth grade class. The new man took over the physical education for the elementary boys, but no grades were given to them.

Each year since she had been on the job, Miss Newland had received some complaints from students that their gym grades had kept them off the honor roll. The girls felt that it was unfair for their gym grades to be averaged in when figuring the honor roll, because the boys didn't have a mark to be averaged also. The honor roll was important to them, and the names of the students making it were published in the local newspaper. In addition, students who made the honor roll three out of four periods in the academic year could be excused from one of their final exams. Honor roll students received free passes to the local theater and a certificate of achievement at the annual Honors Assembly in June. Miss Newland also learned that the students received no credit toward graduation for physical education, although these grades were averaged in with other subjects.

Miss Newland felt that physical education was an important subject in the curriculum and should have the same status as other subjects. She reasoned that the grades given each marking period were a step toward this objective. She became annoyed when other teachers asked that girls be excused from physical education to make up tests or to take part in other activities.

One day, after turning her grades in for the previous marking period, she began to think about the hours spent with this task. It bothered her that the men in the department spent almost no time on this at all. She put as much time or more into planning the girls' program as the men did in planning their work.

Her dissatisfaction with the "double standards" became so great that she decided to approach the principal on the matter. She didn't know whether to ask if she should be allowed to adopt the credit or no-credit system, since she felt that grades do little toward settling discipline problems. On the other hand she believed that grades helped to give her subject status. She wondered if it would be right for her to argue that the boys' department should institute grading each marking period also. She realized that this would not be looked upon very favorably by the men in the department.

Suggested Questions for Discussion

1. Should students be given regular academic credit for physical education?

2. Why do you imagine that no grades were given to the elementary pupils?

3. Why do you think the administration allowed this set-up where a "double-standard" existed?

4. If a grade is given, what should be considered in the evaluation?

5. Do you feel that grades have an effect on class discipline?

6. Do you think that Miss Newland should attempt to rectify the situation so that the boys would be graded also?

7. If so, how should she go about it?

27. RAWLINS HIGH SCHOOL
("Legal Liability")
(As reported by a high school teacher)

Ms. Bolling was hired in April as girls' physical education teacher at Rawlins High School. She was just completing her senior year at Boardman State Teachers College, where she was a good athlete with interest and ability in most sports. Although not a large individual, she was energetic and commanded the respect of the students.

From the time she started at Rawlins, she became instrumental in initiating an interesting and varied program for the girls. Previously, the program had consisted of only a few games. A few girls, as might be expected, were not overly impressed by Ms. Bolling. They were not fond of physical education and felt that they were being overworked in class. Their participation was usually as passive as possible.

Ms. Bolling made an attempt to treat all the girls fairly. What one had to do, all of them had to do. She showed no partiality. Miss Bolling's treatment of students earned her the respect of the students to the extent that some of the teachers sent their discipline problems to her.

Irene Skowron was sent to Ms. Bolling by the study hall monitor because of her misbehavior. Since she arrived very early in the class period, Miss Bolling told her to dress for gym (which she hated) and join the girls on the playing field.

This particular playing field had been created by dumping fill in a low spot behind the school. Occasionally, below surface currents caused a sinking of the surface in spots. This possibility was known and careful checks were made to block off any such areas, until they were repaired.

When Irene arrived at the play area, she was chosen by one of the captains. After playing conscientiously for a while, she began to "showboat" and make a travesty of the game. Ms. Bolling noticed this and replaced her immediately, with the intention of further disciplining her.

Just then MS. Bolling's attention was diverted by another problem with one of the other contests. As she was looking after this matter, a scream was heard from one part of the field. Irene had wandered off and stepped in a hole. Her leg appeared badly hurt.

First aid was administered, and she was taken to the hospital for treatment. The final diagnosis was that Irene's fibula was fractured just above the ankle.

Upon receiving this news, Mr. and Mrs. Skowron consulted their lawyer, who advised that suit citing neglect should be brought against the teacher. The school board furnished Ms. Bolling with a lawyer. During the trial, the prosecution attempted to show that it was the neglect of the instructor that caused the incident. It was stated that the teacher had a responsibility to see that the playing area was free of conditions where a student could be injured. The point was made that Irene should not have been in that class at that time.

The jury decided in favor of the teacher, because the injury had been incurred when Irene went into an area forbidden to students. On the second count, the teacher was within her rights because it was customary at Rawlins to ask other teachers to assist with disciplinary problems.

Because of the unfavorable publicity of the case, Ms. Bolling's contract was not renewed for the following school term. Miss Bolling was upset at this turn of events, but she reasoned that it might be better to start another career in a different community.

Suggested Questions for Discussion

1. Do you think problem students should be sent from the study hall to the gymnasium?

2. How should a dangerous area be blocked off?

3. Do you feel that Ms. Bolling was negligent in any way?

4. Why do you imagine Ms. Bolling's contract was not renewed?

5. Should Ms. Bolling have accepted the final result of the situation?

28. Bolton High School
("Supervision")
(As reported by the woman physical education teacher)

Bolton High School, located in a rural community, needed a new staff member. Several applicants were interviewed, and the position was offered to Bob Franklin. Bob was a likable chap, who had just graduated from college the previous June. The Board of Education was well satisfied with his credentials. After the choice had been made, the Board members were even more impressed as to the wisdom of their choice by Bob's wife Mary, who was attractive and friendly. Everyone felt that they would "fit" into the community, and they were immediately accepted by the community of Bolton after their arrival. They attended one of the local churches, and Bob became a member of the choir. Bob was very witty and was often called the 'life of the party."

Because Bob had a minor in physical education, he was asked to coach basketball and baseball. He was to have a full teaching load during the regular school day. As the school year progressed, complaints were often heard about his method of teaching. He was not getting his subject across. The students said that most of the time was spent "just gabbing about anything-mostly sports."

In the meantime, Bob had become quite the "Good Joe" in town. He entered many of the community affairs and even had an "in" with some of the Board members. Because he was so well liked, the complaints about his teaching went unheeded. There was no adequate teacher supervision, so that Bob received no help as a beginning teacher. The students "griped," but soon forgot their specific grievances, because they liked him so well. Toward the end of the year the football coach left to take a better position. Bob was asked to coach football, also.

Mr. Franklin, the principal, did not feel that Bolton High was very progressive, because they did not have a physical education program. Bob heard about this from him, and immediately began laying the groundwork. He stressed the importance of the program to the Superintendent, Mr. Canton. Mr. Canton was conservative and did not help push the idea.

Bob then took another course of action. He approached his friends on the Board of Education. Finally, two years later, the Board agreed to add physical education to the program on a small scale. It was to be offered only to the boys one hour a day as an elective.

Bob continued to teach some academic subjects. The better students continued to express their dislike for his teaching methods, because they didn't feel they were learning anything. The same students might "back him up" in another situation, because "you just couldn't help liking him."

By this time, the girls also were demanding a physical education program. It was agreed that the next year a full program would be organized. The girls had the use of the gymnasium in the mornings, and the boys would take over the facility in the afternoon. Miss Simmons was added to the staff to teach girls' physical education.

Bob received another honor. He was voted class sponsor for the graduating class. According to the co-sponsors, he gave them very little cooperation. They said that he usually "passed the buck." The rest of the faculty noticed this, but no one seemed to hold it against him.

During Bob's third year he was relieved of the responsibility of coaching football. Another staff member was assigned this duty, and track was added to the list of interscholastic sports. Bob continued to coach basketball, and that winter his team showed unusual promise. They won a large percentage of their games, and it looked as if they might win the district championship.

Unfortunately, Bob's laziness was becoming apparent in his coaching duties, also. He started the season in a most efficient manner. He drilled the boys hard until their basic plays were perfected. One of the male staff members made the remark that Bob had the ability to go a long way as a basketball coach. As the season progressed, however, Bob slackened his effort even though the pressure to win was mounting. He would arrive late for practice, watch the team for a while, give them a little advice, and sometimes leave early.

The week of the district tournament he really let the team down. He didn't show up even though the boys came to practice night after night. They would shoot for a while and then leave because the coach wasn't there. This team with a lot of potential was eliminated early in the tournament. A number of comments were made about Bob, but people soon forgot the basketball season.

During Bob's fourth year at Bolton, he was given a free period to take care of his duties as athletic director. His workload consisted of one classroom subject, a study hall, and three physical education classes. Since his free period was in the middle of the morning, he always went to the school kitchen. This was common practice and acceptable if a teacher had a free period. He would complete his duties such as counting gate receipts, interviewing sporting goods salesmen, or writing letters. After this, he usually chatted with anyone available and forgot the time. He was habitually ten or fifteen minutes late for his next classroom period. Often in the afternoon when he was supposed to be in the gym or on the athletic field, he would go to the nearby drug store. The teachers and students talked about his frequent absences, but nothing was done. It was even disclosed that he was meeting board members at the drug store for coffee during school time.

During this year, Bob's absences from gym classes were not "setting so good" with the boys. They still liked him, but they were finding his laziness difficult to overlook. The first-year students were asked to write essays on the subject "What I Like and What I Dislike about Bolton High." One of the fellows stated: "I wish Mr. Franklin would spend more time in my gym class, so I can learn something."

Bob's trips to the drug store became more frequent, and sometimes he just stayed in the coaches' room. He would use upper-classmen to keep order, hand out equipment and baskets, and referee games. Because so much equipment was lost or stolen (and often broken), the girls' physical education teacher became disturbed. The money to replace this equipment could have been used to add new sports to the over-all program.

That year Bob had a terrific basketball team that won the league championship and went on to take the district title. The student body and the town were greatly excited about having a winning team. The team was rated very high in the state, and many people predicted that they would at least take the regional, if not the state, championship. However, after winning the district title, Bob lost interest. It was rumored that he told the fellows that he was satisfied with winning the district championship. They had defeated a very powerful team in the finals-a team from a larger school that was a perennial champion. Since they had defeated Rumsey, townspeople were confident that the boys would go far in the regional tournament.

Maybe the pressure had been too great. Bob had been working long hours all year trying to complete a new home. Whatever the reason, his interest had vanished. Bolton lost most disappointingly in the first game of the regional championships to a team that was obviously inferior. To make matters worse, the score was lopsided. Many were disgusted and disappointed according to the remarks passed for the next few days.

Bob was slowly losing his prestige in town. The students still liked him, but the former admiration was gone. In informal faculty gatherings there was considerable criticism of his actions. His conference free period was changed to another hour so that he wouldn't always be late for his classroom assignment. Pressure was brought on him to do a better job with his physical education classes. For a time he improved, but by the middle of the winter he was back to his old habits again…

Suggested Questions for Discussion

1. Should Bob have received some sort of supervision during his first few years of teaching?

2. Should friendships exist among board of education members and faculty?

3. What should the co-sponsors (or the students) have done when they failed to get any cooperation from Bob?

4. Whose responsibility is it to see that Bob coaches the basketball team adequately?

5. Should Bob leave the building during regular class hours? Would it make any difference if he were meeting members of the board?

6. What steps could be taken to see that Bob gets to class on time?

7. Should Bob have been condemned because his team lost out in the first game of the regionals?

8. How can a better program be secured for the boys?

29. Morgan High School
("Teacher-Student Relations")
(As reported the woman physical education teacher)

Morgan High School had an enrollment of approximately 700 students, a great majority of whom traveled to school by bus. The superintendent of schools in this city was Mr. Alexander, who had been in this position for four years. In the 12 years previous to his arrival at this post, he had held 11 different positions. He was a very impulsive man. When he came to take up his office at Morgan High, he found a faculty with high morale. The previous superintendent had been well liked and an outstanding citizen in the community. Mr. Alexander let it be known that he saw many educational practices at Morgan High that were "out-of-date." He made some drastic changes in class scheduling, in the appointment and duties of a number of faculty members, and with specific school policies.

Mr. Curtis, the high school principal, was congenial, kind, and easy-going. He was trustworthy and assumed that everyone else had this quality. He seemed to believe that if you closed your eyes to problems, they would not exist. Much of his time was spent in the office making decorative notices for the student bulletin board. He was lax in disciplining students. If, for example, a student skipped school, the principal might pat him on the head and tell him to be good in the future. The student might then agree to this and exit laughing. Some students talked back to him arrogantly and "got away with it." Many of the students had no respect for him. Some members of the faculty felt the same way.

Mrs. Gibbs, aged 24, was the girls' physical activity and health education director at Morgan High. She was enthusiastic and conscientious about her work. Many of the students confided in her and discussed their personal problems.

In April, Flora Shiebler enrolled in Morgan High. She was a 19-year-old junior. Her family moved often because her father was a transitory construction worker. She was "going steady" with a 37-year-old man who lived with the family in a trailer about 7 miles outside the city limits.

Flora was a straightforward and bold individual. On her first day at school, she told the principal to "keep his nose clean" of her affairs when he asked for her home address. When the English teacher accidentally mispronounced her name, she told her to go back to school and learn a bit more.

Flora was in Mrs. Gibbs' physical education class, which met twice a week. When she asked to be excused from class for the second time, she was advised to see the school nurse. She did not come back to class that day. Upon checking with the nurse, Mrs. Gibbs discovered that Flora had not reported to her. One of the girls said that Flora had gone downtown after she left class.

A short time later, Flora said she had a toothache and wanted Mrs. Gibbs to give her a pass to leave the building. Mrs. Gibbs explained that only the principal and the school nurse could issue building passes. Later that day, Mrs. Gibbs learned that Flora had been to the nurse and had received a pass to go to her family dentist in a nearby town. Flora mentioned his name to the nurse. Mrs. Gibbs thought it unusual that a family dentist would be established already, since Flora's family had just recently moved to Morgan.

She mentioned to the nurse that some of the girls were worried about a rumor that Flora smoked cigarettes that were "drugged." In addition, Flora had been missing school quite often. Mrs. Gibbs learned that she spent much of her time in the local "teen-shop." It was rumored that she had bought some expensive pills for which she had a prescription, paying $70 for eight of them. Several of the schoolgirls told their parents that she had bragged about the pills.

Upon checking with Flora's "family dentist," Mrs. Gibbs learned that Flora had not been to him for a visit. She hadn't even been listed for an appointment, and the dentist had never heard of her.

Mrs. Gibbs realized that she should not jump to conclusions, but she could not help wondering about the possible truth of the rumors. She decided to see the school nurse again. After talking the matter over at length, they decided to take their suspicions to the principal. This was one week after Flora had entered the school as a new student.

Mr. Curtis listened to them attentively. Mrs. Gibbs thought the matter worth investigating, although she agreed that it might be a matter of circumstantial evidence. The school nurse agreed; so, Mr. Curtis asked Mrs. Gibbs if she would be willing to follow up on the case. She said that he would do anything possible to help, but she did not want her name used. She was afraid that it would mean being disloyal to the confidences placed in her by students who had informed her of the situation. He said he understood.

The next morning Mr. Curtis called Mr. Ford, a detective with the State Police, and explained the situation. He came to the school immediately and talked to Mrs. Gibbs, the school nurse, as well as to Mr. Curtis. It was decided that it would be best not to say anything to anyone, not even the superintendent, until some concrete proof was available. Mr. Ford felt that they had to get evidence, to be certain that Flora still had any of the "pills." Mrs. Gibbs was asked if she would cooperate with the State Police by obtaining Flora's purse during a gym period. They wanted to check it without Flora's knowledge. Mrs. Gibbs wasn't certain that she should be involved in this way, and she didn't know what to do.

Suggested Questions for Discussion

1. Do you get an insight into the problem from the character description of the superintendent and the principal?

2. What is the basic problem in this case?

3. Is Flora's age of any significance?

4. Was Mrs. Gibbs right in going to Mr. Curtis?

5. Should Mr. Alexander have been consulted before going to the State Police?

6. Why do you suppose the police asked Mrs. Gibbs if she would help?

30. SOUTH BAY HIGH SCHOOL
("Coach-Player Relations")
(As reported by the team captain)

South Bay High School is located in the town of Grayling, that is the business and shopping center of the surrounding rural area. The population of the town is 6,000, of which number 360 are students at the high school. Four varsity sports are played regularly: football, basketball, winter sports, and baseball.

The entire program was administered very carefully by the principal, Mr. Rogers, who had served many years as a coach before assuming an administrative post. The faculty was composed of seven men and four women. Six of the seven men had coaching experience, although they weren't all holding coaching assignments. Mr. Rogers ruled the school's athletic program "with an iron hand." He had recently been elected secretary of the State Athletic Association and felt this responsibility keenly. Many townspeople still talked about his outstanding record as an athlete when he was a student.

South Bay High had reached the point where athletics were a most important phase of high school life. For a period the records of the teams hadn't been very impressive, although the prior school athletic record had been excellent. Now with a good record from the previous year, the whole town was more interested and looked for a good year.

The townspeople were not disappointed, as the football team fought its way to the state championship in its class. Mr. Gary, the football coach, was in his second year at South Bay and could do nothing wrong with such an impressive record "under his belt."

When the basketball season came, Mr. Cole, the basketball coach, was expected to produce a winning team as well. The first five players from the previous year were back, which meant that prospects were excellent. Coach Cole was in his third year as basketball and baseball coach, having assumed this post immediately after graduating from college. He had gotten off to a bad start his first year, but this was not entirely his fault. There was little interest in sports at that point, and the facilities and equipment were inadequate. Team morale was low, and team discipline was poor.

Sensing the situation, Cole had started a "get-tough" policy, which may have been necessary. However, it didn't go over very well with anyone. The regular players resented being "pushed around" and being forced to abide by his training rules. He found it necessary to bench many of his players who had been "stars" the year before he came to Grayling. In their places he used freshmen and sophomores of lesser ability who were willing to work hard for him. At the end of his first year, the team had a losing record (8-11), but things looked good for the future because of the youngsters' potential.

Needless to say, Cole's first-year policy had brought much unfavorable reaction from the players left out, the alumni, and subsequently even Principal Rogers. Cole and Rogers argued quite a bit when Cole asked for better equipment, or when Rogers tried to tell him how to coach. Cole seemed to be temperamental on a number of occasions and told people with responsible positions to "keep their noses out of his business." Even though his team did have a winning season his second year, some people still didn't like him very well. Their respect for him did increase, however.

With such good talent the third season started well, but the boys were expected to improve considerably as the season progressed. They won four of their first five games. Instead of improving, however, they seemed to be having more trouble with each game. They looked especially poor against weak teams. Coach Cole figured that he knew the reason: the boys weren't playing together unless they really had to in order to win.

The team members were fairly friendly off the court and seemed to get along well. A good attitude was apparent during practice sessions, also. When they played a game, however, Bob Sands and Al Snyder wouldn't cooperate with the rest of the players. They tried to do all the scoring and left the defensive work to the others. Cole tried to develop team unity, but it didn't seem to be improving.

One evening the coach visited the team captain, Mike Clark, and asked him to help solve the problem. Cole knew that the captain was liked and respected by all the players and was a good team leader. He figured that Clark could do much to bring the team members closer to each other, and could perhaps encourage Snyder and Sands to play more cooperatively. Clark agreed to do what he could. They discussed the situation at length. In games that the team was winning easily, Sands and Snyder would start playing for themselves, although Sands would work with the captain, also. Snyder was the biggest offender. The coach felt that he couldn't bench him, because he was so much better than the available substitutes. He was averaging about 13 points a game and was rebounding well. When Snyder wasn't in the line-up, Sands wasn't so much of a problem and played well with the team. He was averaging twenty points a game and was the team's playmaker. Coach Cole and Mike Clark agreed that South Bay had a good chance to make the state tournament, if they could just solve this problem.

During the next week South Bay lost a league game by two points after "blowing" a 10-point lead at the half. The next day Mr. Cole found out that six of the team's ten members had gone to a neighboring town the night before the game. They had gone in Al Snyder's car and had arrived home very late because of a snowstorm. At practice Cole "read the riot act" to the whole team, and especially to Snyder who had organized the trip. As this meeting was going on in the center of the gym floor, a few of the "downtown coaches" walked in to watch practice. This didn't stop Cole. He was excited and was swearing quite a bit. At one point in the tirade, Snyder smiled about something. Cole kicked him in the leg, told him "to get the hell out of here," and not to come back until he was ready to play for the team and not himself. Snyder was back at the next practice. One of the onlookers had been his cousin. Cole hadn't known this, but he probably wouldn't have cared.

Two nights later, South Bay lost by 15 points to a very weak team. The next morning two alumni ("downtown coaches") came to see Mike Clark. They wanted to know what he thought of Mr. Cole. They had talked to Sands and Snyder, and both blamed the coach for the team's poor showing. They wanted Clark to help them get rid of Cole by telling certain people about his recent actions. Clark said he simply would not go along with this idea, and that most of the team would stand behind Cole. The attempt to get a petition started was a failure.

South Bay won its next two games by wide margins, and the team's troubles seemed to have cleared up. A short while later an away game was played with Sauter Academy, and South Bay won again. This gave them a record of seven wins and three losses. The trip to Sauter was a short one with private cars used for transportation. Captain Clark drove one of the cars and took five other players with him. After the game Al Snyder went to Clark and told him that he had put a basketball in the trunk of Clark's car. Clark questioned him and learned that it belonged to Sauter Academy. Clark said nothing more until it was time to leave. Snyder had driven off in the other car with Mr. Cole. Clark then told the others in the car what had happened. They agreed that the ball should be returned right away. Clark took it back and said that it had been mixed up with South Bay's balls by mistake.

On the way home, a couple of the boys in Clark's car spoke about the actions of Snyder and Sands. They thought, but could not prove, that the pair had stolen two basketballs from two other schools. This was the first that Mike had heard about the two thefts, as he had been hurt at one game and hadn't made the other trip because of illness.

When they got back to Grayling, Snyder came over to Clark's car and asked for the ball. Mike told him that he had returned it and Snyder became angry. There was an argument, and Clark and the others told Snyder that they didn't want to have anything to do with stealing basketballs. They warned him not to do it again, because the whole team would get into trouble. In the meantime, Sands joined Snyder and told the rest of the players that it was none of their business what he and Al did. The argument broke up with nothing settled.

South Bay lost the next two of the next three games, which made the team's record eight wins and five losses. After the third game, which was lost by one point, everyone was very angry. The game was played away from home, and there had been fights and poor officiating. Principal Rogers was there, and he was angry with Coach Cole and the officials. Most of the players were angry with themselves and with the officials as well.

Just as most of the team members were about to leave the locker room, Rogers came "storming in," pushing the manager, Bud Jacks, and Al Snyder ahead of him. He said, "What the hell is the matter with you, Cole? Can't you even see what's going on in your own locker room?" Rogers had seen a basketball thrown out of the locker room window into a snow bank. He had waited in his car to see who would come and get it. Finally, three boys had come out, looked around furtively, and then pulled the ball out of the snow and wiped it off. Then they let the air out of the ball and put it in one of the traveling bags. At that moment they were "collared and herded" back to the locker room by the irate principal.

The incident upset everyone a great deal. The boys knew there was more to come. Coach Cole said later that he had received letters from two other schools, asking him if a basketball had become mixed in with South Bay's equipment accidentally. Now everyone wondered how many had actually been taken.

The next day at school Principal Rogers held his "criminal court." The members of the team who were not involved had agreed in advance not to tell about the Sauter Academy incident. Instead, they tried to convince Jacks and Snyder to confess what they had done, but they refused. The principal questioned each member separately and finally tricked one of the uninvolved players into telling about the Sauter Academy incident. When pinned down, this player implicated Sands, also.

Coach Cole was asked to check the homes of Sands, Snyder, and Jacks. He recovered five basketballs, one at Sands' home and two each at the homes of the other boys. The balls were returned to the schools with apologies from South Bay's principal.

Public opinion differed greatly over the matter of the thefts. Many blamed the coach for poor supervision. Others thought that he lacked certain character traits himself. These statements probably came mostly from people who had developed a strong dislike for the coach. The principal was undecided as to the punishment for the guilty boys. Cole wanted to cancel the remainder of the schedule and throw the three boys out of high school athletics for good.

Evidently Rogers gave in to public pressure to a certain degree. Sands was allowed to continue with the team. It was discovered that he had not been involved with the stealing, although he had accepted a ball from Snyder. Snyder and Jacks were dropped from the team and forbidden to participate in any more sports at South Bay High.

South Bay won three of its remaining five games and played good ball. The two games that were lost were very close; two of the three wins were over top teams in the league. Team unity improved; all did their best for the coach. They seemed to appreciate his position and what he had been through. The team members agreed that most of it had not been his fault. The local fans, however, jeered him relentlessly at the remaining games. South Bay ended the season with 11 wins and 7 losses. Their conference record gave them a third place tie. It would be safe to say that everyone was glad to see the season end. Considering the personnel, the team had compiled a poor record.

Matters quieted down between the basketball and the baseball seasons. There seemed to be a rift between Coach Cole and Principal Rogers, although it was plain that most of the faculty members sided with Cole.

When the baseball season started, many people were uneasy about the outcome because of Cole's earlier problems. Most of the members of the basketball team played baseball as well. Fortunately, there were no major incidents throughout the season. South Bay won the district championship and went on to win the regional title. They lost out in the state championship, but ended up with a record of 14 wins and 3 losses.

Many people seemed to change their minds about Cole now, as even Principal Rogers seemed more friendly with him. He was offered a contract and raise for the next year, but he was undecided what to do. He knew that many people still did not like him. Several job offers were very attractive, but they were not appreciably better than his position at South Bay High.

Suggested Questions for Discussion

1. Do you agree with Coach Cole's initial "get-tough" policy?

2. Does a coach ever have a right to tell others "to keep their noses out of his business?"

3. Should Cole have discussed the "team unity problem" with Clark?

4. Should either Snyder or Sands have been benched until they agreed to play with the rest of the team?

5. Should a coach ever "read the riot act" in the way that Cole did?

6. Should outsiders be excluded from watching practice sessions?

7. Why do you imagine that Snyder asked Clark to take the stolen ball back in the trunk of his car?

8. Should Clark have reported the incident to Coach Cole at once?

9. When Cole received letters from other schools about missing balls, should he have investigated the matter?

10. What do you think of the punishment meted out?

11. Do you think that Cole should take another position in the light of what has happened, and considering what some townspeople think about him?

Part 3: Ethical Cases for Analysis

Professional Cases (Ethical Orientation)

Adding an Ethical Dimension to Case Analysis. In Part 3 the emphasis will be on professional ethics. By that I mean that the ethical problems considered here will relate primarily to an individual's relations with others at his or her place of employment. This professional category will include 10 case situations of an ethical nature

Initially, we all need to keep in mind that there are values and norms that are basic to life in democratic societies, and that they, accordingly, also relate to the subject matter of ethics. (The term norm here refers to one of a series of standards of virtue that are expected to prevail in this type of society or culture as explained below.) Persons in a responsible world culture can also be expected to be honest, fair, truthful, etc. These are ordinary norms that inevitably also have a relationship to what I call professional norms.

Additionally, over time, certain rights and privileges have been accorded to citizens in democratically oriented countries. In North America, for example, the following norms relating to rights and privileges currently prevail:

1. Governance by law
2. Individual freedom (as much as
   may be permitted in the social setting)
3. Protection from injury
4. Equality of opportunity
5. Privacy
6. Individual welfare (Bayles, 1981, pp. 5-7).

Second, based on a review of the literature, the following five categories or are recommended for a code of ethics for any profession (e.g., a manager/teacher/coach).

1. The professional's conduct as a teacher/coach

(The intent here is that the teacher/coach should in the performance of his/her duties, (a) hold paramount

263

the safety, health, and welfare of the public, (b) perform services only in his/her areas of competence, (c) issue public statements only in an objective and truthful manner, (4) act in professional matters for each employer or student/client as faithful agent or trustee, and (5) avoid improper solicitation of professional employment.)

2. The professional's ethical obligations to students/clients

(The intent here is that the professional should be completely trustworthy and that he/she has the following obligations or responsibilities in his/her relationship with students/clients: To exhibit candor, competence, diligence, discretion, honesty, and loyalty)

3. The professional's ethical responsibility to employers/employing organizations

(The intent here is that the professional should understand and respect his/her responsibility to both the student/client and third parties (e.g., superior and organization represented) by exhibiting fairness, truthfulness, and non-maleficence [i.e., doing no harm])

4. The professional's ethical responsibility to colleagues/peers and the profession

(The intent here is that the professional has certain obligations to the profession in regard to doing research; working for reform; providing social leadership; improving professional knowledge and skills; and preserving and enhancing the role of the profession so that society's respect will be maintained.

Under this category, also, the professional should never forget that he/she has an obligation help with the self-regulation of the profession (a) by encouraging desirable young people to enter the profession and (b) by complying with, and seeing to it that others comply as well, with the established responsibilities and obligations of the profession as explained in the profession's code of ethics)

5. The professional's ethical responsibility to society

(The intent here is that the professional has an ethical responsibility to society and therefore will make his/her full services available to all who need help regardless of age, sex, physical limitation, ethnic origin, religion, or sexual orientation. Additionally, the professional person will make every effort to see that he/she personally, as well as his/her colleagues, will live up to the canons and principles of the profession's code of ethics)

Third, proceeding from Bayles' (1981, Chapters 3-7) fivefold categorization of the basic make-up of any code of ethics proposed, the recommended progression to be followed in the eventual determination of specific rules and regulations moves to a secondary categorization within the heading of professional obligations or responsibilities. Included here as they might relate to any one of a number of professions are (a) standards (virtues or vices), (b) principles (where some latitude is possible), and (c) rules that must be adhered to strictly.

(See Table 1 on the following page.)

TABLE 1

Examples of Provisions for a Code of Ethics for Sport Managers

Categories	Standards	Principles	Rules
a. Bases upon which professional services are made available	A prof. should be <u>fair</u> and <u>just</u> in providing his/her services	A prof. should ensure that all students receive adequate instruc.	A client needing help should receive it as soon as possible

Example: A professional manager shows bias toward a client and offers him/her poor or inadequate management service in a way that might cause the individual to lose interest and to look elsewhere for such service.

Categories	Standards	Principles	Rules
b. Ethical nature of prof.-client relationship	A prof. should be <u>honest</u> in his/her treatment of a client	A prof. should never treat a client as a means to an end	A client must never be forced to take an illegal or unethical action because of fear of loss of status

Example: In sport management, an athletic director urges an athlete to act in a harmful or dishonest way by stating that a scholarship will be lost otherwise.

Categories	Standards	Principles	Rules
c. Conflict resolution when conflict arises between prof.'s obligations to clients and third parties	A prof. has an obligation to be <u>truthful</u> in dealing with third parties	In checking eligibility of a team member, a manager should be most careful not to permit an inaccurate statement to be entered	A manager must never knowingly sign an eligibility form in which an athlete has committed perjury

Example: A manager knows that an athlete's eligibility has been used up elsewhere, but signs the form nevertheless in which an athlete has perjured himself/herself.

Categories	Standards	Principles	Rules
d. Professional	A prof. should	A prof. has a	A prof. has

(Table 1 is continued on the following page,)

obligations to society and to profession (i.e., duty to serve the public good)	be loyal to societal values and those of the profession	duty and responsibility to preserve and enhance the role of the sport management profession	a duty to upgrade and strengthen his/her knowledge by attending one or more conferences or symposia annually

Example: A professional gives the profession a bad name by obviously falling behind on the knowledge of his/her area of expertise.

e.	Ensuring compliance with the established obligations of the professions code of ethics	A prof. should practice his/her profession with honesty and integrity	A prof. should encourage his/her students to be honest within the letter and spirit of the established rules	A prof. who permits his/her client to lie or cheat shall be reported and should be excluded from the profession if found guilty

Example: A manager guilty of flagrant unethical practice shall be reported to the ethics committee of the professional society and subsequently to his/her employers.

267

Note: It should be understood that there always are choices to be
made when an individual acts personally or professionally in situations
that are less than clear-cut. Thus, if one category is that of obligations
(i.e. you must do so-and-so), a second category of available norms may
be designated as permissions (i.e. you have freedom of choice because
any action may be debatable). In this latter case, professionals are
permitted to do (1) what is not prohibited by law; (2) what is not
considered unethical in the society, generally speaking; and (3) what is
not considered to be unethical by the professional society to which one
belongs.

Fourth, and finally then, the listing of eight standards (virtues) should
be implemented above in Categories Two and Three (i.e., candor,
competence, diligence, discretion, honesty, and loyalty under Category
Two; and fairness, non-maleficence, and truthfulness under Category
Three). A brief, hortatory, approved ethical creed is typically placed after a
preamble to a code of ethics. It remains for a somewhat more detailed code
itself to include (a) a listing of the major principles or canons under which
the professional person act, and (b) to show how professional associations
may begin the process of developing a listing of the specific rules of practice
that must be adhered to in daily professional life. (See Table 3 above, also,
for a diagrammatic explanation as to how rules of practice can be derived
in the immediate future.)

What Is a Profession Today? A profession typically includes those people
who are functioning in a professional and/or disciplinary way within the
broad field concerned. Merely stating that a group of people working
within a field of endeavor at the public, semipublic or private levels
represents a profession is a beginning, of course, but there is obviously
much more to be accomplished than that. It can be argued, however, that
there is no generally acceptable definition for a profession today--i.e., it is
impossible to characterize professions by a set of necessary and sufficient
features possessed by all professions--and only by professions (Bayles, 1981,
p. 7). Nevertheless, the following is a brief attempt to define what
constitutes a profession in the last quarter of the 20th century:

> (1) A profession can be defined as an occupation which
> requires specific knowledge of some aspect of learning
> before a person is accepted as a professional person.

(2) There are sub-categories of professions as follows: administering, teaching, supervising, consulting, research, etc. Teaching would presumably represent some combination of teaching, administering, supervising, and consulting duties and responsibilities. However, some within the profession or closely related fields should undoubtedly have a responsibility for scholarly and research endeavor.

(3) The following may be considered as three necessary features of an occupation that can also be designated as a profession: (i) a need for extensive training; (ii) a significant intellectual component that must be mastered; and (iii) a recognition by society that the trained person can provide an important basic service.

(4) Additionally, there are some other features that are common to most professions as follows: (i) licensing by state/province or professional body, (ii) establishment of professional societies, (iii) considerable autonomy in work performance, and (iv) establishment of a creed or code of ethics (Bayles, 1981, p. 7).

Note: One aspect of a comprehensive code of ethics is that the controlling body should establish an code of ethics discipline committee to which infractions of the ethical code may be reported for deliberation and possible disciplinary action.

Cases in Professional Ethics

In this section two characteristic cases in professional ethics will be offered for your consideration. Each case will be described briefly, but sufficiently for our purposes here. (For a recommended approach to case method discussion of professional ethics, including a situation where human relations are involved too, a more-detailed presentation would be needed. (See Phase Four, Chapter 9, for such a discussion.)

Then each case will be analyzed by implementing the steps followed in Phases One, Two, and Three (see the brief "Introduction to Part Three," as well as the longer explanations in Chapters 6, 7, and 8 for possible review).

Following this, a series of 10 case situations, briefly stated, will be presented as exercises for you to carry out as you find the time to do so. At the very least, as recommended previously in Chapter 10, you should follow the three-step plan recommended for Phase One by determining separately on a single sheet of paper whether your proposed decision about a particular case situation (i.e., the three steps) seems reasonable to you after you have "spelled it out."

Finally, I hope that you will also follow through with the steps recommended for Phases Two and Three as well. To this end you will find a sample, incomplete "law-court-format" sheet included below for this purpose. The simplest way to follow through with this proposal would be for you to make 10 copies of this (incomplete) page format. As you do this, you may wish to enlarge the page to 125% on the copier you use (if that is possible).

Sample Case 1. "Honesty in Sport Marketing"

Brad, a university graduate in the sport management program, obtained a position with responsibility for assisting with the advertising and marketing of his firm's products in sport and recreation. His superior, Wesley, appeared to be a real "go-getter." One of the people in the marketing department described him as a person who "wanted to start at the top and work up." Nevertheless, Wes gave every indication of wanting to be very helpful to Brad in a number of different ways. Brad was anxious to do well with his new job, of course, and he appreciated the fact that someone was willing to "show him the ropes." As time passed, however, Brad began to see that he and Wes were really operating on different wavelengths. That evening he told Barbara, his wife, that Wes was really much more realistic and pragmatic than he was. Wes was always trying to cut corners and to get ahead of the other guy (the firm's competitors)--or even the consumer for that matter. "I guess I'm just too idealistic," Brad said to Barbara one evening during dinner, "but in writing advertising copy I try to tell the truth about our products. They are good, of that I'm certain, but Wes is always on me to write what I feel is 'borderline' fraudulent copy." On Barbara's urging, Brad invited Wes out for a beer after work and explained his concerns to him. Wes replied that he knew what Brad was talking about, and he also said that he felt that way once too. "But," he concluded, "I soon learned that the only way to get there is to be as 'borderline' as everyone else is. It's 'dog-eat-dog' out there, and you have to cheat a little here and there and occasionally make wild claims that may not be true--or you'll be left behind in the dust." How should Brad cope with this situation?

Written Analysis. On the surface the problem faced by Brad in the Case 1 example seems pretty much "black and white"--either you practice honesty or not. However, as many of us learn along the way, this question can be a highly complex one in numerous life situations encountered. Human relations at the personal level and at the professional level are rarely simple or "black or white." It is an unfortunate fact that a significant minority of the populace does seem to be ready to be dishonest in small ways--and at times in more serious ways as well. These people of questionable morality tend to rationalize their actions by saying, "Oh, everybody does it; so why shouldn't I?" If we permit even minor dishonesty as a "standard" of virtue either in personal or professional life, it is fundamentally wrong . Also, if we apply Kant's principle of universality to this matter, it is obvious that everyone doesn't cheat and be dishonest. Secondly, think of what the net consequences of "everyone doing it" (Mill's principle) would be. It would not be a very nice world in which to live. Lastly, are there situations (Aristotle's thought) where you might be dishonest and yet be moral? Probably very few, although every day we do run into the so-called "white lie" where you are dishonest in a sense that you lie to someone because you don't want to hurt his or her feelings. And it is true, of course, that a great many people are dishonest in business with their marketing practices when they practice what I call the "We're the greatest!" syndrome even if they know they aren't--if the truth be told. To return to the case at hand, it appears that Brad is going to have to engage in a large measure of soul-searching if he is going to continue and be successful in his present position.

(Continued on the next page)

Table 1
DIAGRAMMATIC ANALYSIS (HONESTY)
(With the Three-Step Approach Superimposed
on the Jurisprudential Argument Layout)

D
DATA

Q
SO, LOGICALLY

C
CONCLUSION

Brad, a graduate in sport management, discovers in his first position in advertising & marketing that his superior is urging him to cut corners and "camouflage" the facts in various ways if he hopes to achieve real success in the advertising game.

Brad will eventually need to decide if he can go along with the morality of the approach that Wes, his superior, says is necessary to succeed in today's "cut-throat" business environment.

(SINCE W)
WARRANT

(UNLESS R)
REBUTTAL
OR EXCEPTION

Since the competition in a strongly capitalistic economy even in a democratic state is such that "survival of the fittest" demands that business people follow an aggressive, "borderline" business ethic as they seek to advertise and market their products, businesspeople are being forced to abandon strict application of a code of ethics.

1. Brad can convince himself that it is possible to go along with Wes and still remain true to his principle of honesty and ultimately achieve sufficient success in his career.

2. Brad decides that his youthful idealism about being completely honest in his business dealings was naively idealistic in the

TEST NO. 1 (KANT)
(universalizability)

(ON ACCOUNT OF B)
BACKING

An approach based on commu-
nistic theory to the business
enterprise, in which there was a large
measure of government ownership
and control, has evidently led to waste,
corruption, and inefficiency typically;
thus, the underlying theory has not
proved to be valid or successful.

TEST No.2 (MILL)
(**net** consequences)

realistic business world
that he is encountering.

TEST No. 3 (ARISTOTLE)
(intentions)

Key: Jurisprudential Argument Terms:

D =   Data (A statement of a situation that prevails including
        evidence, elements, sources, samples of facts)
Q =   Modal Qualifier (adverbs employed to qualify conclusions
        based on strength of warrants (e.g., necessarily, probably)
C =   Conclusion (claim or conclusion that we wish to establish)
W =   Warrant (practical standards or canons of argument designed
        to provide an answer to the question, "How do you get there?"
B =   Backing (categorical statements of fact that lend further
        support to the bridge-like warrants)
R =   Conditions of Exception (arguments of rebuttal or exception
        that tend to refute or "soften" the strength of the conclusion)

Sample Case 2. "Athletic Eligibility"

Sam is a young teacher/coach in Bradford High School, a large inner-city high school. The school principal, Mr. Washington, a former physical educator/coach himself, is enthusiastically behind the idea of Bradford having a fine program of physical education and athletics. Sam likes his position very much and enjoys working with young people of that age a great deal. He does what he can to promote physical fitness for all the boys in his gym classes, although a large minority has difficulty getting into the spirit of the program. The intramural and recreational sport program for all is practically non-existent because of space limitations, however, not to mention that the only teachers available have heavy workloads and commute to the inner city daily. Sam is very enthusiastic about his assignment as coach of the basketball team, however. There is a substantive talent pool with various ethnic groups represented. Cutting the number of young men down to a varsity squad size of 15 is always difficult. It wouldn't be so bad if there were a junior varsity squad too, and they played an extramural schedule. Sam finally got his starting five picked along with those selected for the number two and three slots at each position. Bradford won the first two games, one away and one at home. At midterm Sam realized that a couple of his starting five were having grade trouble. He worried that these two young men were not going to have sufficiently high averages at mid-year and might lose their eligibility. It wasn't as if these two athletes weren't conscientious about both their studies and basketball. Also, both were highly talented and had hopes of earning athletics at a university. However, as the situation developed, both of the young men failed one subject. Nevertheless their overall averages were very close to the standard required for continuation in so-called extra-curricular activities at Bradford. Sam knew "the axe was about to fall" in his young athletes' basketball aspirations. He went to Mr. Washington to see if somehow they couldn't be placed "on probation" and allowed to continue to play for the remainder of the season. Mr. Washington was sympathetic, but couldn't see any escape from the prevailing situation in the city that maintained the tradition that a student's scholastic average has a bearing on his/her athletic eligibility.

<u>Written Analysis</u>. Situations like this are quite typical and will undoubtedly continue. Traditionally a student's scholastic average does indeed have a bearing on his/her athletic eligibility. Students who aren't progressing normally from grade to grade have been barred from athletic

competition. The idea behind these rulings is usually that "intellectual learning" is basic, and that sport and other recreational activities are what has been called "extra-curricular." Also, if students don't do acceptable work, they won't graduate--and diplomas and degrees are required increasingly for entry into the job market. However, those who argue against rigid application of eligibility rules have argued that competitive sport develops desirable personality traits leading to success in life. It is true, also, that society has increasingly been willing to accord competitive sport status as worthwhile activity in youth development. Further, the opportunity to play sport has no doubt kept many young people in school, people who might otherwise have dropped out because of lack of interest.

Table 2

DIAGRAMMATIC ANALYSIS (LOYALTY)
(With the Three-Step Approach Superimposed
on the Jurisprudential Argument Layout)

D DATA	Q SO, LOGICALLY	C CONCLUSION
Sam, a basketball coach at Bradford High School, learns that two of his best players are about to be declared ineligible for the remainder		Students who are not progressing normally through school should be barred from further athletic competition
SINCE W) WARRANT		UNLESS R) REBUTTAL OR EXCEPTION
Students who do not maintain an average that will permit them to proceed normally in their program will eventually not graduate	It is decided that society is willing to accord competitive sport status as a curricular experience	
TEST NO. 1 (KANT) consistency)	and	

(ON ACCOUNT OF B)
BACKING

Graduation diplomas and degree are increasingly necessary for successful entrance into the job market

and

Test scores are indicating that educational competency has been declining in recent years

and

Athletic prowess is not typically responsible for a person obtaining and holding a job

TEST No.2 (MILL)
(**net** consequences)

It can be shown conclusively that competitive sport does develop desirable personality traits leading to successful living

and

It can be shown also that the opportunity to play and take part in other "co-curricular activities helps to keep young people in school for a longer period of time

TEST No. 3 (ARISTOTLE)
(intentions)

Key: Jurisprudential Argument Terms:

D = Data (A statement of a situation that prevails including evidence, elements, sources, samples of facts)
Q = Modal Qualifier (adverbs employed to qualify conclusions based on strength of warrants (e.g., necessarily, probably)
C = Conclusion (claim or conclusion that we wish to establish)
W = Warrant (practical standards or canons of argument designed to provide an answer to the question, "How do you get there?"
B = Backing (categorical statements of fact that lend further support to the bridge-like warrants)
R = Conditions of Exception (arguments of rebuttal or exception that tend to refute or "soften" the strength of the conclusion)

Cases in Professional Ethics

Note: Below are 10 case situations described briefly. In each instance, ethical decision-making seems required on the part of one or more persons involved. After you analyze each case situation, use one "format page" for that purpose. The format for this sample page is provided below after Case 10. Keep the following in mind as you consider each case situation:

Determine "who had a duty or responsibility to do what" in each of the case situations below. Decide whether you believe that there someone had a moral obligation to "do this" or "not to do that" in the situation concerned. As you make this assessment, keep in mind the following questions about the actions (or inactions) of one or more of the major individuals concerned:

1. Is the action basically unfair to a person or group?
2. Does the action or decision (or inaction) impose on another's freedom?
3. Does the action hurt another person's welfare?
4. Does the action impose on an individual's privacy
5. Does the action deny an opportunity to another person?
6. Is the action, in addition to being one of the above, also illegal (thus adding another dimension to the analysis)?

Note: In this instance (i.e., the matter of professional ethics), we should also keep in mind the obligations a professional has (1) to make provide services equally and to make them equally available; (2) to exhibit honesty, candor, competence, diligence, loyalty, and discretion in client relationships; (3) to be truthful, non-maleficient, and fair to third parties (i.e., ordinary not professional norms); (4) to promote values inherent in a liberal society, as well as fulfill obligations to do research, work for reform, and maintain respect for the profession; and (5) to work so that compliance with the profession's ethical norms results (Bayles, 1981, Chapters 3, 4, 5, 6, and 7).

With an ethical obligation, it is probably best to use the word "should" (i.e. or e.g., "As her superior, Joe should not taken advantage of Marie when she was in such a vulnerable position").

When the obligation has been accepted as a societal norm--and has resultantly been instituted legally (i.e., "Joe committed a criminal offense when he assaulted Marie sexually after the office had closed for the day")-- the "should not" can be further strengthened by "must not".

Assume the role of one of the major participants in the case situation, and then make recommendations as to what should be done (ethically)--and what must also be done (legally) if what happened violated an established law as well as a societal norm.

Case 1. "Discipline at Compton High"

Ralph Talbot was a physical education teacher and an assistant coach in both football and wrestling at a large metropolitan high school (Compton High). One of his assigned duties was noon-hour supervisor of the school's indoor recreation area. This included checking on the boys' lavatory occasionally to prevent smoking that is against the state law. On this particular day Ralph was walking across the room to shut off the record player because it was time to close up for the afternoon. As Bob Jones, a tall, well-built young man (a Black) saw him, he moved directly and deliberately in Ralph's path. Ralph stopped and asked him what he wanted. "Nothing." Ralph asked him to move four times, and then stated that he was not going to ask him again. Bob simply smiled. Ralph grabbed Bob's right arm and tried to move him aside. One move led to another, and Ralph stated that they should go to the principal's office. To Ralph's surprise he was hit in the face twice before he started to defend himself. Then Ralph took Bob to the floor with a wrestling take-down. Bob scratched at Ralph's face as he sought to stand up; so, Ralph hit him in the face. Just then a black, ex-wrestler separated them and, as he started to speak, Bob charged Ralph and hit him in the face again. So Ralph went behind Bob with a wrestling maneuver, literally dragged him to the office, and threw him on the sofa there while continuing to hold him down. When Bob agreed to calm down, Ralph released him. However, Bob immediately went on the attack again. Finally several teachers and students got control of the situation. So Ralph, quite shaken by the experience, went to his next class. After the next class the principal, Eric Thornton, called Ralph to the office. He stated that nothing like this had ever happened in his experience. He also said that some students had said that Ralph was prejudiced against Blacks. Ralph denied this vehemently, stating that he had no problems whatsoever with Blacks in either football or wrestling. As Ralph left the office he had the feeling that he was "guilty until proved innocent." That evening Bob's mother called Ralph asking why he had hit her son and also torn his clothes. She explained that she was a single mother with five children and really didn't have time to get overly involved with the entire situation. Ralph tried to tell her that Bob had hit him first, but she didn't seem to believe that. Ralph didn't know what else to say or do. As Ralph thought about the problem later that evening, he recalled that he had reported Bob at the beginning of the school year for smoking in the lavatory. Also, he had stopped Bob and a young woman from doing what he thought was an obscene dance during noon hour a bit later. At school the next morning, it was obvious that the struggle was being talked about. Ralph learned that Bob had a reputation for fighting; that Bob--just prior to the altercation--had received his report card with all failures; and that Bob was actually cutting a class at the time the confrontation took place.

Case 2. "Stealing at Chickamauga Township High School"

Chickamauga Township High School is situated in the suburbs, south of Los Angeles. It is a relatively new high school with an enrollment of approximately 3,500 students. The area's main business concern is auto accessories, and there are a number of other minor industries. The high school's athletic facilities compare with the best in the state of California. The varsity football team at Chickamauga has had an outstanding record, having won their conference six of the past seven years. Head Coach Brogan is 34 years of age and is in his eighth year there. He is assisted by Paul Duthie, who is in his fifth year. The players seem to hold them in great respect. This fall, once again, the football team is off to a great start, having won their first two games with comfortable margins. Townspeople are already talking about another championship team. On Monday morning after the second win, Coach Brogan was checking over equipment and noticed that several boxes of brand new "T" shirts were missing. At practice that afternoon, he and Coach Duthie called the squad members together and explained the morning's discovery. He explain how only people related to the team had access to the equipment room and said how badly he and Paul felt that there must be one or more thieves on the squad. Finally, he said that serious consideration must be given to canceling the schedule for the year if the shirts weren't returned. Then both coaches left for the day. The co-captains, Jeb Stuart and Harry Lee, immediately carried on with the meeting. Some felt that each squad member should chip in three dollars or so to pay for the missing equipment. Others felt that things like this happened all the time, and that it wasn't a very "big deal." Another small group wanted nothing to do with a pool to raise money to pay for the shirts. These team members felt that those who had snitched the shirts ought to own up to the theft. Finally, it was agreed that the co-captains would sit in the room where chalkboard sessions were held. It was agreed further that each person on the squad should report there individually and (in effect) take an oath as to non-involvement with the missing boxes of "T" shirts. This plan was carried out, but no one confessed to guilt in the matter. It had also been agreed further at the meeting with the co-captains that each person should bring back anything further that he might have stolen. When the coaches arrived for practice the next day, there was a huge pile of equipment on the locker-room floor by the entrance--but no "T" shirts. . . .

Case 3. "Breaking a Teaching/Coaching Contract"

Charles Carson came to Central High as a physical education teacher and head football coach in the first year of the school's operation. Although from the first he was popular with the students, faculty and most of the teaching staff, Principal Twombly soon discovered that Carson could create problems. As many policies and procedures were being established, Carson because to cause embarrassment by refusing to do almost everything that wasn't to his liking. He skipped faculty meetings because they conflicted with football practice, never showed up at PTA meetings, and never bothered to initial a sign-in sheet that was started. Carson's philosophy was that "anything that was worth doing was worth doing well." Accordingly he most neglectful of assigned duties other than his football coaching and classes to be taught. He neglected his duty as a class sponsor, a dance chaperone, and as a cafeteria supervisor (one noon a week). Finally Twombly called Carson to his office regarding his persistent dereliction of duty. Although an experienced administrator, the principal was somewhat baffled by Carson's quite good-natured refusal to live up to what had been designated as his ancillary duties. Interestingly, although Carson thought high school sport was very important. Twombly merely tolerated athletics as a relatively unimportant aspect of the school's fine academic program. Twombly ended the session by stating that he expected to see improvement, but Carson only smilingly nodded in agreement. Bob Dixon, the assistant principal, was a man who delighted in accepting responsibilities--but then he had trouble carrying them all out satisfactorily. In Carson's second year at Central, Dixon intimated to Carson that he would recommend him as athletic director when he relinquished the post in a year or two. Carson was excited about this prospect, but there was no further development in this direction by the end of the fourth year of the school's operation. (In the meantime Dixon had changed his mind because he felt that Carson would overemphasize football to the detriment of other sports.) At the conclusion of the football season in Carson's fifth year, he made an appointment with Superintendent Blosdell to talk to him about his future in the system. Carson realized that Dixon wasn't going to give up the post as athletic director. He then told the superintendent that he was ambitious and had even thought about looking for a position at the college level. With his good win-loss record at Central High, Blosdell thought to himself that he should be "keeping an eye open" for other fine young coaches in the region. Carson started looking in earnest for a college post. Although he was interviewed for several positions, he said nothing about this to his superiors. In the spring he did not sign his contract for the following year, intending to leave it unsigned as he had done several times before. (This is known as a teacher's continuing contract--a form of tenure that states that the position is permanent, that he could be dismissed only for cause.) On these occasions he hadn't signed it until late in the fall. But this year the office staff was more careful about getting contracts signed. Having heard nothing definite from any of the three places where he had interviewed for a post, Carson simply signed the contract. However, he "told himself" that he would break it if a college post materialized. During the first week in July, a rumor spread that Carson was going to be hired by Lakeside Community College as head football coach. Superintendent Blosdell called Dixon, who was still the athletic director, because he couldn't reach Carson. Dixon became quite upset because he didn't even know that Carson was thinking about another position. When Carson was finally contacted, he called back immediately and said that he planned to return to Central for the coming year. Blosdell thanked him and said that he knew that Carson wouldn't leave Central in an embarrassing position at such a late date. However, on July 18 Carson was finally informed that he was the choice for the Lakeside post. Evidently another person had finally turned the position down. Later that afternoon Supt. Blosdell received a note from Carson. He said he was very sorry, but he simply could not afford to let such an opportunity go by.

Case 4. "Poison-Pen Letters at Midwestern University"

Midwestern University was a large public university with a growing school of health, physical education, and recreation. When the dean retired, Dr. Carlton Ramsay, a man with a solid background experience, was appointed dean of the school after a nationwide search. This was a challenging responsibility because both the intercollegiate athletic program and the intramural and recreational sport program were under the general supervision of the school. Dr. Ramsay undertook his new position enthusiastically. He gradually became an even more highly regarded person at both the state and national levels in the health and physical education field. He regarded intercollegiate athletics as a program that should be worked into an overall, balanced program. He also stressed the importance of a required physical education program for first-year students, as well as a broadly based intramural athletics program that reached more than half of the students enrolled. He disliked "free-ride" athletics scholarships, arguing more for an "Ivy League approach"--one in which financial aid was provided to any needy student who was truly a bona fide student. When an opening for a new basketball coach developed, Dr. Kyle Brammel was finally selected from the outside. Brammel had a dynamic personality and was regarded as a highly effective coach. Players respected him, but feared him too because of his explosive temperament. Part of Brammel's responsibility was the teaching of several theory and practice courses in basketball. It turned out that his philosophy of athletics was diametrically opposed to that espoused by Dean Brammel. Faculty members and students soon were arguing on both sides of the question, but the coaches were solidly behind the position being expressed by Brammel. Many thought Ramsay was a high-principled educator whose views were somewhat dated. As it developed, it became obvious to Dr. Ramsay that his leadership was being challenged in several different ways, also. After thinking long and hard about continuing in office, he finally decided to step down from the dean's post to "concentrate more on writing and research"--an oft-heard phrase in academic circles. A committee was struck to find a successor and make a recommendation to the president. Dr. Brammel submitted his credentials for consideration and was picked by the committee as one of three names who would be acceptable to the school's faculty. The president chose Dr. Brammel to succeed Dr. Ramsay. As might be expected, due to prevailing social influences and the enthusiasm of Dean Brammel, the program of intercollegiate athletics seemed to take on new life. This is not to say that the other programs "suffered" in any way.

However, when significant changes occur, there are always those who are opposed to the change and show their disapproval in a variety of ways. For example, the president and members of the board of governors began to receive unsigned letters explaining that the faculty wanted a de-emphasis in intercollegiate athletics. The complaints were typically about football and basketball. They took special notice of the fact that varsity athletes were being paid for part-time jobs, jobs at which they never actually worked! As time went by, these "poison-pen" letters kept coming to the same people about all types of irregularities and inconsistencies that presumably were occurring within the intercollegiate athletic program. Eventually the governor of the state heard about these letters and called for an official investigation. Proceedings were started to determine who, or what group, was responsible for writing the letters. Interestingly, many faculty members had to admit generally that a great many of the charges being made were true. It was rumored that the ex-dean, Dr. Ramsay, was behind the attack on the current administration of the school. Dean Brammel stated that the charges being made were actually preposterous, actually the work of a disgruntled person who had become almost psychotic about a perceived injustice. How should this matter be resolved both legally and ethically?

Case 5. "Keeping Up Professionally"

Henry is a high school teacher/coach who has been doing quite well in this capacity for 12 years since he received his teacher certification. In addition to teaching both physical education and health education classes, he coaches three sports: football, basketball, and baseball. He is married with two children. To make ends meet, his wife has been working half time as a librarian. All of this adds up to the fact that he and his family are extremely busy, often tired, and have great difficulty finding time for most leisure pursuits in which they are interested. Additionally, Henry realizes that he is falling behind professionally in several ways. To make matters more difficult, Frank, another teacher/coach in the same school, is a "whirlwind" in the sense that he seems to be able to do it all and still have time for professional involvement. Frank attends seminars and symposia to keep in touch with advancements in his areas of interest and involvement. The physical & health education profession always seems to be battling for its "rightful" place in the curriculum, and Frank feels he is doing his bit to help out. He also goes to the state conventions and national conventions of his professional association almost every year. To make matters worse for Henry, Frank is always waving information sheets and articles at him saying, "Have you seen this piece by Morgan on stress?" or something of that sort. Henry figures that Frank is gunning for the department head's post when "old Pete hangs it up" in a few years. However, Frank believes that he is handling all that he can cope with reasonably well. "I do my job as well as I can," he stated the other day, "someone else is going to have maintain departmental 'PR' with the other teachers, the principal, the school officials, outside colleagues, the profession association, and the public." Can we truly argue that Henry is being unethical in the way he is handling all of his responsibilities and duties to his family, his teaching position, his profession, and to his community ?

Case 6. "Athletic Recruiting at Midwestern University"

Midwestern is a large prestigious state university with a fine academic tradition, as well as a fine tradition in many sports. Glen Mather is the elderly, quite successful head wrestling coach at Midwestern University. One of his onerous responsibilities every year involves recruitment of high school wrestlers to attend Midwestern. Bob Reston had a fine record in high school wrestling, but his grades were not high because of the need for him to work two different part-time jobs in his senior year in high school. This, along with injury and illness, brought his high school average down to the point where he barely graduated from high school. Somehow, due to these extenuating circumstances, Coach Mather was able to arrange for a "special" exam so that Bob was finally admitted to the first-year class. There was an agreement that Bob would receive an athletic tender (grant-in-aid) to cover in-state tuition. If he maintained sufficiently high grade to maintain athletic eligibility, and his performance in wrestling was satisfactory, Coach Mather stated verbally that Bob would shortly receive a "full ride" (i.e., room, meals, tuition, and books). Bob was smaller than the top limit of the lightest weight class in the sport. This meant that Bob was always wrestling against heavier opponents in both practice and regular competition. However, in Olympic wrestling there was a lighter weight class that suited Bob perfectly. Coach Mather was delighted when Bob won the Olympic trial in his region, but unfortunately Bob injured his ankle and had to withdraw from further competition at that time. At the beginning of his sophomore year, Bob did not receive the "full ride" that he had been promised because his grades were not "sufficiently high." Bob had to look for part-time work. Then he learned that two other members of the team were getting the "full package" even though they had lower averages than Bob. During Xmas break Bob had a minor operation that set back his conditioning program. Also, this operation meant that he missed the tournament that the team took part in every year. Bob was released from the hospital the day before classes started up again. Realizing that Bob's operation was not of a nature that prevented him from practicing, Coach Mather got him started immediately because of matches scheduled for that very weekend. Bob lost close matches on Friday and Saturday. Two weeks later wrestling with a much heavier man at the coach's suggestion, Bob dislocated his right elbow severely. Bob was in the hospital for two weeks, and several doctors told him that his wrestling career was over. The coach visited him and was very glum about the bad news. Because his financial situation was so bad, Bob asked the coach if the university athletic association could help him somewhat to tide him over. This was evidently not possible and, since Bob had fallen behind in his schoolwork, he felt there was no alternative but to drop out of school. For the next year and a half Bob worked to recover normal use of his arm. At the same time he took a full-time job and saved every cent possible to that he could complete his university education. He was determined to pay his own way completely, because he felt that his coach hadn't treated him fairly. Also, he didn't want to be obligated to wrestle for Midwestern if he ever went out for wrestling again. When Coach Mather heard that Bob had returned, he called him right away and urged him to come out for the team again. Bob felt that he ought to re-establish himself academically first. This status was accomplished, and Bob got married in August after his first year back was completed. Bob discovered at the beginning of what he thought was his final year that he really had three semesters of academic work left to receive his bachelor's degree. Coach Mathers knew about this too, and he had already made application so that Bob might have two full years of eligibility left if he took the absolute minimum of credit hours each semester. Bob's former desire to make good at wrestling returned. He realized further that a truly successful record in competition would help him obtain a better position as a teacher-coach. The coach offered him a tuition waiver, but Bob and his wife decided not to accept the offer. She was working; they had their savings; and Bob knew about a good part-time position. It turned out to be a good year in all ways. He had a good academic average, and he wrestled in all the meets--and then finished third in the conference finals. The future seemed bright again. As luck would have it, the summer before Bob's senior year was a disaster. Bob could find only part-time work. His wife became ill and required hospitalization. So in August, with much hesitation, Bob asked his coach for the proverbial full ride again. Others were receiving it, and Bob felt that he had truly earned such compensation.

However, Coach Mather said that at this late date all commitments for the year had been made. He said that he might be able to put him on the full-ride roster for the second term. It turned out also that a new lower-weight class had been added, and Bob was the only man on the squad who could make the weight by losing 15 lbs. Bob did it; he mad the weight for the early meets. At the beginning of the second term, Coach Mather said that he was sorry but the expected opening on the full-ride roster had not materialized after all. Bob didn't know what to do. . . .

Case 7. "A Deluxe Counseling Program"

Bill Reardon is an assistant professor in a department of physical education and sport studies in a large university that offers an intercollegiate athletics program in a major athletic conference. He, along with Roger and Jim, are responsible for the educational counseling of all undergraduate majors in the program. Many of these young men are scholarship athletes who are "marginal students," often because of attitude. Toward the end of the academic year, the assistant director of athletics invited Bill to coffee. They talked about a variety of subjects, one of which had to do with athletes running afoul of university regulations because of their indifference to such matters. As the discussion developed, the assistant director told Bill that the athletic director would like the assistance of a counselor in this regard (e.g., to look after the "blue-chippers" in regard to such things as, for example, dropping courses after the prescribed deadline). He offered Bill $5,000 a year as an "unlisted" honorarium if he would take on this assignment for the division of intercollegiate athletics. Bill could really use this extra money, especially since it would be in essence for doing the sort of service he is already providing--but typically within the established regulations. However, he told his colleague, the assistant athletic director, that he just "wouldn't feel right" about taking unreported money in this way. The following week Bill by chance learned that Roger Barton, his office associate, seemed to have taken on the responsibility. From an ethical standpoint, should Bill report Roger to the department head?

Case 8. "Sportsmanship at Midwestern University." The co-captain of the Midwestern basketball team, Sandy Slews, volunteered to serve as coach of his fraternity's basketball team in the university's intramural program. Early in the contest a technical foul was called when Sandy, in his capacity as coach of the Mu Gu team, protested a referee's decision too vehemently. He was said to have quieted down after the call, but erupted again late in the game when another technical foul was called on him for walking on the court and using obscenities. As the game ended with Mu Gu losing by two points, Slews, according to several people present, chased one of the referees while shouting obscenities at him. He finished by making an anti-semitic remark at the referee too. Finally, Slews grabbed the referee and spit in his ear. Then, after releasing him, he rushed over to the sidelines, picked up one of the benches and threw it at the basketball backboard. (Interestingly, the referee was actually of Iranian heritage.) At a meeting the next day, Slim Paterson, Intramural Supervisor, stated that such violent action and verbiage was the worst that he had ever seen or heard of. He felt that Slew's most serious offense was his "anti-Semitic outcry" and action toward the referee. "Religious or racial prejudice has no place in IM activities on this campus," Paterson continued, "and it simply will not be tolerated on this campus." Both referees of the game agrees with Mu Gu's representatives at the meeting that the incident really was not the fault of the team. Dave Spanich, Mu Gu's president, said, "The team members were reasonably well behaved. There just wasn't anything they could do with Slews at that point." The following day Coach Cecil Smythe, Midwestern's head basketball coach, decided that Sandy should sit out varsity game to think about his outburst at the intramural game. Stating that "this has been a difficult season for us," Coach Smythe added, "and this is the culmination of many different things. Sandy will still have an opportunity to play in the final two games, and we expect him to be at practice on Sunday. This is all most unfortunate."

Case 9. "Breaking Training Rules at Slocom High"

The Slocom Board of Education was asked at its meeting last evening to rule on a petition by parents to overrule a recent action by the high school administrative and coaching staff to suspend 10 football players and a member of the track team from athletic participation for the remainder of the school year. The disciplinary action taken again the nine seniors and ten juniors was the result of a drinking party held after Slocom's 33-0 football victory over Dedham High on Sept. 29. The 11 suspended athletes admitted that they had been drinking at a lakeside cottage, and also that two automobiles had been damaged by gunfire during the party. Last night's special meeting of the school board was called at the request of Trustee Paul E. Munn. Mr. Munn asked Chairperson Howard Franszen to hold the session in response to mounting pressure from members of the community and parents of the boys for a more lenient policy. Community concern appeared to be divided between alarm on the part of one group at the revelation that underage teen-agers had been involved in such an affair, as well as further alarm from a second contingent at the impending absence of the varsity team from this year's highly rated football team. The latter group really began to protest when the "depopulated" squad was only able to tie winless Blanton High School on October 6. Thus. some 36 people arrived at 7:30 p.m. as the "audience" for the school board meeting However, they had to wait two hours in the high school library to learn what the decision of the appeal would be as the result of a closed-session meeting of the board's executive committee. Chairperson Franszen had explained that the closed session was necessary because of the delicate nature of the matter, as well as the presence of members of the press. Franszen emerged at 9:30 p.m. to the meeting of the entire board and stated: "The Executive has discussed the Board's policy in camera and now feel that they have achieved some unanimity on the subject at hand. We are now ready to entertain a motion to resolve the petition that has been submitted to us by members of the community." To himself Franszen wondered how the issue would be resolved. He himself had no doubt as to how it should be settled.

Case 10. "A Realistic Approach to Promotion"

Bruce is an assistant professor at a large state university. He is on tenure track which means that he has a maximum of seven years in which to convince the promotion and tenure committee of his department that he should be granted a permanent position there (i.e., tenure). The achievement of such status presumably provides Bruce with a "life appointment," because tenure when earned can only be broken because of (1) proven incompetence, (2) proven immorality, or (3) proven dishonesty. (If a university can prove "financial exigency," tenure can be revoked with a "pay-out" to the professor concerned.) A professor's work assignment is typically a 40-40-20 proposition (i.e., 40% of his time should be devoted to teaching, 40% to scholarship and publication, and 20% to service in the university, the profession, and/or the community. However, at the "better" universities, if is generally recognized that solid publication, research grants, and "citation-index" recognition will get a person tenure and a subsequent "clear track" to the rank of full professor and the accompanying perquisites. Of course, practically no one will admit that fine teaching at both the undergraduate and graduate levels doesn't really count for all that much "when the chips are down." It can help somewhat, of course, but "marginally acceptable" teaching will do the trick if the research component of one's dossier is strong. The same can be said for the service component of one's overall promotion and tenure folder that is evaluated-- i.e., it helps a bit, but barely nominal effort along that line will fill the bill. Returning to the case of Bruce, a bright assistant professor in his second year of a tenure-track appointment, he assessed the situation carefully and decided very quickly what approach he was going to take. As he told his wife after dinner one evening, "There's no question but that research grants and publication are "the name of the game here. So that 40-40-20 division of workload time for me is going to be 70-20-10. Seventy percent of my time and effort is going to be devoted to scholarship, applying for grants, and publication. I will teach as well as I can, just enough to 'keep the students sullen but not mutinous,' and I'll duck every time-consuming committee assignment that I can. Also, my only concern with professional associations and scholarly societies will be to find opportunities to present the results of my research as often as I can." Is Bruce's proposed "realistic" approach an ethical one?

Additional Topics for Discussion (and Possible Formal Debate)

1. Resolved that a student's academic average should have a bearing on his/her athletic eligibility.

2. Resolved that an unacceptable level of violence is an inevitable component of contact/collision sport.

3. Resolved that living up to the "spirit" of the rules is outmoded and Incongruent in today's competitive sport.

4. Resolved that coaches have too much interpersonal power over athletes in today's competitive sport.

5. Resolved that the use of any and all stimulants, painkillers, and bodybuilding agents should be banned for athletes at all levels of sport competition.

6. Resolved that highly competitive sport develops desirable personality traits.

7. Resolved that a teacher/coach should never go out on strike.

8. Resolved that a comprehensive national code of ethics should be developed and enforced for the coaching profession.

9. Resolved that athletic scholarships should only be one component of a university's plan to help needy, scholastically able students to attend university.

10. Resolved that until the needs of all students for physical activity education are reasonably well cared for, the physical education profession should take a strong stand against the idea of elite sport at all levels of education.

(Continued on the next page)

Table 3

SAMPLE FORM FOR USE WITH ANALYSES (PHASES ONE, TWO, AND THREE)

(Name of Case: _____)

D
DATA

Q,
SO, PROBABLY?
(NECESSARILY?)

C
CONCLUSION

(SINCE W)
WARRANT

UNLESS R)
REBUTTAL OR
EXCEPTION

1.
2.
3. etc.

TEST No. 1 (KANT)
(consistency)

TEST No. 3 (ARISTOTLE)
(intentions)

(ON ACCOUNT OF B)
BACKING

TEST No.2 (MILL)
(net consequences)

Key: Jurisprudential Argument Terms:
D =   Data (A statement of a situation that prevails including
        evidence, elements, sources, samples of facts)
Q =   Modal Qualifier (adverbs employed to qualify conclusions
        based on strength of warrants (e.g., necessarily, probably)
C =   Conclusion (claim or conclusion that we wish to establish)
W =   Warrant (practical standards or canons of argument designed
        to provide an answer to the question, "How do you get there?"
B =   Backing (categorical statements of fact that lend further
        support to the bridge-like warrants)
R =   Conditions of Exception (arguments of rebuttal exception that
        tend to refute or "soften" the strength of the conclusion)

PART 4

THE GOAL: A SUCCESSFUL ADMINISTRATOR

By the time you read this summary selection, you will probably have read and discussed many of the cases in this text. You have now been exposed to the case method of teaching human relations and administration as applied to the field of sport and physical activity education. It is not possible for the author to know if his hopes for this teaching method have been realized. This final part is an effort to summarize some of the beliefs and reactions that have come from other groups similar to yours who have used this material and these cases.

The reason for this text was the belief by the author that the typical administration course in physical activity education (including athletics) has not given students an opportunity to face the sort of problems that will be encountered on the job.

The book started with something that actually was contrary to the case method approach: we attempted to characterize administrators into types such as strong, fairly friendly, weak, friendly, conservative, and democratic. Of course, we realized that no person can be made to fit into a particular mold-that is, each administrator is unique and faces problems in a way all his own. We defined a competent manager by saying that he/she would employ wise leadership in such a way that a complex department would function effectively, making possible maximum learning on the part of the students.

Inductive Versus Deductive Approach to Administration

Delving into the theory of administration, it was reasoned that it might be possible to employ an inductive approach to administration where an examination of facts led to general concepts about possible action. Deductive reasoning, conversely, is an approach where we operate on the basis of principles that lead us to the identity of specific facts involved in a problem situation. Thus, an administrator acting on the basis of the application of guiding principles to an administrative problem would apply a definite action pattern to all situations. But this is not the way life situations occur, as anew pattern of rules seems to be needed with each administrative problem because of the variables introduced by the human personality factor. Some administrators seem to fail by attempting a combination of these two methods of procedure. The ever-present human relations factor seems to favor the use of the inductive approach, if an administrator hopes to achieve long-term success in his complex undertaking.

Learning by the Case Method

The primary objective of a course in administration and human relations was to increase the student's capacity to work effectively with others. The hope was that through this experience you have been helped to develop an attitude and a point of view toward administrative practice. If you, who have presumably had experience with team sports, can see that group effort means literally "team effort," perhaps you will become a more efficient administrator in a society which stresses the importance of "democratic administration."

Although this book does not minimize the importance of factual knowledge, we do maintain that the important qualities for a successful administrator are: the ability to work cooperatively with others; the ability to think and act responsibly; and the ability to provide an "atmosphere" where co-workers will have an opportunity to work effectively and with true satisfaction as members of the group.

No Fixed Formulas for Specific Situations

By now you undoubtedly realize that the case method is no easy way to learn, although some may disagree. In addition, it is not an easy method for the teacher. There are no fixed formulas to use in specific situations. The need is for the administrator to devise with his associates a step-by-step pattern to bring the various factions in a situation into some sort of harmony, so that progress can be realized. Some general suggestions were called to your attention that might be helpful in analyzing a case. They have stressed the importance of knowing all the available facts thoroughly and discarding the irrelevant ones quickly. We should decide for ourselves what the exact question at issue is. Furthermore, we should learn to ask the right questions to get at the basic problem.

Once we have settled upon what we think is the main issue in a case, we may then broke it down into sub-issues or sub-questions. Formulating and answering these sub-questions are, we believe, the best ways to arrive at a solution to the basic issue. We prefer this approach to another method where pro's and con's are listed on opposite sides of the 'ledger" at the outset, although this technique may be helpful later in the analysis. Now that you have come to this point in this course on sport and physical activity management, have you found that there are a number of ways to approach the analysis of an administrative problem?

In most cases we have found that there are one or more alternatives that could conceivably guide our actions. If these alternative courses of action seem plausible, their possibilities should be exploited for what they are worth. We found that it is neither necessary nor even desirable to memorize conclusions or available facts from a case. What we are encouraging you to do is to continue to develop is the power to think and to plan in a constructive, orderly manner when confronted with a problem that must be met. Of course, it is necessary to study a case carefully before discussing it, but it is just as important to think through the results of discussions and to understand what critical questions have been raised.

Currently Useful Generalizations

You have become aware that it is not possible to consider a particular case in a vacuum. Prior experience with other problem situations sharpens your discriminatory powers. We form "currently useful generalizations" continually. They serve as indispensable guides. Before leaving any case, we should always ask ourselves, "What have I learned that will help me in a general way in facing future situations?"

That some may still have some doubts about the wisdom of this approach is acknowledged. The hope, of course, is that this experience that has been shared with your classmates and instructor will help you to realize the goals that you have set for yourself in this challenging field of human endeavor.

Difficulty of Communicating With Others

You may agree that through the case discussions you have achieved a certain basis of understanding. The class knows a bit more about each other's reactions to certain problem areas in the field; yet, still further steps could be taken to achieve genuine understanding. It is difficult to convey our real thoughts to others and to get them to trust the sincerity, much less the wisdom, of our words.

Keep in mind that a basic managerial function is the development and maintenance of a communications system. The establishment of a sound organization with accompanying executive personnel is fundamental. The processes needed to accomplish this include the selection of men and women who are offered incentives to join the enterprise. Then, in addition to application of techniques of control permitting effectiveness in promoting, demoting, and dismissing staff, the manager must secure an informal organization that is compatible. This informal organization is responsible ultimately for the establishment of an organizational scheme where free and easy communication prevails, one that helps to minimize undesirable influences as it promotes desirable ones.

Others Have Difficulty With This Approach

If you found some difficulty with the "ethos" of the case method approach at first, you should not be too disturbed. Students evidently found difficulty with this method at Harvard when it was first originated. This appeared to have a direct relationship to their maturity and prior practical experience. Each student must determine his or her own strengths and weaknesses and must use them in the best way possible.

When students realize that they are indeed on their own, they eventually relinquish the established habit pattern of relying on the teacher for answers. Ideally, you should be looking forward to the challenge of more administrative problems or cases in which you can test your mettle. In the vicarious experience provided by the case method, you have been able "to stick your necks out and have them stepped on." In time, the "neck muscles become conditioned to the tread of many heavy feet." Fortunately, only rarely does an individual become discouraged through this vicarious experience, where the risk of failure is at an absolute minimum.

Writing and Analyzing Cases

Certainly one of the most interesting experiences for you has been to write a case and then analyze the situation. It represented a challenge to your intellect as well as to your power of observation and your ability to tell a story factually. Naturally, the best cases are written by experienced case writers. Actually, this is a technique that you might continue to use in the future as you face administrative problems. As was stressed, we need to keep in mind that a good case writer is a good reporter, although every effort should be made to disguise the identity of each participant. As you can appreciate, one of the best preliminary indices of the usefulness of any case is the extent of interest that you have in it.

Basically, the case writer should report just what he/she sees and hears-no more. He should make every effort to obtain a broad perspective on the problem, while at the same time looking for commonplace statements and incidents that may hold significance. No one can ever know all the relevant facts of any case.

Writing Examinations

You may now be facing a final examination in this management course. It would seem wise to reiterate information as to what may constitute a satisfactory examination paper in the case method. It may be more difficult for your instructor to tell you clearly and specifically why a paper is superior, satisfactory, or unsatisfactory, than if he were teaching, say, algebra. Perhaps it will help to repeat how superior students approach the material at hand. Basically, they are concerned with the problem of communication and the achievement of a common basis of understanding. They take a carefully defined clinical approach, but they realize that no one can hope to learn all the facts in a given situation. They realize that a person responds not to the facts, but to the facts as he sees them. They believe the attitude of the administrator to be most important in determining the behavior of the various staff members.

In addition, people making superior case analyses stress the point that action taken too fast can trigger adverse reactions on the part of subordinates. They refrain from recommending "principles" of administrative action and suggest instead the adoption of basic assumptions that have to stand the test of verification in specific situations. Finally, they realize that people's behavior is governed by many different factors, and that staff members will not always be affected by logical thinking. Hence, any given action on the part of a staff member might be taken in the light of the assumed favor or disfavor of the group.

Poor students, on the other hand, tend to see things as either "black" or "white." Many of them accept any and all opinions of the participants in the cases as fact. Some go to the other extreme and immediately discount any statements or opinions as unverifiable. These students do not help to analyze the problems evident in the cases. When some students find that they are making no headway in the analysis of a case, they "reason" that the particular case does not offer them enough information to gain the insight sufficient to formulate a solution.

From the standpoint of the "science of meanings," the language and logic of poor students show deficiencies. The words and phrases they use in their answers carry no real meaning. They tend to make statements like "the whole answer to this problem lies in the fact that the department head didn't establish good communications," or "that coach needs to lie on a couch and tell his troubles to a psychiatrist." Some seem possessed with the idea that a manager has two choices: he can get efficiency by being tough, or he can keep his staff members happy by being a "softie." The problem appears to be that students come to examinations prepared to think, to feel, and to act in the same old habitual ways. Students who have truly absorbed the lessons to be learned through the case plan of instruction have learned a new behavior pattern.

Examinations bring with them a greater pressure. Poor students revert to their basic ways of thinking, because they have not yet mastered this new approach. They tend to concentrate on one small area of the total problem. They rarely show an understanding of the administrative process that has developed because of the problem explained in the case. They grasp for a solution-any solution-that will come to them at the moment. Because they are confused, they resort to an authoritarian approach, thus losing the precious opportunity to propose a solution that might better the administrative process in operation.

Some poor students see that a definite problem exists; hence, it must be solved immediately. They fail to see all the alternatives possible. "Either the coach should be dismissed, or the "recalcitrant" should be put on probation." They often set themselves up as "little Gods" and proceed to arbitrate in sepulchral tones. On the other hand, some qualify their statements to such a degree that their proposed solutions are meaningless. Others develop "should" complexes. "The coach should realize that he has been too strict with the boys." "The boys should understand that winning the Harvard game means everything." "The athletic director should be able to see that the coach is under great pressure."

Implications for Clinical Research

With the ever-increasing number of students in sport and physical activity management, there are ample opportunities for research in human relations and administration through the use of the case method. Although methods of research differ a great deal in their specific application, basically this clinical research would follow similar methodology involving (1) observation; (2) recording observed data; (3) generalization to theory formulation; and (40 testing the new generalizations by further clinical observation. Since little experimentation of this type has been conducted in sport and physical activity management, students would, of necessity, need to acquire a background in clinical research and case writing. Some students, particularly those who have no special talent in statistics and its methodology, may find the case method of research intensely interesting. This is so, because here the concern is with the analysis of qualitative factors that simply cannot be measured by statistical treatment. This type of research has been recognized by many social scientists and gained favor rapidly. Here we understand that there may be a danger in attempting to discover a coefficient of correlation for everything in life.

Sport and physical activity management is in need of a great deal of research that would contribute to fundamental theory and practice. Such research should provide detailed observation of management in process, including events and subsequent decisions as they unfolded. Careful and skillful recording of observations of numerous ongoing administrative situations should be recorded. Such analysis of the data should then be compared with data from other observations. Finally, when uniformities in the managerial process appear, it will be possible to construct generalizations of a tentative nature about uniformities that appeared. Such uniformities can be tested by continued analysis.

This approach could be applied easily to the many aspects of sport and physical activity management in which elements of administration exist. The working relationships between men and women often become more complex when aims and objectives seem to differ. Supervision and similar problems are in evidence with the various administrative areas. These areas all present a great many problems in human relations. The evidence in from the field of business research proves that immeasurable help can be gained from the case method.

The "Tough-Minded" Approach

McNair's "tough-minded" approach dating back to mid-twentieth century seems essential to serve as a reminder that you cannot consistently straddle the fence in an administrative problem situation and survive (1954). The case method is the "hard route," for you must tell others what you have decided should be done in a particular case. Naturally, others stand ready to challenge any statement that you make-that is, if they feel it represents a belief that they cannot accept.

It should be obvious why instructors generally do a minimum amount of challenging at first in this type of course. It seems necessary for an instructor to refrain from too stringent questioning until the student understands fully the instructor's position. It would be easy for the instructor to use the authority of his position to get you to accept his beliefs.

McNair stressed further the instructor's responsibility to see that the class settles down to a "tough-minded analysis of the facts and issues" in the various cases. This is most difficult for an instructor if he is still to keep in front of him the goal of the nondirective approach. After the issues have been determined, it is possible to formulate critical questions and to reach a reasonable percentage of answers by considering the evidence pro and con.

The Complexity of Any Administrative Situation

Any administrative situation may be unusually complex. Hower offered a diagram that can be of considerable help titled "Influences on

Behavior." A brief study of it will show just how many relations and determinants influence a person's behavior in any given situation (in K. B. Andrews, 1953. p. 96).

From this diagram it can be seen how many factors are involved in individual behavior. In some circumstances direct orders from the administration or economic incentive would be the most important determinants; yet, on other occasions they could easily have very little influence. The task as you analyze a problem situation is to gain as much perspective as possible. But you must, while responding to the facts as you see them, keep in mind that each person sees a situation differently. Such a realization should make administrators often hold back a little before initiating quick action to meet a problem.

Attitude Is Important

The manager's attitude toward his or her staff is most important. When things go wrong and unrest prevails, almost anything that he does will be looked on with disfavor by skeptical eyes. Thus, any action taken to rectify difficulties will have to be considered most carefully in light of the reactions that this "remedy" may cause. If the line of communication has not broken down completely, the administrator may be able to predict with a good chance of success what effect his intended words or deeds will have. When you assume a new position with managerial duties, make your moves carefully and with considerable forethought.

Most people are willing to admit that they have certain bad habits. Unfortunately, although they often know what is right, they do not do it. When you assume an administrative post, you will need to improve your "batting averages" with the typical managerial practices that you will apply to problems. It is usually wise, for example, to seek the counsel of others on the staff before setting a policy, but administrators often go ahead on the basis that "the boss knows best." Other false notions are (1) staff members will work hard only when driven; (2) the staff will generally respond to what the boss calls "logical thinking"; and (3) what the administrator thinks about them is more important (to the staff) than what their colleagues think.

Don't Leave Cooperation to Chance

With every passing year, education is becoming increasingly "bigger business." This means that managers cannot expect cooperation among staff members and between staff and administration to develop by chance. Why is it that some coaches perennially have teams where fine team spirit is evident to all? Can this be achieved by telling the boys that they must cooperate with others? Or is this team spirit developed by the coach because he has promoted an atmosphere favorable to esprit de corps?

Such an atmosphere can be developed by: delegating responsibility and authority; by allowing subordinates to participate in policy formation, which of necessity brings about emotional acceptance to necessary decisions; and by keeping the lines of communication open. In this way the administrative burden on top will be lightened, and all of the workers will develop a feeling of belonging to administration.

True Democracy in Action!

Perhaps now you are finally ready to take another step forward—to agree that administrators or managers are made, not born—that they can be developed in a democratic atmosphere. Certainly there are risks to this approach, but at least everything is not being staked on the qualifications of one individual, who, for any number of reasons, may not hold his position for long. The encouragement of this type of participation by staff members prepares for a succession of administrators capable of carrying on efficiently their predecessors' work.

Moving from the realm of the practical to the theoretical, here is a way to come much closer to the goal of democratic education for which we have been striving. Now that you have made a good start in this direction, continue to use this approach in your work and strive constantly to develop all those attributes that will help to make you a better manager of sport and physical activity education.

References and Bibliography

Andrews, K. R., ed. (1953). *Human Relations and Administration*. Cambridge, MA: Harvard University Press.

Barkley, E., K. P. Cross and C. H. Major.(2005). *Collaborative Learning Techniques*. Jossey Bass.

Boehrer, J. 1990-91. Spectators and gladiators: Reconnecting students with the problem. *Teaching Excellence* 2. No. 42, Summer 1990. Jossey-Bass Inc.

Boehrer, J. 1994. On teaching a case. *International Studies Notes* 19:13-19.

Boehrer, J., & Linsky, M.. 1990. Teaching with cases: Learning to question. *New Directions for Teaching and Learning*. No. 42, Summer 1990. Jossey-Bass Inc.

Bransford, J. D., Brown, A.L. and Cocking, R.R., (eds.). (1999) *How People Learn: Brain, Mind, Experience, and School*. National Research Council (U.S.). Committee on Developments in the Science of Learning. Washington, D.C.: National Academy Press.

Brakke, M., T. Dunrud, R. Peterson, M. Reicks, and S. Simmons. 1994. Decision Cases for Secondary Education. *College of Agriculture Program for Decision Cases*, University of Minnesota, St. Paul, MN.

Christensen, C. R., D. A. Garvin, and A. Sweet (eds.). (1991). *Education for Judgment: The Artistry of Discussion Leadership*. Boston: Harvard Business School Press.

Christensen, C. R., A. J. Hansen, and L. B. Barnes. (1994). *Teaching and the Case Method*. 3rd ed. Boston: Harvard Business School Publishing Division.

Cliff, W.H., and L. Nesbitt Curtin. 2005. An Open or Shut Case? Contrasting Approaches to Case Study Design. *Journal of College Science Teaching* 30(1):14-17.

Cliff, W.H., and L. Nesbitt Curtin. 2005. The Directed Case Method: Teaching Concept and Process in a Content-Rich Course. *Journal of College Science Teaching* 30(1):64-67.

Colber, J.A., K. Trimble, and P. Desberg. 1996. *The Case for Education: Contemporary Approaches for Using Case Methods*. Boston: Allyn & Bacon.

Copeland, M.T. 1958. The case method of instruction. In *And Mark an Era: The Story of the Harvard Business School.* Boston: Little Brown.

Corey, Raymond (1998), Case method teaching, *Harvard Business School* 9-581-058, Rev. November 6, 1998

Christensen, C. R., A. J. Hansen, and L. B. Barnes. (1994). *Teaching and the Case Method.* 3rd ed. Boston: Harvard Business School Publishing Division.

Colber, J. A., K. Trimble, and P. Desberg. (1996). *The Case for Education: Contemporary Approaches for Using Case Methods.* Boston: Allyn & Bacon.

Copeland, M. T. (1958). The case method of instruction. In *And Mark an Era: The Story of the Harvard Business School.* Boston: Little Brown.

Corey, Raymond (1998), Case method teaching, *Harvard Business School 9-581-058*, Rev. November 6, 1998..

Daft, R.L., and K.M. Dahlen. (1984). Guide to case analysis. In *Organization Theory: Cases and Applications.* R.L. Daft and K.M. Dahlen, editors. New York: West Publishers.

Duch, B.J., S. Groh, and D. Allen. (2001). *The Power of Problem-Based Learning.* Stylus Publishing. LLS.

Easton, G. (1993). *Learning from Case Studies.* London: Prentice-Hall

Fitch. B. and Kirby, A. (2000). Students' Assumptions and Professors' Presumptions: Creating a Learning Community for the Whole Student. *College Teaching* 48 (2): 47-54.

Guyer, R. L., M. L. Dillon, and L. Anderson. (2000). Bioethics cases and issues: Enrichment for social science, humanities, and science courses. *Social Education* 64(7):410-414.

Hammond, J.S. (1976), Learning by the case method, *HBS Publishing Division, Harvard Business School*, Boston, MA, Case #376-241, doi:10.1225/376241

Herreid, C.F. (1997). What is a case? *Journal of College Science Teaching* 27:92-94.

Herreid, C.F. (1997/1998). What makes a good case? *Journal of College Science Teaching* 27:163-165.

Herreid, C .F. (1998). <u>Return to Mars: How not to teach a case study.</u> *Journal of College Science Teaching* 27:379-382.

Herreid, C. F. (1999). Dialogues as case studies: A discussion on human cloning. *Journal of College Science Teaching* 28:245.

Herreid, C. F. (2001). <u>When justice peeks: Evaluating students in case method teaching.</u> *Journal of College Science Teaching* 30(7):430-433.

Hutchings, P. (1993*). Using Cases to Improve College Teaching: A Guide to a More Reflective Practice.* Washington, DC: American Association for Higher Education.

Hammond, J. S. (1976). *Learning by the case method*, HBS Publishing Division, Harvard Business School, Boston, MA, Case #376-241,

Herreid, C. F. (1997). <u>What is a case?</u> *Journal of College Science Teaching* 27:92-94.

Herreid, C. F. 1997/1998. <u>*What makes a good case?*</u> *Journal of College Science Teaching* 27:163-165.

Hutchings, P. 1993. *Using Cases to Improve College Teaching: A Guide to a More Reflective Practice.* Washington, DC: American Association for Higher Education.

Johnson, D. and Johnson. R. (1992). *Creative Controversy: Intellectual Challenge in the Classroom.* Interaction Book Company.

Leenders, M. R., and J. A. Erskine. (1989). *Case Research: The Case Writing Process.* London, ON: Research and Publications Division, School of Business Administration, The University of Western Ontario.

Lundeberg, M. A., B. B. Levin, and H. L. Harrington. (1999). Who Learns What From Cases and How? *The Research Base for Teaching and Learning with Cases.* Lawrence Erlbaum Associates.

Lynn, L. (1996). *What is the Case Method? A Guide and Casebook.* Foundation for Advanced Studies on International Development (FASID), Japan.

Lynn, L. (1999). *Teaching and Learning with Cases: A Guidebook.* Chatham House Publishers. Seven Bridges Press, LLC.

Leenders, M. R., and J. A. Erskine. (1989). *Case research: The Case-writing Process.* London, ON: Research and Publications Division, School of Business Administration, The University of Western Ontario.

Lynn, L. (1999). *Teaching and Learning with Cases: A Guidebook.* Chatham House Publishers. Seven Bridges Press, LLC.

McAninch, A. R. (1993). *Teacher Thinking and the Case Method.* New York: Teachers College Press.

Mackenzie, R. A. (1969). The management process in 3-D. *Harvard Business Review,* 47, 80-87,

McNair, M. P., ed. (1954). *The case method at the Harvard Business School: Papers by present and past members of the faculty and staff,* New York: McGraw-Hill, pp. 139, http://www.questia.com/PM.qst?a=o&docId=28506390

McAninch, A. R. (1993). *Teacher Thinking and the Case Method.* New York: Teachers College Press.

McNair, M. P., and A. C. Hersum. (1954). *The Case Method at the Harvard Business School.* New York: McGraw-Hill.

Millis, B., and P. Cottell. (1998*). Cooperative Learning for Higher Education Faculty.* Phoenix: Oryx Press.

National Center for Case Study Teaching Partnership with Dept of Education at Michigan State University. This is a website summarizing the literature at http://edr1.educ.msu.edu/references/

Rogers, L. A. (1978, 1981). *Business analysis for marketing managers.* Heinemann

Simon, H. A. (1960). *The New Science of Management Decision.* NY: Harper & Row.

Schwart. P. , S. Mennin, and G. Webb. (2001). *Problem-Based Learning: Case Studies, Experience and Practice.* Kogan Page Ltd.

Shulman, J. H. (1996). Tender feelings, hidden thoughts: Confronting bias, innocence and racism through case discussions. In J. Colbert, P. Desberg, and K. Trimble, eds., *The Case for Education: Contemporary Approach s for Using Case Methods pp.* 137-158. Boston: Allyn & Bacon.

Silverman, R., and W. M. Welty. (1990). Teaching with cases. *Journal on Excellence in College Teaching*.

Silverman, R., W. M. Welty, and S. Lyon. (1991). *Case studies for teacher problem solving*. New York: McGraw-Hill.

Smith, B. L. ed. (1993). *Washington Center Casebook on Collaborative Teaching and Learning*. Olympia, WA: Washington Center for Improving the Quality of Undergraduate Education.

Wasserman, S. M. (1992). A case concerning content: Using case studies to teach about subject matter. In J. H. Shulman, ed., *Case Methods in Teacher Education* 64-89. New York: Teachers College Press.

Wasserman, S. (1994). *Introduction to case method teaching*. New York: Teachers College Press.

Welty, W.M. (1989). Discussion method teaching. *Change:* July/Aug. 1989, 41-49.

Wren, D.A. (2003). *The History of Management Thought*. NY: Wiley.

Yin, Robert. (2003). *Case Study Research: Design and Methods*. Sage publications.

Yadov, A., M. A. Lundeberg, K. Dirkin, N. Schiller, and C. F. Herreid. (2006). National Survey of Faculty Perceptions of Case-Based Instruction in Science. Paper presented at the Annual Meeting of American Educational Research Association. San Francisco, Ca.

Zeigler, E. F. (1959). *Administration of Physical Education and Athletics: The Case Method Approach*. Englewood Cliffs, NJ: Prentice-Hall.
Zeigler, E. F. (1959). *The Case Method Approach: Instructor's Manual*. Englewood Cliffs, NJ: Prentice-Hall.
Zeigler, E. F. (1982). *Decision-making in Physical Education and Athletics*. Champaign, IL: Stipes.
Zeigler, E. F., and Bowie, G. W. (1983). *Management Competency Development in Sport and Physical Education*. Philadelphia: Lea & Febiger.
Zeigler, E. F., Bowie, G. A., & Paris, R. (1988). *Competency Development in Sport and Physical Education Management*. Champaign, IL: Stipes.
Zeigler, E. F. (1992). *Professional Ethics for Sport Managers*. Champaign, IL: Stipes.

Zeigler, E.F. (1994). *Critical Thinking for the Allied Professions: Health, Sport & Physical Education, Recreation, & Dance*. Champaign, IL: Stipes.

Zeigler, E. F. (2007). *Applied Ethics for Sport and Physical Education Professionals*. Victoria, Canada: Trafford.

Zeigler, E F. & Bowie, G. W. (2007). *Management Competency Development for Physical Activity Education & Educational Sport; A Laboratory Manual*. Victoria, BC, Canada: Trafford.

Zeigler, E. F. (2010). *Management Theory and Practice in Physical Activity Education (including Athletics)*. Bloomington, IN: Trafford.